The Irish Penitentials

AND THEIR SIGNIFICANCE FOR THE SACRAMENT OF PENANCE TODAY

Hugh Connolly

FOUR COURTS PRESS

This book was set by Seton Music Graphics
in 11.5 on 13.5 Ehrhardt, for
FOUR COURTS PRESS LTD
Kill Lane, Blackrock, Co. Dublin
and, in North America,
FOUR COURTS PRESS LTD
c/o ISBS, 5804 NE Hassalo Street, Portland, OR 97213.

ISBN 1-85182-161-9 hbk
1-85182-203-8 pbk

A catalogue record for this book is
available from the British Library.

Printed in Ireland by Colour Books Ltd, Dublin

Nobody can help the man who has fallen beneath a burden, unless bowing down he gives him a hand: no doctor can heal wounds, if he is afraid of infection. Likewise, no priest can heal the wounds from which a sinner suffers, or take away the sin, if he does not suffer and pray and weep with him.

Haltigar of Cambrai

CONTENTS

ABBREVIATIONS

PRIMARY SOURCES

Ad.	Canones Adamnani
Aq.	Synodus Aquilonaris Britaniae
Bi.	Paenitentiale Bigotianum
Ca.	Tres Canones Hibernici
Co.A,B.	Paenitentiale S. Columbani A,B
Co.Reg.Mon.	Regula Monachorum S. Colombani
Co.Reg.Coen.	Regula Coenobialis S. Colombani
Co.Inst.	Instructiones S. Colombani
Cu.	Paenitentiale Cummeani
Da.	Excerpta de Libro Davidis
Gi.	Praefatio Gildae
Hi. I-VI.	Canones Hibernenses I-VI
Lu.	Synodus Luci Victoriae
OIP.	Old Irish Penitential
OITC	Old Irish Table of Commutations
Pa.Conf.	Confessio S. Patricii
Pa.I	'Synodus I S. Patricii'
Pa.II	'Synodus II S. Patricii'
Te.	Paenitentiale S. Teodori
Vi.	Paenitentiale Vinniani
Wa.A,P	Canones Wallici, Textus A, Textus P
tit.	titulus
pr.	preambula, prologus
ps.	postscriptum
ssc.	subscriptio

SECONDARY SOURCES

CHR	*Catholic Historical Review*
CSEL	Corpus Scriptorum Ecclesiasticorum Latinorum
DACL	*Dictionnaire d'Archéologie Chrétienne et de Liturgie*

GS	*Gaudium et Spes*
IER	*Irish Ecclesiastical Record*
ITQ	*Irish Theological Quarterly*
JEH	*Journal of Ecclesiastical History*
LG	*Lumen Gentium*
MSR	*Mélanges de Science Religieuse*
NRHDFE	*Nouvelle Revue Historique de Droit Français et Etranger*
Ordo	*Ordo Paenitentiae*
RHLR	*Revue d'Histoire et de Littérature Religieuse*
RP	*Reconciliatio et Paenitentia*
T.I.	*Theological Investigations* (K. Rahner)

PREFACE

It is with gratitude and a sense of indebtedness that I present this book. Special thanks are due to my Bishop, Dr Francis G. Brooks, whose personal interest and support made my initial studies in Rome possible. No less important are my family and friends, who have all been generous, patient and supportive throughout my years of study.

I am deeply indebted to my moderator Fr Ivan Fucek S.J. of the Gregorian University for the gift of his experience, patience and wisdom. I also owe a special debt of gratitude to the many professors, colleagues and friends at St Patrick's College, Maynooth, and the Irish College, Rome, whose counsel was most valuable in the preparation of the original thesis.

I acknowledge the services rendered to me by the various libraries, especially those of the Gregorian University, Rome; Queen's University, Belfast; St Patrick's College, Maynooth, and the Bibliothèque Nationale, Paris. My thanks are also due to Michael Adams and the staff of the Four Courts Press, who had the unglamourous task of adapting my dissertational research for a wider readership.

A final word of thanks to all those who have supported me in very different ways throughout the preparation of this book.

Fad ar bhur tsaolta agus laethanta geala.

CHAPTER ONE

CELTIC PENANCE: AN INTRODUCTION

This study has been undertaken in the belief that the priests and people of the early Irish Church had a unique and vivid understanding of man's relationship with God, on the one hand, and of his awareness of his own sinfulness, on the other. It is primarily a theological enquiry and, as such, does not seek to significantly add to our historical knowledge of the period in question nor to contribute specialist scientific scholarship to the ongoing literary and linguistic scrutiny of the various penitential manuscripts.

Any theological assessment of the Irish Penitentials, however, cannot be undertaken in complete isolation from the historical context out of which they emerged. Clearly there have been key junctures in the history of the Church where individuals and groups of Christians have had extraordinary lucid insights into the mystery of divine forgiveness, insights which have in turn profoundly affected the development of the theology of penance.[1]

The basis of this present study is the argument that the Irish, monastic Church represented one such key moment and its aim is to examine and identify the theological fruits which it has bequeathed to present-day Christians. Accordingly, our efforts must be rooted firmly in an awareness of the history, culture, structure and spiritual motivation of the Irish, monastic Church.

Evidently, the Celtic monks, had a very detailed and particular understanding of the moral life as laid down by Christ. Further, they had equally concrete views on precisely which behaviour was in accordance with the Christian life and which was not.

Although there was no systematic elaboration of a complete code of morality in Ireland, many of the issues with which moralists concern themselves today also formed the basis of the writings of these ancients. There was, in fact, a very keen awareness of the spiritual diseases which hamper and, indeed, often rupture our relationship with God. As a remedy to this, they compiled well documented lists of penitential exercises designed to restore this relationship to full spiritual health. But before venturing into the sixth-century Celtic monastic enclosure let us first explore the sociological and historical landscape from which it was born.

THE HISTORICAL CONTEXT

The Evangelisation of Ancient Ireland

Whilst it is certainly true that the Church which Patrick founded in the fifth century was fundamentally at one with the Church in continental Europe, in terms of structure and organisation the early Irish Church diverged considerably from its European counterpart. Patrick was familiar with the language and institutions of his adopted people, yet the Church in Ireland remained, to a considerable extent, a foreign body, with its use of the Latin language and Roman institutions. Despite having made a great beginning, the Church was being introduced to a society which was very different from any yet encountered in the spread of Christendom.[2] The Roman armies had never set foot in Ireland and their influence, therefore, would only have been very slight and indirect.

For all intents and purposes, then, Irish society was still largely pagan. Furthermore, whereas elsewhere in the Empire the Church had taken root in the great cities and centres of population, in Ireland, by contrast, cities were largely unknown. And, whereas even in Celtic Britain the Latin culture had become much more naturalized, Ireland, having never been a Roman colony, lacked the structure upon which the Church had so successfully capitalised in previous expansions.[3] Little wonder then that Patrick's mission to Ireland has been viewed as somewhat unconventional.

It appears likely, in fact, that given the aristocratic nature of early Irish society, Patrick logically sought to first convert the kings and noblemen. This conversion achieved, it was then a reasonable hope that their followers should follow suit.[4]

Patrick's whole missionary campaign may be described as a very mobile one. Despite describing himself in his *Confession* as a 'bishop' who is 'resident in Ireland', it seems that the idea of a centralised ecclesiastical seat never really materialised in Patrick's time. In essence, however, the Church which Patrick strove to establish was that with which he had already been familiar in his native Britain and in Gaul. And his writings leave us in no doubt but that the message he preached was a faithful and full rendering of the Gospels. The words of the *Confession* indeed are replete with vocabulary which was drawn from both the Old and New Testaments.[5] It was the unusual structure of Irish society which was to be the distinctive factor that allowed the Irish

Church to grow into a markedly different version to its Gaulish and British sisters.

Society in Ancient Ireland

The Ireland which Patrick encountered in the middle of the fifth century was a country comprising many petty kingdoms. Each of these was governed by a king who was, in turn, directly answerable to the high king.[6] The kingdoms themselves were referred to by the Celtic term *tuath* and they were mainly tribal in origin. Each tuath represented a separate political entity by virtue of its king and subsequent strata of social classes. Society, in fact, had a five-tiered structure. First in rank was the king who was followed in turn by nobles, non-nobles with property, non-nobles without property and finally slaves.

The language, customs and religion, however, were largely the same from one tuath to another. In this way, pre-Norman Ireland managed at once to combine political fragmentation with cultural unity. The king, despite being the royal leader, had very little power. Instead, in this largely autocratic society the individual nobleman bore the weight of responsibility for his kin.

Ancient Irish law or 'brehon' law was largely based on custom.[7] Crimes against individuals had to be paid for through compensation of the injured party. A principle of compensation, in fact, was firmly enshrined in brehon law, whereby all compensation had to be commensurate with the extent of the injury and the status of the injured party. These details are of interest to our present study since many of the penitential texts contain canons from the civil law, and indeed the Irish monastic authors may well have used the Brehon codes as models for their own texts.

A further feature of interest in brehon law was the stipulation that a person who undertook a contract should pledge some item of treasure by way of an initial guarantee or deposit. This came to be known as the honour-price. In the event of failure to honour a contract, the honour-price was forfeited together with the contractor's status. The forfeiting procedure was enforced through an *eric* or compensation fine. In this manner, the guilty person forfeited both material wealth and rank on account of his wrong-doing. The law sought thus to discriminate between acts which simply contravened the law and those which were carried out with malice aforethought. The Celtic penitentials were later to exhibit a similar concern for determining the intentionality behind a particular act.[8] They also cite a similar principle which prescribes the loss of material wealth and the forfeiture of clerical rank as punishment for particular classes of sin.[9]

Early Irish society did possess a rational process for maintaining the rule of law. Indeed, even by today's standards some elements of Brehon law seem quite enlightened. The law, for example, made provision for malicious personal injury. The victim of such a crime could claim medical and nursing attention from the guilty party as well as recompense for his family throughout the period of his incapacity. This provision also found an echo in later penitential discipline.

Also, every man had, under the law, the right to demand hospitality, within certain limits, from an equal or a superior. Hospitality, although already a hallmark of monasticism elsewhere in Christendom, was to become particularly typical of Celtic monasticism. Failures in this matter were viewed as a very serious issue by the penitential authors.[10]

We may say, then, that the provisions of brehon law augured well for the welfare of the whole society and for the protection of its weaker members. Each citizen was motivated not only negatively, out of fear of censure, but also positively, through the desire to increase his own prestige. This too, was an area of legislation which lent itself readily to adaption within a clerical or monastic system. The Church, with her various grades of ecclesiastical office from abbot and bishop through to novice, had always accepted that those in a higher position of authority had a proportionately greater responsibility to act wisely and virtuously. This point of view, of itself, was not peculiar to Irish monasticism, but Irish, penitential literature did display a keen interest in the various degrees of knowledge which might be expected of the different clerical ranks. To this end, they adopted a clearly defined grading system so that penances might be individually tailored according to age and rank. Hence clear differentiation is made between laymen, clerics, deacons, priests and bishops.[11]

A further area of Celtic legal procedure which seems to find a reflection in penitential practice is the provision for so-called 'fasts of distraint'. This provision came into play when a person failed to honour the principle of compensation. The defendant would then undertake a 'fast of distraint' before the plaintiff's dwelling place. This fasting process was held in great awe as an act which commanded considerable moral power thus compelling the plaintiff to consent to proper legal redress.

The practice resembled that of the Hindus which is known today as 'sitting *dharna*'. It serves to show that the institution of *purposeful* fasting was familiar to the Irish mind before the arrival of Christian ascetical theology. It may also help to explain the zeal and application with which the Irish monks gave themselves to penitential fasting.[12]

Druidic Cult and Culture in Ancient Ireland

The religion of pre-Christian Ireland is commonly referred to as Druidism. Although not priests, the druids were an important class involved in most of the important religious rites and observances. As well as having a reputation for great learning, for possessing magical powers, and for being prophets, historians, poets and even physicians, the druids also had an important role to play as teachers and counsellors. They were often employed to teach the children of kings and of chieftains, and it is said that even St Columcille (521–97) may have begun his education under a druid.[13]

Druidism, indeed, in some of its more sophisticated expressions, did elaborate quite a comprehensive body of doctrine. For example, Gaulish druids had quite a complex theory of ethics based on the notion of the 'Bardic triads'. According to this, the great truths and laws of the universe were believed to assume a threefold structure.[14] Three rules had to be adhered to in order to ensure harmony between mortals and the divine: (a) Adore God; (b) Do no wrong to anyone; (c) Act justly toward everyone. Similarly, druids shared three great fears: offending God, contravening the love of another, unduly accumulating riches. There were also three snares or vices: pride, hatred, and cupidity. There was, finally, a body of positive teaching based on this triadic system. Every druid had three duties to perform: to love, to create and to learn. These in turn derived from the triad of druidic virtues: knowledge, love and courage.

It is difficult to say with certainty which particular expression of druidism was in vogue in Ireland prior to the foundation of the Church and to assess its uniformity from one place to another. We can be sure, however, that, at the very least, druidism made early Irish religious consciousness a receptive terrain in which the seed of Christianity would later flourish.

In its more sophisticated expressions druidism adhered to an ideal of non-violence. Accordingly, the use of force was to be severely curtailed, as was any form of irrevocable condemnation. Thus, if the individual should somehow fail in his pursuit of spiritual fulfilment, there was *always* the possibility of making a fresh start, providing that he was disposed to submit to the prescribed triad of suffering, choosing and self-renewal.[15]

It would, of course, be a mistake to draw facile conclusions from these parallels of druidic and Christian practice and unfortunately, our lack of accurate historical information renders such speculation very tenuous indeed. On the other hand, it does seem quite probable that the Celtic and druidic mind was already familiar with some form of conversion experience before the Christian doctrine of penance gained the upper hand. Hence, it is not so surprising that this same Celtic mind was later to play so important a role in shaping the development of that doctrine.

Apart from the druids' own beliefs, however, it is doubtful as to how much their ideas were understood or adhered to by the common folk. Despite the druidic belief in non-violence, for example, we know that the early Irish were particularly bellicose and, indeed, often revered and venerated their warriors.[16] Irish monasticism was later to capitalise on this zeal for warfare by urging young men to come and do spiritual battle inside the monastery.

Learning in Ancient Ireland

Because druidism had never been crushed by force in Ireland as it had been in Gaul and Britain, druids, bards and brehons continued to function up to, and beyond, the coming of Christianity. The brehons were judges who determined the laws and adjudicated in matters of dispute. Bards, on the other hand, together with *fili*, were poets and philosophers who gave themselves to learning and schooling.[17] Their schools were quite highly organised. Usually families would specialise in particular professions from one generation to the next. Thus, there would have been specialists in poetry, history, medicine, building and law. Each of these areas was, in turn, promoted by professors who were qualified to teach it. These were known as *ollaimh*, and in order to attain this rank the student had to apply himself to a twelve-year period of disciplined study. These druidic schools were also to have a profound effect on the Irish monastery in terms of how it saw itself as a centre of learning and knowledge.[18]

Another area of learning in which druidic culture may have influenced later monastic tradition is that of medicine. The druids saw human kind as an integral part of the universe. Accordingly, man was but the human microcosm of a great macrocosm—the universe, and human life corresponded to certain great natural cycles which man could discern. This world-view affirmed that there were no exclusive opposites in the natural order; there were just two poles, each of which represented different extremes of one and the same reality. The goal of druidic medicine was to find the mean-point, the point of harmony, between these two poles whereat human life would flourish to the full.[19]

The Irish penitential authors were later to adopt the imagery of medicine and healing in their discussion of penance and the remission of sins. They frequently invoked the principle of 'cure by contraries', drawn from patristic sources, to demonstrate that vices must be healed by practice of the corresponding virtue. Thus, to each vice there was a corresponding virtuous activity or disposition, which was seen as an antidote. Although the principle of cure by contraries would have undoubtedly come to the Irish monks via the writings of John Cassian (*c*.360–*c*.435), the Celtic mind was already favourably disposed here toward the application of this type of medical imagery.[20] Indeed, the likeness between the druidic principle of the harmonious mean-point and the patristic principle of cure by contraries is striking. It too helps to explain why the Irish so readily adopted Cassian's principle and why the medicinal metaphor was to become the predominant imagery of the penitential literature.[21]

Beyond their teaching office, the druids also had a consultative role, in that they acted as counsellors to kings and high kings. It is reported, for instance, that King Laoghaire who was high king at the time of Patrick's mission, had two druids as principle advisers.[22] The druid too was often called upon as an arbitrator, but, in addition to this role as mediator between men, he was also held to be an intermediary between men and God by virtue of his religious knowledge. This, of course, gave him a very high standing in Celtic society. It was said that no one could speak before the king, but that even the king had to humble himself before the druid. In this way, the druids gained a reputation for being counsellors and guides and soul-friends to the decision makers.

This was to be another area of Celtic culture which foreshadowed later monastic developments. Historical research now shows that directors of conscience were a regular feature of Indo-European cultures and, indeed, many parallels may be traced between the Irish brehons and the Indian brahmans in this regard.[23] The latter also had recourse to spiritual guides whose functions so closely resemble that of the Irish monastic *anamchara* 'as to point with reasonable probability to a racial institution of great antiquity'.[24]

Evidently, many of the pre-Christian elements and institutions of Irish society were to have far reaching effects which would endure long after the foundation of the Church.

Whilst not seeking in this brief survey of early Irish society to attempt any manner of historical proof of the various links between the druidic and monastic cultures, we have observed, nevertheless, how certain areas of native life and culture lent themselves to (and indeed often foreshadowed) subsequent, Christian development.

II. THE IRISH MONASTERY AND CELTIC PENANCE

History of Irish Monasticism

The Church which Patrick established in Ireland was in complete accordance with that to be found elsewhere in Christendom, insofar as the diocese was the territorial unit, and this, in turn, came under the jurisdiction of the bishop. The diocesan episcopacy did not, however, flourish in Ireland. Despite its initial solidity, it began to rapidly diminish as the popularity and importance of monasticism grew. The Christianisation of Ireland had happened at a time when monasticism, as a movement within the Church, was spreading from Egypt, Palestine and Asia Minor to all parts of Western Europe.[25]

Patrick was hampered, as we noted earlier, by the lack of large population centres, such as were to be found in the Roman world. The contents of early Church documents pertaining to this period give a good illustration of the problems he faced. For example, the collection of canons known as the *First Synod of St Patrick* paint a picture of a nascent Church still coming to terms with order and organisation.[26] Concern is expressed that clerics make sure to determine which church they are to serve in. There are regulations for those engaged in travel, and rules concerning the status of clerics who arrive from Britain informing them that they must first register with the local bishop (Pa.I 27–34). The general impression given, then, is one of a young Church which is gradually getting on its feet. The central thrust, however, remains focussed on all authority deriving from the bishop. For instance, canon 30 reminds any bishop who travels outside his own diocese that he cannot ordain in another diocese unless he first seeks permission to do so.[27] Here the diocese is quite clearly the unit of ecclesiastical jurisdiction.

A century or so later, a very different situation was to obtain. The penitential manuals of Finnian, Columbanus and Cummean are all squarely situated in a Church which is centred upon the monastery. Evidently, there was quite a rapid transition within the Irish Church between the late fifth and early seventh centuries. Places which had been important ecclesiastical centres in Patrick's time lost their importance. Contemporaneously, monasticism began to flourish and abbots and learned monks increasingly assumed the role of Church leaders. Undoubtedly, social and historical factors played an important part in this transition. The Celtic world had always set great store by its schools of learning, wise men, counsellors and heroic warriors. The new monastic foundations appealed to this aspect of the Celtic imagination, and young men, eager to emulate the heroism of their forbears, flocked to the cloister.[28]

Instead of fighting as warriors in the *Fianna* (the Celtic army), these young men saw themselves as enlisting in a *Militia Christi* for the purpose of fighting against the Devil and Sin. The founding fathers of Irish monasticism thus appealed to the native bellicose instinct of the Irish and sought to transform it into the service of Christian ideals. This imagery of spiritual warfare and Christian soldiery was not, of course, unique to the Irish—it had found frequent expression in the writings of Cassian[29]—but it did find a ready and eager listenership among the Irish, who always relished the idea of doing battle, irrespective of whom the foe might be.

There was never, however, any formal repudiation of bishops or of the role of the episcopacy within the Irish Church. Bishops continued to be held in great esteem and to have clearly defined duties and powers which they alone could exercise.[30] The penitentials of Gildas, David and Cummean[31] all make reference to the office of bishop and the collection of *Irish Canons* devotes a lengthy section to personal injury of a bishop (Hi.IV:1–731). Notwithstanding this, the tribal and rural nature of Irish society seems to have favoured a monastic rather than an episcopal Church. One historian describes the situation thus: 'The bishop stood in a similar relationship to his diocese as did the petty king to his tuath; but the head of a great monastic *paruchia* was like a king over kings.'[32]

In this way, the abbot became the administrative head of the Church and was often referred to in fact as a *princeps*. He became the centre of power in a loose, disaggregated system, which had as its base the great monastic family. Significantly, the word for family in the Irish language remains to this day *muintir*, a derivative of the latin *monasterium*. The Irish Church, then, took a form which due to monasticism was markedly different from the older European Churches.[33] Furthermore, this monastic Church was to be the *locus theologicus* out of which the penitential manuals were born. It is therefore opportune at this juncture to take a closer look at the nature and organisation of the Irish monastery.[34]

Structure of Irish Monasticism

As elsewhere, the head of the Irish monastery was the abbot. Next, in terms of administrative power, were the *seniores*, who generally had the responsibility of correcting and directing the junior monks. From the ranks of *seniores* would then usually be drawn other key personnel among whom were to be found the vice-abbot, economo, cellarer, guest-master and various other minor officials.[35] The abbot had wide-ranging jurisdiction, ruling over all people within the bounds of the monastery and also over those from the surrounding district who came to worship at the monastery church. Also under his rule were those who periodically came to the monastery seeking help, advice, penance and reconciliation.

The Irish monastery was always quite a populous place and the inhabitants could usually be divided into the following categories: monastic, clerical, scholastic and penitential. Clearly, not everyone within the monastery was a cleric nor even a monk. Only a few monks, in fact, were promoted to priestly orders for the purpose of celebrating mass and the administration of the sacraments. This meant that there was actually a predominance of non-clerics in the Irish monasteries.

Large numbers of students came to study there because of the strong reputation of the monastic schools. There were also large groups of laymen known as *manaig* without whose help the day to day running of the monastery would have been impossible. Whereas in the later Benedictine, monastic system, the tenants of the monastery remained outside the monastic family, in the Irish system the *manaig* were firmly within it. The penitential manuals themselves give us ample indication that these lay people were an essential part of the fabric of the Irish Church.

> So intimate indeed was the union between monastic principality and its lay clients that the latter are called like the community

> *manaig*, and in many regards are distinguished only with difficulty from the religious family.[36]

Many of the lay people to be found in the Irish monastery were penitents attached to the monastery for longer or shorter periods. There were always guests too, coming and going, and for these a special guest house. Even beyond the bounds of its enclosure the monastery would have continued to exert an influence: the folk from the surrounding countryside would have frequented a church served by the monastery and they too would have looked to the monks for spiritual care.[37] Jonas of Bobbio, a disciple of Columbanus who recorded that great saint's life, recorded that crowds flocked to receive the healing power of the '*medicamenta penitentiae*', in rather the same way as people today might go to hospital to regain their health.[38]

From the earliest times, therefore, lay people formed an important part of that theological context which was the Irish monastery. It was in this context, moreover, that the penitential literature was shaped and fashioned and therefore it was quite natural for authors to distinguish between penances for clerics and those for the laity. Finnian, in a set of canons concerning intent to kill, discriminates thus between categories of penitent:

> If anyone has decided on a scandalous deed and plotted in his heart to strike or kill his neighbour, if a cleric he shall do penance for half a year . . . but if he is a layman he shall do penance for seven days; since he is a man of this world, his guilt is lighter in this world and his reward less in the world to come. (Vi.6–7)[39]

Asceticism and Irish Monasticism

The Irish monk saw himself especially as a servant of Christ and as a soldier who had to fight against the many evils which threatened his spiritual life. In this regard, Irish monasticism gradually developed its own distinct theological viewpoint, perhaps best encapsulated in the Irish teaching on martyrdom. According to this teaching there were three distinct forms of martyrdom; known as white, green and red martyrdom.[40] The first entailed forsaking all worldly possessions for the love of God; the second was seen as a kind of purifying process whereby a person gave himself to the monastic life and purged himself of all evil through a life of prayer, fasting, work and study. Finally, the third form, or red martyrdom, describes what we would more usually associate with the term, namely suffering persecution on to death for the sake of Christ and his Gospel.

Ireland, as we have said, was unique in that it had been evangelised without bloodshed. There was, therefore, no tradition of the more usual expression of martyrdom within the Irish Church. The great Irish religious leaders were very much aware that no clear-cut victory had ever been scored over the druids and their cult. They feared that the people had instead adopted Christianity while still holding on to some elements of druidic superstition and belief. Hence, the preponderance throughout the penitentials of canons which condemn the practice of magic, contact with the barbarians and 'keening' — wailing for the dead.[41]

Having never had the opportunity to offer themselves for red martyrdom, the Irish monks revised and expanded their understanding of martyrdom. This allowed them to give themselves to a life of rigorous asceticism and mortification and thus become, in some sense, living martyrs. In so doing, they sought to renew and purify the faith of the Irish Church, so that once it had passed through the filter of purgative suffering, it would be cleansed for ever of its pagan impurities. Irish or green martyrdom envisaged the core of the monk's relationship with Christ in terms of penitential activity and renunciation of sin.

In a very real sense, this Irish interpretation of the term 'martyr' was very close to the original significance of the Greek *marturein,* that is, to bear witness. The Irish monks chose to bear witness to Christ *not* through a martyr's death and persecution but rather through a life dedicated to penance and mortification. In his *Rule* Columbanus refers to the 'happiness of martyrdom' and it is clear from the context that he does not mean death but a life of penance and austerity.[42]

And there is no doubt but that the Irish monks interpreted penitential activity in the most severe and rigorous terms. Fasting was a regular feature in all the penitential manuals. Work too was usually very demanding and the amount of time allowed for sleep meagre. Conversation was severely restricted and some penances even made provision for corporal punishment using the rod or strap. Among other typically Celtic forms of penitential activity we find immersions in cold water, repeated genuflections and the distinctively Irish *crosfigell* (*crucis vigilia*).[43] The latter practice, involving praying for lengthy periods with the arms outstretched in cruciform shape, was greatly valued since it imitated the posture of the crucified Christ. Indeed, these are just some of the many ascetical practices which the monk would undertake throughout his 'living martyrdom'.

Nevertheless, the fact that the Irish placed the emphasis on martyrdom in terms of a way of life rather than death may be taken as further evidence that they considered penitential activity to have a life-giving, curative and healing power and, therefore, not a purely negative pursuit. In this sense, the simple monk could be justly called a martyr before God and men. His mortified life bore testimony to the healing power of Christ, in overcoming sin and purifying the individual from all evil.

This life-giving aspect of penitential discipline was later to be developed still further by the eighth century reforming 'Culdee' monks. They often referred to themselves as 'sons of life' and recommended that if one of their number neglected penance, he should have the *Penitential* and the *Rule* read to him in order that the power of sin and death would not gain the upper hand.[44] The penitentials too were seen to be, in their own way, inspirational and life-giving, due, in the main, to their frequent recourse to Scripture and their delineation of the virtues to be practised and the vices to be avoided. Finnian sees his penitential as representative of this position and he describes it as being: '. . . adapted for the sons of his bowels, out of affection and in the interests of religion, overflowing with the waters of the scriptures, in order that by all men all evil deeds might be destroyed' (Vi. ps.).[45]

Ascetical activity, however, was always subject to some form of control; and the young monk in the early part of his career was placed in the charge of a senior, who would lead the novice wisely, urging him to 'cleave to God and to Him alone'.[46] The ideal put before the monk was to reproduce the likeness of Christ within himself. The monastic system, in turn, was geared toward bringing this about; it aimed at purging the soul of all worldly desires and rendering it truly Christ-like. It was not sufficient for the ideal to remain merely an ideal; instead it had to become a reality.

Spiritual Direction in Irish Monasticism

Sin and failure had to be overcome so that the monk could truly become an image of Christ. An important part of the battle against sin was the identification of particular areas of weakness and their subsequent confession. It was to this end that Cummean and some of the other penitential authors set out Cassian's octade of the eight principle vices in their manuals (Cu.tit. passim).[47]

Cummean's writings also show us that there was a profound spiritual theology underpinning the prescriptions of these manuals. As well as stipulating the penances for the various sins, there was also a considerable body of positive teaching. Cassian's schema of virtues and vices was set forth as an indication of the pitfalls to be avoided and the goals to be striven after in the monastic life. At a later stage we shall use this schema to investigate more fully the Celtic understanding of sin and forgiveness. For the present, it suffices to note that the penitential authors produced their manuals because they believed that if spiritual disease could not be avoided or prevented, then it would have to be cured. To do this, however, the vice which was the root cause of the sickness would have to be correctly identified and diagnosed. The young monk was obliged throughout his life to make full and regular confession of all his faults, whether in thought or in deed.

In the Irish monastery such 'confessions' were usually made to a spiritual guide known as an *anamchara*, a Gaelic word which literally means soul-friend. The soul-friend was greatly esteemed within the monastic system. An ancient Irish saying comments that 'anyone without a soul-friend is like a body without a head'.[48] Every monk was expected to have an *anamchara* to whom he could make manifest his conscience (*manifestatio conscientiae*).

It seems that the origins of the *anamchara* tradition may be traced to two sources. The first was that of pre-Christian Ireland. The druids, we have already noted, were respected for their wisdom as teachers, counsellors and judges. They had long fulfilled the role of soul-friend to kings and decision makers.

The second source was Eastern, namely that of the Desert Fathers of the fourth century who engaged in the practice of *exagoreusis*, that is, the opening of one's heart to another which was believed to lead to *heyschia* or peace of heart. These two religious influences, one pagan, the other Christian, gelled into the Celtic anamchara tradition of heart speaking to heart. In leaving this legacy they also introduced to Celtic monastic practice the notion that man's relationship with God could take the form of effective dialogue.[49] This marked a special juncture not alone in the development of the doctrine of penance but also in the whole growth of Christian spirituality generally. This intimate encounter between man and God was to pave the way for the future developments concerning indulgences, private masses and the voluntary undertaking of penance for the salvation of souls.

Since many lay men and women were in regular contact with the monastery, they too would have had recourse to a particular monk for help and advice. We know this to be the case from an eighth-century *culdee* text which warns the *anamchara* to refuse to accept gifts from lay clients lest this in some way should undermine the balance of their relationship.[50]

But the role of the soul-friend was initially not a judicial one. Instead, he was seen as a guide who helped the individual through all the trials of his spiritual life. This provided him with a unique context in which to discuss and reveal his conscience, for the purpose of healing the wounds of sin and progressing in his relationship with Christ.

In the development of penance what was undoubtedly most significant was the introduction, in the context of soul-friendship, of what we have referred to as 'effective dialogue', of a type which was neither contractual nor constraining but which bore testimony, instead, to a God who was always willing to forgive. It was not as though one somehow earned forgiveness through penitential activity; rather, in the practice of therapeutic sacrifice one re-discovered in one's heart God's call to forgiveness.[51]

While it would be misleading to assert that Christians prior to this did not have sufficient awareness of their sins, it is nevertheless true that they did not have available to them the same possibility of personal and intimate confrontation of their spiritual lives as did the Irish. Under the older canonical system of penance Christians relied on the prayers of the Eucharist to express their common confession of sinfulness and their plea for divine mercy. Individually, there was much less opportunity for the penitent to take stock and rigorously examine his conscience.

Since communal practice of reconciliation had never reached the Celtic world, the anamchara was the only means to reconciliation which was known in this region. The practice did not, at the outset, represent an official act on behalf of the Church. No ecclesial judgement was made as to the individual's relationship with the Christian community.[52]

The later lives of the Irish saints and the later monastic Rules are generally replete with advice regarding the soul-friend. By this time, the office seems to be understood both in the narrow sense of direction of souls and the broader sense of hearing confessions of the faithful. 'As the floor is swept every day, so is the soul cleansed every day by confession.'[53]

A truly wise soul-friend was deemed to be one who had learned humility. The choice of a 'humble, learned, soul-friend' was recommended to all, and to the soul-friend himself the following advice was given:

> You do well to correct. You do *not* do well to reprove. The mind rebels against reproof. It is humble at being corrected. Wisdom without learning is better than learning without wisdom.[54]

Within the context of effective dialogue, there was also another principle at work, namely that of healing. Cassian's 'principle of contraries' (*contraria contrariis sanantur*) was wedded to the older pre-Christian, druidic notion of the harmonious equilibrium, and together they found in the Irish monastery a *locus theologicus* wherein a powerful new expression of penance as curative and medicinal was forged. Columbanus, throughout his writings, uses language which is reminiscent of both traditions.

> Thus between the little and the excessive there is a reasonable measure in the midst, which ever recalls us from superfluity on either side . . . For we must always restrain ourselves from every side according to that saying 'keep yourselves from the right and from the left'. (Co.Reg.VIII)[55]

The anamchara tradition, which so profoundly shaped the Irish understanding of penance, introduced not only the idea of dialogue but also that of *healing* dialogue. Further, I believe it is only in the context of this healing dialogue that a theological reading of the Irish penitential literature can properly take place. To make the criticism, as some commentators have done, that the penitential books were mechanical and impersonal is, I think, to ignore their true *Sitz im Leben* and thus to read them out of context.

We will return to this argument at a future juncture; for our present purposes it suffices to note that the Irish penitential authors all wrote from within a particular context and that that context embraced the anamchara tradition as well as a rich spiritual tradition regarding the healing aspects of penitential activity. This heritage is always quite evident throughout their writings and they take care to advise confessors and soul-friends that it is in this light that they are to understand their role:

Let the power of the physician become greater in the degree in which the fever of the sick man increases. Hence those who take care to heal the wounds of others are to observe carefully what are the age and sex of the sinner, what instruction he has received, what is his strength, by what trouble he has been driven to sin, with what kind of passion he is assailed, how long he remained in sinful delight, with what sorrow and labour he is afflicted and how much he is detached from worldly things. (Bi.1–2)[56]

III. THE ADMINISTRATION OF CELTIC PENANCE

Original Context

The aspects of Celtic attitudes toward sin and forgiveness considered so far give us some indication of the esteem which the early Irish Church held for personal sanctity and how the individual was to foster and maintain it. Given the emphasis which was placed on martyrdom within the monastic life, that is a life of truly bearing witness to the Gospel, it was clearly very important that the sinner should always have the possibility of rehabilitation. He needed to be freed from social censure in order that he could return to harmony with the Church and God. The Irish expected their monks to be living saints and, judging by the severity of their penitential practice, there is no doubt but that they took their living sainthood very seriously.

This was important to the Irish Church because in Ireland the lives of the monastic ascetics was to take the place occupied elsewhere by the cult of Latin martyrs. There is a clear contrast between the Celtic and Latin practices here; one was a cult of living saints, the other a cult of dead saints.[57] Given their rigorous quest for sanctity the Irish monks evidently needed to have frequent recourse to a penitential system. In this way, each monk could then be challenged to an inner moral change and thus set about a process of personal rebuilding, such that the sinful areas of his life could be identified and overcome. Penance, in other words, had to become a frequent event from which all could benefit. Such development, however, would only be possible within a theoretical and theological framework which expanded the rite of pardon out of its old canonical boundaries. We must now take a closer look at the shape of that expanded framework.

Assuming that the Irish monks were not familiar with the older canonical form of penance, they would, consequently, have had to create their own signs and symbols regarding the penitential process. I believe we can best discover the nature and novelty of these signs and symbols by juxtaposing them with those of the older canonical method.

Salient Features of Celtic Penance

Unlike the older Latin practice, there was no 'order of penitents' within the Celtic system. Hence, anyone could request divine pardon. Further, public embarrassment was not a feature of this system; rather, penance entailed fulfilling a series of prescribed exercises which the penitent carried out privately. These exercises usually involved fasting on bread and water, which, on the one hand, could be rendered more severe by the imposition of a limited allowance, or, on the other hand, could be relaxed to a simple abstinence from wine and meat, after a certain period of time had elapsed. In the early penitentials, in fact, the term *poenitere* (i.e. to do penance) is used interchangeably with *jejunare* (to fast).[58] The forty-day fasts are also a salient feature of this type of penance. These were carried out during the three annual lents or *quadragesimae* which comprised the forty days of Lent, Advent, and the forty days following Pentecost Sunday. However, fasting was not deemed to have much penitential value, unless also linked to prayer.[59]

Just as penance did not have a public character in the Celtic system, neither did reconciliation. The penitential manuals do inform us that after the requisite penance had been carried out, the penitent would be restored to the altar; but this reconciliation does not seem to have been marked by any public ceremony or pronouncement. In practice too, it appears that the prescribed acts of satisfaction may have been somewhat less severe than is set down in the manuals. Indeed, some scholars hold that there was a deliberate departure from the strictness of the rule and that reconciliation was granted after a part of the period of penance had elapsed.[60]

The minister of penance in the Irish system, unlike the Latin, was not usually the bishop. Instead, priests became the more usual ministers of penance, given that many people were frequently availing of the medicine of penance. Section 'B' of the *Penitential of Columbanus* makes explicit reference to the role of the priest in the process of reconciliation (Co.B.25).[61]

A fourth characteristic of this Celtic mode of penance was the fact that clerics could have recourse to the penitential process. Following the decree of Callistus at the beginning of the third century, this had ceased to be a possibility in the older canonical system. In Ireland, by contrast, clerics could seek forgiveness as often as the laity. Most of the penitential manuals provided separate canons which were specially tailored for the sins of clerics. Similarly, whereas in the canonical system civil rulers and officials were not frequently found among the penitents, in the Celtic practice there were no such restrictions.

In the Latin system, because of the civil disabilities which accompanied penance (that is, exclusion from clerical service and public office, as well as occasional prohibition of marriage or marital rights), not many young people were numbered among the penitents. The Irish system, on the other hand, attracted great numbers of young people because it appealed to their strong sense of idealism and determination to overcome sin.

A further characteristic of Celtic penance was its reiterability. In the canonical scheme the penitent had been received into an order of penitents where he persevered in fulfilling acts of penance until he had satisfied the judgement of the bishop. Once restored to full communion, there was generally no further possibility of forgiveness of subsequent sin, until that which was offered on his death-bed. All this changed with the Celtic scheme, where the Christian was encouraged to frequently avail of the healing powers of penance that he might worthily approach the Lord's altar. No limitation was placed on the number of times that the penitent could seek forgiveness through the ministry of the priest.[62]

Yet another feature of Celtic penance was the fact that confession of one's sins now became a much more detailed and explicit recounting of one's failures. In this understanding of penance, with its provision of special penitential exercises for every individual offence, much more emphasis was, quite naturally, laid on the actual 'confession' than in the older system. Indeed, from this time onward, the term *confessio* began to be used to describe the act of penance itself. The historical influence of the *manifestatio conscientiae* is evident here, for monks would always have been encouraged to give a full and frank account of themselves to their soul-friend.[63] In the earlier Latin tradition however, the penitent, even when applying to be received into the order of penitents, was not expected to make a formal and precise account of his sinful deeds. Instead, the sinner would confess his sinfulness and his need for forgiveness in a general manner. This kind of confession was not intended to be the revelation of particular sins but rather a public acknowledgment of sinful activity and need for divine pardon.

We shall attempt a more systematic analysis of the topic in a later chapter. For the present we may say that the principle differences between the two models of penance are as follows. Penance was not restricted to any kind of person nor to any type of sin. Anyone could seek forgiveness whenever they needed it without exclusion on account of age, sex or social position. In seeking forgiveness one came to a greater awareness of the particular areas of sinfulness within one's own life and how these could be best tackled. The Irish system thus proved more flexible than its Latin predecessor and was therefore more easily adapted to the needs of all kinds of people: 'men and women, young and old, weak and strong'.[64]

The Antecedent Virtues of Celtic Penance

We have already seen how early Irish society was shaped by two distinct influences, the one Celtic and indigenous, the other Latin and Christian. This twofold influence was also very much a part of the background to the moral scriptures of early Ireland. On the one hand, the Irish monks were heirs to the great sagas of Celtic heroic society, so that they even set down the legendary deeds of heroes such as Concubhar and Cuchulainn, whose history and lives were set centuries before in an age when Ireland was still pagan. On the other hand, they were also, evidently, situated squarely within the Judaeo-Christian tradition. They had studied the Scriptures at length and also had available to them the writings of some of the Fathers of the Church.[65]

Each of these cultural *Weltanschauungen* had its own moral order and system of moral evaluation in which various virtues and vices were set down as the different poles of human ethical behaviour. The Irish monks found themselves in a society which had changed its focus from one centred on the tuath or petty kingdom to the monastery which was now the natural hub of administrative power. A once pagan, heroic society was now being transformed into a medieval, Christian society.

The monastery thus inherited two distinct evaluative systems. Celtic monks lost no time in assuming for themselves the role of moral protagonists, slotting themselves into that space which had on the one hand been occupied by the Celtic mythical hero and on the other by those who had offered their lives in Christian martyrdom. As we have seen already, they not alone borrowed from these two models of moral behaviour but in fact re-defined and rehabilitated them so that the notion of Christian martyrdom could now coexist along with that of

Celtic valour in a new spiritual philosophy of green martyrdom which united both of these traditions in the fight against sin.

In this way, the Irish monastery became the *locus* wherein the Christian theological virtues of faith, hope and charity encountered the native Celtic traits of loyalty, courage and acceptance. The penitential literature reflects the efforts of the early Irish Church to evaluate and guide the moral behaviour of all the faithful. In common with all moral codes it recognised and valued certain qualities of mind and character which were deemed to correspond to the ideal behaviour of a true follower of Christ; it also saw a need to identify those actions and dispositions, the espousal of which would be detrimental to the fundamental tenets of the Christian life. The penitentials situated themselves within this latter enterprise. They were handbooks for confessors or physicians of souls who were to use them in order to steer the faithful away from behaviour which was spiritually harmful, to heal them from the effects of sin, to instruct them in the virtues which were to be sought after and to indicate a means by which this virtuous state might be achieved.[66]

It is clear, then, that early Irish monasticism, in common with many other religious schools of opinion, understood human life as a progression through harms and dangers, both moral and physical, which had to be confronted and overcome, in one way or another, in order to achieve eventual union with God. A closer examination of what exactly was considered to be harm or danger, success or failure, good or bad, virtue or vice, and the inter-relation of these should yield us a much more precise picture of how Irish monasticism understood this pilgrim's progress from a sinful to a virtuous state.[67]

In this regard, Irish monasticism did not invent its own categories but adopted the notion of the eight principal vices which, as we have already seen, figured prominently in the writings of John Cassian. These vices—gluttony, lust, covetousness, sorrow, anger, spiritual disgust, vanity and pride—had first been listed by Evagrius Ponticus (d. 399) in his *Antirhetikos*. Gennadius informs us that this was a work which comprised of suggestions against the eight principal sins. He investigates the causes of each of the vices as well as the evil forces at work within them. His purpose is, evidently, to provide a useful vademecum for the monk engaged in the daily spiritual battle against evil.

It seems probable that if Ponticus was not the original author, he was at least the first literary witness to the doctrine of the eight vices, which was in turn to be followed by Gregory's more celebrated doctrine of the seven capital sins.[68] We shall, during the course of the next two chapters make use of this *ordo disciplinae* as a key to understanding the ethical categories of Celtic Christianity. There are, of course, other and more comprehensive contemporary categories we could use. By retaining, however, those of the penitential authors we shall, I believe, gain a more authentic insight into their particular understanding, emphasis and evaluation of the cardinal points of human moral conduct.

Despite the fact that these eight categories were borrowed from patristic times, we would be mistaken to assume that in the encounter between the value systems of the Celtic and Christian cultures the Christian virtues somehow emerged victorious, thus persuading the Celts to repudiate forthwith their own ethical guidelines.

Instead, what seems much more likely is that those traits of the Celtic model which were deemed praiseworthy and noble would have been gradually assumed into a new Celtic, Christian morality, which, whilst being in harmony with mainstream Church thought and teaching, differed considerably in the emphasis it gave to various aspects of the moral life. Likewise, some of the attitudes and actions considered to be offensive or taboo by the Celtic predecessor culture would have clearly had a bearing on the early Irish Christian's perception of sin and vice and may also thus find an echo in the penitential material.

IV. THE PROTAGONISTS

Pre-Monastic Writers

Although the penitential literature is situated squarely within the monastic Church its roots run deeper into the earliest days of Christianity in Ireland. But before venturing into the sixth-century Celtic monastery let us explore the sociological and historical landscape of that time. Two further tasks obviously await us before our analysis of this theological context can be complete—an introduction to the penitential authors, and a general outline of their writings. We shall first turn our attention to some of the great saints who initiated Irish monasticism.

Patrick (d. 461)

We have already seen how Patrick, who first came to Ireland in the year 432, is now credited with founding the Church there. Although his autobiographical *Confessio* does not belong to the *genre* of penitential material, it does give a good illustration of Patrick's ascetical life style — a trait which he was to bequeath to the fledgling Irish Church and which was to have important implications for its future development.

Furthermore, Patrick almost certainly received a monastic training at the island of Lérins in Gaul.[69] He had been trained as a monk and loved the monastic order, although it was to be as a cleric that he would begin his work among the Irish. Already in Patrick's own spiritual life are to be found some of those features which were later to become hallmarks of Irish monasticism:

> In one day I said about a hundred prayers and in the night nearly the same; so that I used even to remain in the woods and in the mountain; before daylight I used to rise in prayer, through snow, through frost, through rain and felt no harm; nor was there any slothfulness in me; as I now perceive, because the spirit was then fervent within me.[70]

There is, quite definitely, here some traces of the rigorous asceticism which was typical of the penitential manuals. Patrick had a keen sense too of his own sinfulness, a vivid awareness of being wounded and in need of healing. Indeed, this is the most striking feature of his *Confessio* which is infused with his acute, and at times painful, awareness of his own limitations. It begins thus: 'I Patrick, a sinner the rudest and the least of all the faithful and most contemptible to many . . .'[71] This attitude of profound humility was later to be adopted as an important ideal by Irish monasticism. Patrick himself refers to this disposition as '*paupertas*'. It represents a poverty which is not alone material privation, but also a spiritual understanding of poverty illuminated by the light of the beatitudes. Further, it expresses a humble self-awareness which was 'full of the hope and joy of going forth to preach the Gospels'.[72] This notion of *paupertas* is, therefore, an essential key for properly understanding the spirit and context in which the penitential manuals were later written with their emphasis on prayer, fasting and humbling exercises.

Welsh Monastic Writers

Gildas (516–70) Gildas has been described as the Briton who 'most powerfully influenced Irish ecclesiastical affairs'.[73] Born in Scotland, he was placed, for a time, in a monastery as a young man. Monasticism existed at this time within the British Church; however, it was probably of a rather loose kind, such as that associated with St Martin when he was bishop of Tours. Gildas quickly earned for himself the reputation of being a most able and venerated teacher, as well as being an ardent critic of the iniquities of his fellow Christians and countrymen.

While he was not directly responsible for the foundation of any British monastery, Gildas did found a monastic community at Rys in Brittany, having moved there late in life. Earlier he appears to have travelled extensively throughout Britain, where he preached reform, and throughout Ireland, where he helped the fledgling Church to grow and develop.

Gildas' legacy to the Church is quite considerable. In his sermon *On the Ruin of Britain* he fiercely attacks the British bishops of his day for their ambition and upbraids them, in the manner of an Old Testament prophet, for risking their eternal salvation in order to gain an episcopal see.[74] He sees much corruption among the clergy but acknowledges that there is one group of truly holy men within the British Church, namely those who have abandoned the world to live the quiet, ascetic life of the monastic cell. In so doing, they had to decide to forego any position of prominence, since the monastery in Britain, unlike the later Irish version, did not occupy a pivotal or central role in Church affairs. Gildas sees these monks as truly holy, the exceptions in a Church which is otherwise reprobate, false, dishonest, lazy, indolent and wicked. He begs pardon from the monks for his harsh words. He praises the goodness of those who have left everything and humbled themselves and he looks forward to the day when he too might retire to a monastery and there spend the last of his days in seclusion, obedience and contemplation.[75]

Gildas' longest and fiercest attack on his fellow churchmen is reserved not for their failings but for their pride. He lambasts those who adopt an ascetical life, but who simultaneously treat their brothers with contempt. All the fasting and vigils of such people benefits them not, for they lack humility. They must learn to base their lives on what the Lord teaches and not what pride teaches. Instead of scorning the sinner they must weep for his sins as well as their own.

> The Lord calls the poor blessed, not the haughty poor, not those who despise the brethren, but the meek. Not the envious but those who weep for their own or for other's sins; not those who hunger and thirst for water with scorn of other men, but those who hun-

> ger and thirst for righteousness; not those who condemn others, but the merciful; not the proud, but the peace-makers; not those who excite discord, but those who support persecution for justice's sake, shall possess the kingdom of heaven . . .[76]

The life of the holy man is seen, then, as being founded above all on a disposition of true humility. The monastery must be free from haughtiness and pride, and the correct attitude for the good monk is a sorrowful awareness of one's own sins and those of one's brothers. There can be no place for those attitudes which are condemnatory, scornful or superior.

Gildas travelled extensively throughout Ireland rebuilding churches, instructing the clergy and advising future monastic leaders; his thoughts and ideas were well known there and held in great esteem. A letter from Columbanus to Gregory IX records that Finnian consulted Gildas on matters of monastic discipline.[77] Also, the later collection of Irish canons (*Collectio Canonum Hibernenses*) makes extensive reference to the *Preface of Gildas*, quoting it by way of a reliable authority. Evidently, Gildas had a profound effect on the development of monasticism and monastic spirituality in Ireland. His emphasis on the need for humility echoed and developed the Patrician concept of *paupertas*, and thus found a ready listenership among the Irish monks who would later expand it still further in tandem with their own penitential theology.

David (d. 589) Of the life of David little is known except that he lived on the south-west coast of Wales, a region which had much commerce with Ireland.[78] Further, it was ruled by Irish petty kings from about the third to the tenth centuries. Despite scanty information, it is known that David founded a monastic settlement at Tyd Dewi (David's House) and that his rule was known for its asceticism and its considerable emphasis on work and prayer. The foundation of David's monastery seems to mark the first step toward greater asceticism in Welsh and Celtic monasticism.

In this context, it is interesting to note that Finnian, the great founder of Irish monasticism, is thought to have studied there. It is also likely that the first forerunners of the penitential manuals were compiled at Tyd Dewi. Extant texts include the *Penitential of David* as well as the penitential canons of *Grove of Victory* and those resulting from the *Synod of North Britain*. David held synods at Llandewi-Brefi (569) and at Lucus Victoriae (569) and it is the records of these synods which form this early penitential material. Furthermore, it is thought that David, together with Gildas and Cadoc, may have undertook a mission to Ireland somewhere between the years 544 and 565, with the intention of renewing the faith and discipline of the Irish Church.[79]

In any event, the mission is important for two reasons. Firstly, it demonstrates that there was an intimate connection between the Welsh and the Irish Churches at this time. Secondly, it illustrates that the Welsh Church was the teacher rather than the taught.[80] Through Finnian, its most celebrated pupil, the Welsh monastic Church was, in turn, to exercise a huge influence on the development of monasticism in Ireland and, by extension, on the history of Christendom in Western Europe.

Irish Monastic Writers

Finnian (d. 549) The era of Finnian represents an important juncture in the history of the Irish Church. Having trained under David, Gildas and Cadoc in Wales, Finnian returned to Ireland and founded Clonard in 520. In terms of influence and location, this was to be the most important monastic establishment. Huge numbers are said to have flocked here attracted, not only by Finnian's own personal sanctity but also by his great talent as a teacher. Traditionally, he is believed to have had twelve leading disciples each of whom later founded monastic centres of their own.[81] Whether the number is correct need not unduly concern us here; what is certain is that Finnian's first settlement at Clonard was in large measure responsible for the moulding of the structure and spirituality of future Irish monasteries.

Unfortunately, despite his leading role in the Irish Church, little concrete information is available concerning Finnian's character or his spirituality. At the end of his penitential, however, he does address the reader directly giving some insights as to his personal motivation and piety. From this brief description it is clear that he is a humble and self-effacing monk, in the manner of Gildas and Patrick before him. He explains that his penitential has been written out of love for his fellow monks. He fears that in so doing he may seem to have strayed beyond his ability and authority. He apologises for his lack of talent and says that, because of this, he has been unable to give a fuller treatment of his subject. He immediately pledges his support and agreement to anyone who might subsequently undertake to elaborate further upon his ideas.

Finnian concludes his *apologia* by reminding his readership that the work was undertaken so as sinners would be saved and would enjoy the remedies of penance (Vi.ps.).

The impression given here is one of a humble, holy and humane legislator whose principal concern is to help his brethren in their quest for holiness. Given too the extensive influence which Finnian was to have on all the later Celtic penitential material, it will be important for us, when we come to evaluate that literature, to bear in mind this statement of motive, by the first Irish penitential author.

Columbanus (c.543–615) Columbanus is, perhaps, the best documented of the early Irish saints. The principle sources of information concerning his life and spirituality are the biography written by an Italian disciple, Jonas of Bobbio, and a collection of the saint's own writings comprising his letters, sermons, poems, monastic rule and penitential.[82] Columbanus first encountered the monastic life at Comgall's monastery in Bangor. Possibly because of Bangor's location near a great sea port the young monk resolved early in life to be a missionary. Therefore, in the year 573 he set off together with twelve others for Gaul, where he founded monasteries at Annegary (573) and later at Luxeuil. After a dispute with a local king he was obliged to abandon Gaul and he sailed up the Rhine to Bregenz on Lake Constance, where he founded another community. Two years later, perhaps with the eventual intention of travelling to Rome, Columbanus crossed the Alps to Italy. After a short stay at Milan, he founded yet another monastic community at Bobbio on the Trebbia (613). It was in the same community on 23 November 615 that the great saint died.

The writings of Columbanus give a good indication of his zeal and strength. He frequently challenges his monks to build their spiritual lives on the rock of Christ. His spirituality, typical of Celtic monasticism, is rooted in a rigorous asceticism. Yet it is never a facile or semi-Pelagian interpretation of penitential activity. Instead Columbanus reminds his followers that 'idle is a religion decorated with prostrations of the body (and) equally idle is the mere mortification of the flesh' (Co.Inst.II:2).[83]

He affirms that the good monk must always die to himself, that he might live in Christ. His *Rule* is undoubtedly hard, but must be considered in the context of the severity of the time and of the violent Merovingian Gaul in which he and his disciples found themselves. Like other Rules of the same period it does not give a detailed account of the regulations which govern daily, monastic life but, instead, takes the form of a meditation on the vices and virtues and on the moral life.

In this context, the term 'discretion' (*discretio*) is given particular prominence by Columbanus. According to him, the good moral life demands discretion and moderation. Thus, mortification of the flesh must be carefully balanced with due spiritual progress and the excessive pursuit of virtue is frowned upon.

> For . . . if abstinence is pushed beyond right measure, it becomes a vice and not a virtue; for virtue sustains and maintains many good things . . . For if temperance exceeds measure it will be a vice and not a virtue; for virtue maintains and retains many goods. (Co.Reg.III)[84]

To discover and learn to cultivate true discretion the monk must first become truly humble. According to Columbanus, it is only in emptying himself that the individual learns wisdom. He recalls St Paul's celebrated christological hymn (Phil 2:5–8) where the apostle points out that although Christ was in the form of God he did not 'snatch' at this equality but instead humbled himself through obedience onto death. Columbanus sees in this passage a great source of inspiration for the monastic life. The monk must learn to humble himself as his Saviour humbled himself; through this act of *kenosis* he will discover and exhibit true discretion. He will then learn that the virtuous course of action is always to be found at the mean-point between two opposing extremes. 'For those who live without discretion intemperance is at hand, and this is always the opposite of virtues which are placed in the mean between each extreme' (Co.Reg.VIII).[85]

This is an important point in Columbanus' thought and one to which we shall return later. This view of human moral behaviour is echoed in his penitential manual and is thus passed on both to the monks and confessors of his communities. Sinful behaviour was judged to arise where too much or, conversely, too little emphasis is given to a natural human propensity. For instance, moderate eating was seen to be virtuous but over-indulging one's appetite constituted gluttony and excessive fasting was also a transgression. Similarly, the human tendency toward self-preservation could be sinned against by uncontrolled ascetical and punitive behaviour and by covetousness and greed. The task of both monk and confessor, then, is to find the mean-point. The implication seems to be that this mean-point differs from person to person.

Thus, the confessor is to exercise due care and judgement in carrying out his ministry. In this way, then, human moral conduct is to be regulated and sinful behaviour to be detected and remedied. Given the thrust of Columbanus' thought here it is not difficult to see why both Cassian's *Principle of Contraries* and the imagery of healing are readily adopted. The individual is seen as subject to sinful forces on either side, but, through proper exercise of discretion by his confessor, his spiritual disease may be accurately diagnosed and the correct penitential antidote prescribed in order to nurse him back to full spiritual health.

Columbanus' thought is dominated, then, by these two distinct but related concepts, discretion and humility. The latter concept is referred to using the term *humilitas* and in essence it is very much akin to the thought of both Patrick and Gildas.[86] This typically Celtic emphasis, however, does not represent some form of self-deprecation or self-abasement purely for their own sake; rather, it is a striving after Christian lowliness, a humility which results from placing oneself totally in the service of Christ. Moreover, it is evident from his life that Columbanus strove to practise that humility and self-denial which he preached with such eloquence.

Like Patrick before him, people were drawn to him because they perceived him as sharing in their lot. And despite finding favour at four royal courts, Columbanus remained steadfast in leading a life of extreme self-sacrifice. He and his monks set before themselves the model of Christ, humble, obedient and abased, and, in so doing, attracted great numbers of people to their monasteries who came seeking compassion, forgiveness, healing and peace.

The names of *Cummean* (591–662) and *Adamnan* (624–704) are closely associated with the Irish penitential literature, though biographical details on both are scarce. Cummean (Cumine Fota) was one of the successors of Brendan of Clonfert (486–578) who, in turn, studied under Finnian at Clonard. His main influence was through his manual *The Penitential of Cummean*, which itself borrows extensively from other Irish penitential material.[87]

Adamnan may well have studied at Clonard as he is known to have received an excellent education. His principle writings were a biography of Colmcille, *Vita Sancti Columbae*, and a book on the Holy Land, *De*

Locis Sanctis.[88] The evidence, however, for linking those penitential canons which bear his name to Adamnán is very tenuous indeed.

Anglo-Saxon Writers

Although somewhat removed from the Celtic tradition, the Anglo-Saxon literature will prove useful at several junctures in our study as a point of reference or comparison.

Theodore (602–90) Though not strictly speaking within the ambit of this study, Theodore is of some interest since the Anglo-Saxon penitential bearing his name draws heavily on Irish sources.[89] Born at Tarsus in Cilicia he journeyed to Rome a sixty-five-year-old monk, in the year 667. He was then chosen for the distant English see of Canterbury after the original candidate turned it down. He travelled to England in 668 where he was duly consecrated Archbishop of Canterbury, an office he was to hold until his death in 690.

Bede the Venerable (673–735) Bede also produced a penitential and this is likewise of cursory interest to our present study since he too had recourse to Celtic sources.[90]

Egbert, Archbishop of York (732–66) The penitential ascribed to Egbert may have been penned by an unknown disciple. Its principal sources are Celtic and Anglo-Saxon.[91]

V. THE TEXTS

The penitential literature with which we are concerned in this study was compiled in the sixth, seventh and eighth centuries. These texts were intended as handbooks or manuals for the use of all priests who were engaged in the 'cure of souls'. They attempt to outline rudimentary elements of pastoral care and to resolve difficulties regarding various sins and misdemeanours. Their main significance is that they show us the old penitential discipline being replaced by new procedures. They demonstrate that the system of penance which was practised in the British and Irish Celtic Churches at this time was private. In other words, the penitent confessed his sins to a priest who, in turn, prescribed a penitential activity which was to be performed in private.

The penitential literature takes the form of a number of diverse texts which concern the administration of penance. While some of these documents are penitentials in the true sense, others are mere lists of penitential canons drawn from the acts of various Irish provincial synods or from the *dicta* of Irish prelates. In most of the texts, however, private penance is portrayed as the efficacious means to obtain remission of one's sins both grave and less grave.

What follows is not intended as an exhaustive analysis of the penitential material, but rather a description and over-view of the principal texts. The subject matter of these texts is consequently not examined in detail here as this shall be the task of the next chapters. This summary description will, on the other hand, furnish us with some information concerning their chronological and geographical origins as well as details concerning emphasis, form and composition of the texts.

Celtic Penitentials of British Origin

Celtic literature, and therefore penitential literature, may be divided into that which is British that is coming from the island of Britain and that which is Irish, coming from the island of Ireland.

The *Preface of Gildas on Penance* (Prefatio Gildae) As with the following three 'British' documents it is probably of Welsh origin: the *Synod of North Britain* (Sinodus Aquilonaris Britaniae), the *Synod of the Grove of Victory* (Sinodus Luci Victoriae) and *Excerpts from a Book of David* (Excerpta de libro Dauidis). These four texts are the earliest Celtic penitential manuals.[92]

Gildas' penitential, as its title suggests, is associated with that saint, whereas the other three texts are thought to be connected with David. The Gildas document and at least a portion of the *Excerpts* are intended for the use of both monks and priests. As such, they are purely monastic codes and no provision is made for those not under the monastic Rule. The penances prescribed here, moreover, may all be carried out in private, and reconciliation is understood to have taken place after the lapse of a particular period in which the penitent fulfils the assigned penance.

The Welsh Canons (Canones Wallici) These are to be found today in two distinct documents. Bieler has labelled these the 'A text' and the 'P text'.[93] The canons, however, are not really penitentials in the true sense, but rather a collection of laws pertaining to some rural community. The main concern of these texts is the punishment is to be enjoined for the crimes of murder, personal injury and theft. On the whole, these documents hold little interest for our present study; being primarily concerned with secular issues and matters of civil legislation they consequently contain no formal reference to the nature of penance itself.

Celtic Penitentials of Irish Origin (Major)

The First Synod of Saint Patrick (Synodus I S. Patricii) *c.450* This is not, strictly speaking, a penitential does contain penance-related material and is therefore of interest to our present study. The document is, in fact, a joint letter to the clergy of Ireland from the bishops Patricius, Auxilius (d. 459), and Isernius (468).[94]

In reading the text, we must bear in mind that the Church to which it was addressed was not yet fully organised. In all, there are thirty-four canons which refer to a wide variety of issues. The following are among the more salient features: clerics are not to hoard possessions, nor to wander through the countryside; they are to have their hair shorn in the manner of the Roman tonsure; it is recognised that clerics may be married; belief in vampires, witches and the various forms of magic are strongly denounced; similarly denounced are those who forsake the responsibilities of the marriage bond to live in irregular unions. In general, despite the wide range of sins and misdemeanours accounted for, the penances remain reasonably lenient. Of the thirty-four canons, seventeen concern the clergy.

The Penitential of Finnian (Paenitentiale Vinniani) *c.590.* It seems the earliest extant Irish penitential. Moreover, Finnian, as abbot of a monastery, intended his work primarily for the use of his own monks. In the main, the text is original, although on occasions the author does refer to scriptural and other learned sources. It is not immediately clear what exactly these learned sources are but it is widely believed among scholars that strong echoes of Cassian are to be found here.[95] The text itself can be divided into two main sections. The first, comprising canons 1–30, refers to the sins of clerics. The second section, which comprises canons 31–48, concerns itself with the sins of the laity. This, of course, immediately marks a development from the Gildas text. Penance is now seen to be available to all whether within or without the cloister walls. The catalogue of sins begins with the lesser misdemeanours and moves on then to the more serious offences. The importance of the text is its originality, for, despite the references to biblical and patristic sources, the book is, for the most part, original. As such, it is the first comprehensive, discriminating and precise penitential produced in the Irish Church. It is much fuller in content than the Gildas and David texts, but less systematic than Cummean's manual.

Throughout the document penance is seen to be of a private character; private confession is presupposed and reconciliation is not marked by any public ceremony. Further, it seems that the priest, rather than the bishop, is the usual minister of reconciliation; however this is not expressly referred to. Finally, in providing penances for the sins of all types of people, one and the same manner of administering penance applies whether the penitent be monk, lay or cleric.

The Penitential of Columbanus (Paenitentiale S.Columbani) *c.608* This shows considerable dependence on Finnian's work. Despite this dependence, Columbanus text was to have the wider sphere of influence, since it was used not only in Ireland but also in continental Europe.[96]

Here again Cassian's principle of *contraria contrariis curare* is much invoked, and again there is much precision and attention to detail in the various canons. The text may be divided into three distinct parts: Section A, 2–8 is intended for the use of monks, Section B, 1–12 is designated for the secular clergy, whilst Section B, 13–23 contains canons which deal with the sins of the laity.[97]

As in the other penitential texts already examined the scope is rather wide-ranging. Also, there is considerable effort here to ensure a fair measure of justice and equitability. Although there is substantial evidence that Columbanus may have compiled his penitential in continental Europe, as opposed to Ireland, there can be little doubt that this text is firmly rooted within the Celtic tradition.

An interesting feature is the breadth and wide range of sins and misdemeanours which are to be confessed. Here the priest-confessor, who is explicitly referred to, finds himself confronted by a vast array of sins over which he must exercise some form of judgement. We can conclude that under the Celtic system of penance, as portrayed by Columbanus, not only did the penitent enjoy a much greater individual attention than ever before, but the role of the confessor was considerably revised and expanded. The principal importance of this text is that is the earliest Celtic penitential to have been used in continental Europe. It was to have a profound influence on the later theory and practice of penance there.

The Penitential of Cummean (Paenitentiale Cummeani) *c.650* Unquestionably the most comprehensive of all the penitentials. It may be divided into two principal parts. The first comprises a prologue which takes the form of a homily on the remission of sins, an extract from earlier patristic sources. Reference is made here to the healing and medicinal power of penance as a remedy for the salvation of souls.

This is followed by eight chapters in which penances are set out according to the eight capital sins as described by Cassian.[98] These are: gluttony, fornication, avarice, anger, dejection, languor, vainglory and pride. The author decides to follow the principle of cure by contraries and, since there are known to be eight vices, he proposes to outline the eight remedies which will restore the sinner to full spiritual health (Cu.pr.15). The canons of these eight chapters bear a strong resemblance to those we have already studied in other penitential material. Here, however, since each chapter deals with a particular vice and the opposing virtue which is its remedy, there tends to be a greater unity of theme than in the other texts.

The second part of the penitential comprises three chapters dealing with lesser offences, the misdemeanours of boys, and questions concerning the sacred host. It concludes with a postscript.

Along with that of Columbanus, this manual was one of the great models for transmitting the strict practices of Celtic penance to England and Western Europe. Compared with earlier texts it shows a marked increase both in depth and accuracy of knowledge. As well as its patristic sources the document also has rich affiliations with Scripture, various Irish sources, both secular and ecclesiastical, the Welsh Canons and possibly an Irish monastic Rule.[99]

Celtic Penitentials of Irish Origin (Minor)

The Irish Canons (Canones Hibernenses) *c.650* Six in number, these describe themselves, for the most part, as decrees from various Irish synods. Worthy of note is the fact that the penances here are much more severe than any we have hitherto encountered. Another interesting feature of this text is that here payments may also be made in atonement for particular crimes.

The second document entitled *De Arreis*, meaning 'of commutations', is also noteworthy. Here the notion of commutation means the reduction of a lengthy penance to a shorter more severe one. We have already noted a similar practice in the *Penitential of Cummean*. The headings of the six texts, are as follows: 'On Penances', 'On Commutations', 'On Tithes', 'On Punishments', 'On Hospitality' and 'On Regulations concerning Dogs'. Each text, except the second, purports to be the acts of synods at which both clergy and laity would have assisted. There is much doubt, however, as to whether the synods ever officially sanctioned these texts.[100] Authorship, therefore, is completely unknown.

The Canons of Adamnan (Canones Adomnani) This is a collection containing a total of twenty canons. Almost all of them concern themselves with alimentary regulations. There is a strong resemblance here to similar precepts which are to be found in the Mosaic law. There is no substantial evidence however, to link these canons with Adamnan, and scholars are of the opinion that their attribution to him is entirely legendary.[101]

The Second Synod of Saint Patrick (Synodus II S. Patricii) Also referred to as the *Pseudo-Patrician Synod*, for it appears that the canons herein have little or no connection with Ireland's national apostle, there are a total of thirty-one canons. The majority of these purport to be acts of a Synodus Romani, although the background and authorship of the documents are extremely uncertain.[102]

The Bigotian Penitential (Paenitentiale quod dicitur Bigotianum) Taking its name from the library in which the original manuscript was formerly kept;[103] there is a close connection between this penitential and that of Cummean as well as further links with the *Old Irish Penitential.*

The document may be divided into two sections. The first takes the form of a preface giving a schedule of commutations by which lengthy penances may be replaced by shorter, more severe ones. This preface cites by way of authorities Paul, Jerome, Isidore, Benedict, Ambrose and Cassian. The second section is divided into eight chapters according to the eight vices (and their remedies) as devised by Cassian: gluttony, fornication, avarice, anger, dejection, languor, vainglory, and pride. The material, however, is very similar to that which we have already examined in the *Penitential of Cummean.* Again, penance is graded here according to the age, status and level of education of the penitent. On the whole, penances are reasonably light.

This penitential shows a greater unity and coherence than many of the other texts we have previously examined. This is largely due to the grouping of sins and their penances under specific headings.

The Old Irish Penitential So-named because it is the only penitential written in the Irish language,[104] much later in origin than any of the Latin texts, is undoubtedly a product of the *culdee* reform movement and, as such, chronologically outside the scope of our present study. Nevertheless, it is drawn almost exclusively from earlier Latin texts and for that reason merits our attention. As is the case with the

Bigotian Penitential the text is divided into eight chapters representing the eight principal vices and the penances which are to be their remedy. Each chapter is also preceded by a preface which offers further advice on the evil of sins. Otherwise the treatment of the material is the same as that to be found in both *Cummean* and the *Bigotian Penitential.*

The Old Irish Table of Commutations As its title suggests, this was also written in the Irish language. It too, belongs to an era outside our immediate area of interest. It is noteworthy in that it makes provision for lengthy penances to be commuted to shorter, less severe, ones and also for its specific reference to the soul-friend within monastic life.

The Anglo-Saxon Penitentials

The Anglo-Saxon penitentials namely those of Theodore, Bede the Venerable and Egbert Archbishop of York fall outside the range of this work from both a geographical and chronological point of view.

Given, however, that Theodore's manual does make extensive use of Irish material we shall have cause to refer to it occasionally. The preface is addressed to all English Catholics and the remainder of the penitential displays a profundity and systematization not seen in Celtic material. It adopts the provisions of Finnian and other Irish authors, but also shows familiarity with Roman law and discipline and various eastern sources.

CHAPTER TWO

TEXTUAL ANALYSIS: THE SINS OF GLUTTONY, AVARICE, ANGER, AND DESPAIR

It may seem to the reader that an evaluation of human morality which takes as its starting point eight vices must be regarded as something of a *via negativa*. Whilst this criticism is, to some extent, true, the fact remains that the penitential material is our only substantial record of moral scripture at this key juncture in the history of the Irish Church.

As penitentials these manuals were necessarily written in some sense on the 'under side' of moral theology. They were not intended primarily to be primers or text-books for the student of human moral behaviour, but rather as practical aids to the confessor engaged in the cure of souls. Our task then is one of reconstruction: by sifting through these penitential writings we hope to arrive at a more complete understanding of how the early Irish monks perceived the Christian moral life.

By taking as their starting point the sinful condition of humankind, diagnosing the various spiritual ailments and prescribing a remedial activity, the penitential authors sought to arrive at a living expression of Christian virtue, thus becoming more faithful witnesses of Christ's message and moulding themselves ever more closely into authentic images of God. This enterprise is, of course, precisely that of all truly Christian behaviour and is the *raison d'être* of moral theology.

The aim of this present study is to evaluate how Irish monasticism came to terms with and corrected human sinful behaviour in order that we, who belong to a very different, era may in turn benefit from their wisdom and insight in this matter. For that reason, we shall now accompany the monastic penitent on his journey from the morass of sin and vice through the purificatory experience of penitential activity and toward the virtues which the Scriptures and Christian tradition set before us.

The *modus operandi* of all penitential literature is perhaps best described in the introduction to the later *Old Irish Penitential* where the author explains:

> The venerable of Ireland have drawn up from the rules of the Scriptures a penitential for the annulling and remedying of every sin, both small and great. For the eight chief virtues, with their sub-

divisions have been appointed to cure and heal the eight chief vices, with whatsoever springs therefrom. Moderation with abstinence against gluttony and drunkenness. Continence with chastity against lust and adultery. Generosity with charity against avarice; and benevolence of heart against envy and hatred. Meekness with gentleness against anger and strife. Spiritual joy against worldly sorrow. Fear of death and perishing against vainglory. True humility with the fear of the Lord against haughtiness and pride. (OIP.pr)[1]

We can see, then, that a three-part process is envisaged, at least theoretically, by this system. The first part entails diagnosing the spiritual illness or identifying the vice by which the sinner is assailed; the second is the prescription of a suitable remedy or penance; and the third is the cure, being the restoration of the sinner to a virtuous state. We too shall follow this tripartite approach in our analysis of the eight major categories of sin which form the ethical divisions of the penitentials.

At the outset, however, it is well to note that no vice or virtue exists in what we might describe as a 'chemically pure' form. Each contains elements of related virtues or vices.[2] Hence, in our analysis of Celtic moral theory we shall see that divisions are not strictly applied and some sins will be deemed to be the product of more than one vice. Therefore, it was not unusual for sins resulting from one vice to be considered as manifestations of a more deep-rooted vice. Further, it must be acknowledged at this juncture that the penitentials do not devote equal space and attention to each category of sin: for example, the number of canons concerning sins deriving from some form of lust is far in excess of those which deal with any other single category of sinfulness.

Since the categories of vice and sin take the form of an octade, we shall analyse them in two groupings of four. To the first of these groupings which may loosely be described as those vices whose effects are most readily discerned, in the subject's own behaviour, namely greed, avarice, anger and despair we shall devote the remainder of this chapter. The following chapter shall deal with the remaining four vices which may, equally loosely, be described as those vices which are perceived above all in the subject's relations with others.

I. THE SINFUL DISEASE: GLUTTONY

The first of the vices, set down by Cassian and subsequently by the penitential authors, is that of gluttony.[3] In its most general form the vice is referred to as *voracitas*, *manducare/bibere ad vomitum*, *gula* and *gastrimargia*.[4]

Almost all of the penitential texts prescribe that eating or drinking be morally ordered. They are anxious to ensure that sins of intemperance are corrected by fasting and abstinence. Cummean (Cu.I.1) sets down the following exhortation from Saint Luke's Gospel as a guiding principle in this matter: 'But take heed to yourselves lest your hearts be weighed down with dissipation and drunkenness and cares of this life, and that day come upon you suddenly like a snare; for it will come upon all who dwell upon the face of the whole earth' (Lk 21:34–5), as also that of Paul to the Ephesians: 'And do not get drunk with wine for that is debauchery' (Eph 5:18).[5]

Gluttony: the Symptoms

Each of the penitential authors is acutely aware of the risk for every Christian of over-stepping the limits of right order to such an extent that he eats exclusively for pleasure rather than simply to satisfy the demands of his bodily health.

Cummean's choice of citation from Luke demonstrates his own belief that excessive eating or drinking is sinful insofar as it dulls the senses so that the mind is turned away from Christ and his message. Thus, the individual's mind becomes literally dissipated instead of being focussed on the Lord. This phenomenon is referred to in turn by the Bigotian author as dullness of sense (*hebitudo sensus*) and he argues that this leads to new expressions of sinfulness such as carelessness and immoderate sleeping (Bi.pr.40).[6] Hence, there are various sub-categories of sin which are brought about by the sinner's original submission to Gluttony.

Excessive eating The most obvious sin prompted by gluttony is that of eating to excess. The vocabulary used to describe this activity suggests over-eating to the point of sickness. The texts also make mention of the pain of satiety and distension of the stomach as indications of excessive eating.[7] Thus, the degree to which the penitent has over-eaten is measured in a rather crude fashion and depends to some extent on the body's ability to digest the additional food.

At another level, however, gluttony and the penitentials' response to it may be seen as representative of the whole penitential process. The 'pain of satiety' must be countered by the curative and healing 'pain of penance' and thus this penitential activity is set squarely within the imagery of healing, a theme which in fact is a recurring feature throughout many of the penitential texts.[8]

Excessive drinking and drunkenness Just as excessive eating is a sin of gluttony, so too is excessive drinking. The usual term to denote this in the penitential literature is *ebrietas* and it receives much mention from the various authors.[9] The early Welsh text of Gildas takes a somewhat lenient approach to the subject (Gi.10). Thus, the monk who has drunk so much as to be benumbed and speechless (*stupens elinguis*) is chastised with a mere privation of his supper. In this instance the monk's inability to discharge his office and not his over-indulgence in alcohol seems to be the principal factor in determining his penance.

Another early text, *Excerpts from a Book of David*, offers perhaps the best classification of the various sins in question here, but the penances it prescribes are considerably more severe (Da.1–3). It distinguishes between those who allow themselves to get drunk (*inebriare se*) and those who are responsible for another's drunkenness (*inebriare aliquem*).[10] The first category is sub-divided into three distinct levels of guilt: those who become drunk out of ignorance, out of negligence and out of contempt for a superior.[11] The penances prescribed for these sins are fifteen days, forty days and three forty day periods respectively. Obviously the third level is considered the most grave sin, since the term *per contemptum* connotes a deliberate and malicious intention on the part of the offender.

These prescriptions are, as yet, directed mainly at monks and clerics. When Colombanus later deals with the same sin among the laity he prescribes the more lenient penance of a week on bread and water (Co.B.22).[12] The *Book of David* also makes a special reference to those who are about to minister in the temple and through their own greed (*gulae gratia*) indulge in excessive drinking. These are to be punished quite severely.

On the question of those who cause another's drunkenness distinction is made as to the reason underlying their behaviour. Thus, someone who is the cause of another's drunkenness for reasons of good fellowship (*humanitatis gratia*) is to be chastised with the same penance as the person who causes his own drunkenness. He, however, who in order to confuse or ridicule a friend (*confundere vel irridere*) causes him to get drunk is to be considered as a killer (*homicida animarum*) and must do penance accordingly.[13]

Importantly, here the vice of hatred is seen to over-ride that of greed and the resultant sin is, therefore, deemed to be much more serious.[14] The author of *Cummean* likewise adopts this distinction, thus underlining the seriousness with which the penitential authors considered the deliberate use of a potent substance in order to harm another person (Cu.I.2–3).[15]

The much later *Bigotian Penitential* draws heavily on *Theodore* in its treatment of the sins of gluttony. As well as enjoining different penances for monks, clerics and laymen it also seeks to clarify some points of confusion.[16] The writer, for example, explains that sickness may result from eating or drinking when the individual is suffering from an illness or when he has just finished a lengthy period of fasting (Bi.I:2,3).

He thus detects a weakness in the previous criteria for determining gluttony and he rules that if one is sick merely for the above mentioned reasons, then there is no transgression at all (*nihil nocet*). Similarly, it may happen that a monk becomes ill as a result of the good fare which is provided at the feasts of Christmas and Easter and which has been consumed with the permission of the *superiores*. Again in this case, no sin is deemed to have been committed.

Another interesting category evoked by the *Bigotian* author is that of the habitual drinker. Here the main preoccupation is with the offender who is in holy orders. The reference demonstrates an awareness of the difference between the penitent who has occasional lapses in the matter of temperance and the one, on the other hand, who has the problem of habitual (*in consuetudine*) drinking. The remedy proposed, however, by the same penitential is a rather severe one. The penitent is to be confronted with the stark choice of breaking his habit immediately and completely or else being deposed (Bi.I:1).[17]

Vomiting the sacred species The desecration of the sacred host as a result of excessive eating or drinking is also classified under the sins of gluttony. All the penitentials consider this a very serious offence.

Gildas seeks to distinguish between various putative scenarios. Thus a severe penance is prescribed for the offender who vomits forth the host as a direct result of his gluttony; if, however, the action is deemed to be the result of a separate illness, the penance is almost halved. If, again, the host is not lost during the sickness, then the penance is still more lenient (Gi.7–8).

Columbanus retains these categories of Gildas but prescribes penances which are considerably more severe (Co.B.12). His tougher approach is, in turn, echoed by Cummean, who also envisages further situations where the host may be destroyed by fire or consumed by dogs. (Cu.I.10–11). The most comprehensive treatment of the subject is offered by the *Bigotian* author, who includes all the aforementioned categories. He also considers the related offence of those who break their eucharistic fast and he rules that they are to do a penitential fast for seven days (Bi.I:3,1–4).[18]

Eating unlawful food The inclusion of this category is at first somewhat surprising.[19] In contrast to Old Testament teaching, there are no unclean foods in the New Testament. Frequent allusions to this subject by the various penitential texts would seem, therefore, at first glance to be at odds with Christ's teaching that 'nothing defiles man which enters into his stomach from the outside' (Mk 7:14–19). Instead, one would expect the only regulations concerning food and drink to be those which would serve the demands of temperance, health and hygiene in order that the individual would not be unduly impeded in his daily activity.

The penitentials, nevertheless, retain the notion of unclean food and drink and, in fact, often make oblique references to the Old Testament in order to support their teaching in this matter.[20] One of the clearest instances of this is to be found in the *Canons of Adamnnan* which prohibits the eating of carrion. It explains that this also rules out the eating of drowned animals since in drowning the blood remains coagulated (Ad.14). It then goes on to demonstrate how this has been expressly forbidden by Scripture, at which point there is a reference to Genesis and, in particular, to the Lord's advice to Noah: "You shall not eat flesh with its life, that is its blood" (Gen 9:4).[21]

Cummean also gives a hefty penance for transgressions of this nature: he rules that the penitent should live for the third part of a year on bread and water and for the remainder of the year abstain from wine and meat (Cu.IX.16). Likewise, in the *Bigotian Penitential* severe penances are enjoined for those who consume human blood, urine or sperm or liquids which have been contaminated by various birds or beasts (Bi.I:5,1–3).

The immediate impression here is one of a set of guidelines which is seeking to suppress some of the more bizarre and macabre, druidic practices, rites and customs, which would have been inherited from the pre-Christian Celtic culture. It is known, for example, that the ancient Irish when making a solemn contract would ratify it by drinking a drop of each other's blood expressly shed for this purpose.[22] This contract then became known as a blood covenant and was regarded as one of the highest forms of sanctioning a promise or treaty. Similarly, a concoction containing human sperm seems to have been used as an aphrodisiac in pagan times. The practice is expressly referred to in the *Penitential of Theodore* (Te.I:14–15).[23]

There was also a practice in vogue among the druids which entailed cooking the flesh of dogs and horses as part of a rite of destruction of one's enemies. Moreover, at a celebration known as the 'bull feast', a bull would be killed and a druid would eat the cooked flesh and drink the broth in order to predict who the next king might be.[24] This link with other forms of illicit cult is more explicitly evoked in the *Penitential of Columbanus* which condemns those lay people who have eaten or drunk beside 'temples' or who have communicated with the followers of Bonosus (Co.B.24–25). In each instance, the transgression is deemed to warrant a penance of three years' fasting, if it is done wilfully in honour of idols (*pro cultu daemonum*).[25]

On the other hand, the consumption of food and drink which has been rendered unclean by small household pests, or by someone with unwashed hands, is considered a much lesser offence. Here the penances are much lighter and the over-riding concern seems to be one of inculcating a keen sense of hygiene and cleanliness among the monastic brethren. In such cases, if the action is judged to be accidental (*si casu*), no offence is deemed to have been committed (Bi.I:5,8–12; Te.I:7,11).

Excessive talking Excess consumption of food and drink are not the only sins to be dealt with under the general category of greed. The vice of garrulousness is also included here. Columbanus, in a short reference to the subject, describes sinners of this kind as '*verbosus*' and recommends that they be punished with an imposition of silence (Co.A.12).

The same remedy is prescribed by Cummean but he also points out that this vice may sometimes be linked to wilful injury of character. Accordingly, he makes a distinction between those who detract from a brother's character and standing, by reason of their excessive talk (*verbositas*) and those, on the other hand, who do so accidentally, in the course of conversation (*confabulationem*) (Cu.VIII.14–15). The first category of sin is considered the more serious and is to be remedied by a period of imposed silence lasting one or two days. Offences belonging to the second category are more easily atoned for by singing twelve psalms.[26] As was the case with causing another's drunkenness, here too that action which is damaging to another person's dignity is considered to be the more serious.

Whilst this offence approximates to what we might today term defamation of character, detraction or tale-bearing, it is true to say that for the most part, the penitential authors would also have recognised these areas as categories in themselves. In this instance, however, their concern is to chastise that area of human sinfulness which is brought about as a distinct result of personal greed. Thus, the transgressor's principal fault here is to indulge in idle talk or gossip, in so doing he not alone gives way to a sinful indulgence of the senses but also as a by-product damages another person's honour and dignity.

Similar but distinct offences are also dealt with under the general headings of *avaritia* and *superbia*. In these instances the transgressor is described as a false witness and a detractor respectively.[27] This serves to illustrate more clearly a point we have already made: vices and *eo ipso* their concomitant sins do not exist in a pure form but, instead, also express a further aspect of other vices.

Conversely, by codifying similar areas of sinfulness under various and different headings the penitential authors demonstrate a keen attention to detail which should not be too lightly dismissed. Evidently, they recognised that in making his confession a sinner would recount sins which may have been committed for any one of a number of sinful motives.

By listing similar sins under diverse headings the penitential authors also sought to impress upon the priest the importance of diagnosing the underlying vice which was the root cause of the sinful behaviour. The confessor could not simply read off a penance for a given sinful act; he had to judge for himself which category best described the sin in question and on the basis of this decision he could then, and only then, prescribe a penance.

Excessive merriment Further categories of sin which fall under the general heading of *gula* are those of *commessationes*, which we may describe as carousing, or revelling and *inepta letitia* which describes a state of immoderate mirth or foolish joy. Neither category, however, is provided for in the penitential canons.[28] The reason for this may be that the offences were considered sufficiently minor as to be left to the discretion of individual confessors or, as seems more likely, they may have been seen as sufficiently dealt with already in the canons concerning excessive eating and drinking. In the latter instance the confessor could then deal with the matter by having recourse to these same canons.

Gluttony: the Penitential Cure

The penitential literature envisaged a process whereby the individual penitent was restored to a virtuous state in a gradual manner. The sinner did not instantaneously cure himself upon confession of his sin. Instead, the confession was the first step toward his recovery. The confessor using Cassian's eight categories would then be able to pinpoint the particular vice assailing the penitent's moral life and prescribe a curative penance, involving a virtuous activity or disposition directly opposed to the sinful one.[29] Whilst this manner of deciding the type of penance to be undertaken was not always so well adhered to in practice, with regard to sins of greed the theory and practice do, in fact, coincide.

Abstinence and self-control Cummean prefaces his discussion of the vices by reminding his readers that the eight principal vices are to be healed by the eight remedies which are their contraries (Cu.pr.15). Columbanus spells out more clearly what precise form this remedy must take with regard to the sins of greed. He ordains that the talkative person be punished with silence, the gluttonous (*gulosus*) with fasting; and the sleepy (*somnolentus*) with watching (Co.A.12).

His choice of language here is quite severe and he deliberately speaks in terms of punishment of the sin. This, however, must be set against his overall description of the confession of sins as the 'healing of the heart' and the 'cleansing' of internal vices and sicknesses.[30] Thus, whatever about the particular choice of vocabulary, it is at least clear that Columbanus does not see the confessor's task as simply a punitive one; instead, he is to prescribe a penance which will serve to heal or rehabilitate the sinner.

The *Bigotian Penitential*, drawing as it does on the thought of Theodore and Cummean, tends to coincide with the views of the earlier authors and also seeks to correct excessive consumption of food and drink by fasting alone (Bi.I:1–10, passim).

Abstinence and activities which are 'other-centred' The much later *Old Irish Penitential*, which in many aspects represents a compilation of the foregoing material, gives the most comprehensive treatment of this subject. It recommends that gluttony and drunkenness be countered with moderation and abstinence and it goes on to identify other activities which will also help to eradicate the vice of greed, including 'remorse of heart, rare meals, frequent self-questioning, feasting the poor and solacing the hungry' (OIP.I,c).[31]

This later material, evidently, marks a further development of Cassian's approach. Appeal is now being made to the plight of those who are poor and hungry through no choice of their own, so as to help the penitent to grow out of the self-centred concern which leads him to excessively indulge his bodily appetites.

Abstinence as a 'type' for penitential healing As we have suggested above, gluttony and the penitentials' treatment of this vice may be seen as archetypal of the whole penitential process. The sinner transgresses right order by exceeding the amount and form of food which serves the preservation of his bodily health as well as the continuing progress of his spiritual activity. In transgressing thus he not alone sins but also renders himself physically sick.

In this instance, fasting and abstinence become not alone a spiritual cure but a physical one as well. The cure for over-eating through fasting, in order to attain the virtuous state of temperance, may, therefore, be seen as a 'type' or definitive example for the curative process which is involved in all penitential activity. The passage from the physical sickness of excessive eating to the healthier, temperate state by means of the healing power of fasting is a metaphor which mirrors the passage from the sickness of sin to the wholeness of virtue through a curative penance.

Gluttony: the Wholesome Antidote, Temperance

The *Old Irish Penitential* also identifies most clearly those virtues which represent the healthy dispositions and actions of one who has overcome greed (OIP.I,c). Included in these are temperance, abstinence, silence, and application to the mysteries of God.[32]

Temperance and the moral life The sins of greed are to be seen as part of this larger framework. Within this framework there are two opposite poles, the one a virtue, the other a vice. The penitent's activity is best described as a journey toward the virtuous pole; in confessing his sin he is not just purified, as it were, by the confessor, but also through dialogue together both come to an awareness of the penitent's particular weakness and, on the basis of this, a course of penitential activity is prescribed.

The purpose of the activity is twofold: it expiates the penitent's greed and promotes his personal growth into the virtuous dispositions of generosity, temperance and care of the poor and needy. There is at once, then, a retrospective and a prospective dimension to the sinner's confession.[33] The sins of the past are called to mind to remind him of his personal greed; but the confessor must also try to steer the penitent toward a new, more generous and temperate spirit.

Temperance as curative Penance which promotes temperance, thus, cannot be seen solely in terms of punishment for gluttony or drunkenness or talkativeness since, by its very nature, it is also curative in that it helps to foster a greater degree of abstinence and self-control in these areas.[34] In practice, however, it seems that individual canons do not fully exploit the richness and wealth of the theology in which they are couched. Therefore, while there is an awareness that feasting the poor and solacing the hungry are potent antidotes to personal greed, the penitentials often stop short of prescribing these measures and opt instead for fasting and enforced silence.

The reasons for this are not explained by the respective authors. We may surmise, however, that fasting and silence insofar as they were readily calculable in terms of hours days and weeks were more attractive to the penitential writers. Moreover, by increasing the penance by days or weeks he could distinguish and demonstrate the various degrees of sinfulness with relative ease.

There was also the further advantage that such penances could be applied equally to all penitents. A penance of feeding the poor and hungry would, by contrast, have to be modified according to the individual's personal resources. Consequently, the penitentials could only recommend this course of penance in very general terms (which in fact they do) and leave its particular application to the discretion and judgement of the confessor.

Temperance and asceticism By placing significant emphasis on fasting and silence the penitentials do, of course, run the risk of overemphasising ascetical activity. Penitents could be tempted to fall into the error of pursuing a rigorous asceticism for its own sake, as an end in itself and thus try, as it were, to merit divine forgiveness.

This danger was all the more likely for, as we have seen, the early Celts had already within their tradition the practice known as fasting by distraint, as a means of obtaining redress from someone who had wronged them.[35] Even in pagan times, however, this practice was only resorted to as a means of restoring justice. Furthermore, the Irish monastery took care to discourage and penalize any over-zealous penitents in this regard. Several texts, for instance, censure those who, due to negligence mistakenly undertake a fast on the sabbath. Such canons demonstrate the belief that there was an appropriate time for fasting and silence and also an equally appropriate time for refraining from all such ascetical activity.[36]

Temperance and discretion Columbanus develops this thought further in his *Regula* where he points out that all penitential activity must be subject to the correct use of 'discretion' (Co.Reg.Mon.III). Thus, it is the function of discretion to moderate ascetical activity as well and to always act so that 'food and drink may both maintain life and not harm'. Fasting may not, then, be pursued as an end in itself; that would be to rob it of its virtuous goal and to render it an instrument of sin: 'For if temperance exceeds measure it will be a vice and not a virtue; for virtue maintains and retains many goods.'[37] Nor were all fasts of the same severity; for example, the *Penitential of Gildas* (Gi.1) describes one fast in rather generous terms as allowing for:

> . . . bread without limitation and a titbit fattened slightly with butter on Sunday; on the other days a ration of dry bread and a dish enriched with a little fat, garden vegetables, a few eggs, British cheese, a Roman half-pint of milk in consideration of the weakness of the body . . . , a Roman pint of whey or buttermilk for his thirst and some water if he is a worker.[38]

It must be said, however, that the penitentials would have usually envisaged much more severe fasts than this. The typical description of a penitential fast is one which enjoins fasting on bread and water and salt (*peniteat cum pane et aqua et sale*) for a given number of days, months or even years (Vi.5. passim). This was to be interpreted strictly and was distinct from a period of abstinence from wine or meat (*abstinere se a uino et carnibus*) or abstinence from other nutritive delicacies (*abstinere se a cibis suculentioribus*).

Temperance and other sins Indeed, fasting was also by far the most common means of doing penance, even for those sins which fell outside the category of *gula*.[39] The term *penitere*, thus, often took the place of *ieunare*, so that, where no other particular form of penance was specified the confessor could assume that fasting was the recommended measure.

The penitentials also make use of the term *superpositio* to indicate a special fast which entailed forgoing the main meal of the day. Columbanus later uses the same term metaphorically when enjoining a penance of silence (Co.A.9).[40] Fasts also become stricter according to the certain times. Thus, there are two major fast days in the week as well as three forty day periods or special penance known as the *quadragesimae*.

Temperance and prayer Despite the preponderance of fasting exercises, the penitential authors did take care to remind the confessor that fasting was to be linked to other spiritual activities, such as seeking pardon from those who had been offended, and from the Lord. Prayer was also encouraged in this way.[42] The penitential manuals, therefore, sought to maintain the focus of the penitent upon the spiritual goal which lay beyond the penitential act in itself.

In adopting the measure of fasting, as a remedy for the sins of intemperance and related vices, Irish monasticism managed to wed traditional Celtic heroism with the early Church's teaching on asceticism. This achievement in itself has, over the years, caught the attention and imagination of several historians of penance.[43]

II. THE SINFUL DISEASE: AVARICE

The vice known as *avaritia* is equated by the penitential authors with the term *filargia*.[44] Both are condemned in the strongest terms. The *Old Irish Penitential* goes so far as to describe it as the root of all vices and it argues that it is on account of this vice that most souls are lost (OIP.III:1,b).[45]

The same penitential resorts to a somewhat poetical turn of phrase to describe the power and intensity with which this vice may besiege the individual Christian. One of the most striking of the images evoked here is that of a hell or great abyss. Avarice, the penitential argues, may be compared to this infernal image since it is capable of swallowing up everything and afterwards; 'it gives up nothing that is cast into it.'[46] The text goes on to employ equally striking and terrifying metaphors in its effort to convey the power which is unleashed by avarice. It is thus variously described as a burning fire, a raging sea, a coiled serpent, a strong dungeon, a poised sword, a hungry lion, a pitfall, a fettering chain, and ultimately the destruction of body and soul.[47]

The earlier Latin penitentials are more restrained in their use of imagery, but remain, nonetheless, equally vehement in their denunciation of the vice. The Bigotian author (Bi.III.pr.) prefaces his treatment of the subject with St Paul's pithy aphorism that: '. . . the love of money is the root of all evils.'(1 Tim 6:12). In this passage, the apostle uses a register of language similar to that of the later penitentials in which the love of money is condemned as a snare into which many people fall and which in turn gives rise to "many hurtful and senseless desires that plunge men into ruin and destruction" (1 Tim 6:9).

Avarice: the Symptoms

There is a common awareness, then, of the pernicious nature of this vice and this is also reflected in the severity of the penances which are enjoined. Cummean, for example, as well as requiring penitents who have stolen property to make due restitution, also prescribes almsgiving, enforced exile, confinement and even, on occasions, excommunication (Cu.III.passim). Let us now examine more closely the sub-divisions of *avaritia* as described in the penitentials.

Stealing Theft is dealt with at length in the course of the penitentials. *Furtum* is the more usual term used to describe the offence but *rapacitas* is later adopted by the Bigotian author and seems to apply as much to the sinful tendency to misappropriate property as to actual instances where this, in fact, has been done.[48] Gildas, who is usually more lenient than his Irish colleagues, prescribes a two-year fast on restricted diet for a junior who steals and a year's fast if the offender is a senior (Gi.6).

The document known as the *Synod of North Britain* develops the subject further and makes provision for recidivists, or repeated offenders. Thus, whereas the simple theft of food here incurs a fast of forty days, a second offence warrants fasting for three forty-day periods, a third a year, and a fourth incurs permanent exile under the direction of another abbot (Aq.4). The author is evidently allowing here for the fact that a penitent may steal more than once. Hence, by gradually increasing the mandatory penance he seeks to eradicate the vice before it has the chance to become firmly enrooted in the sinner's heart.

With the *Penitential of Finnian* comes the first mention of a duty, on the part of the repentant thief, to return what has been ill-gotten (Vi.25). As well as concurring with Gildas' penance of a year's fasting for theft, Finnian also obliges the penitent to make four-fold restitution to the injured party, whom he must in future regard as his neighbour (*proximo suo*).

The inclusion of the latter term is significant. It demonstrates Finnian's anxiety that the sinner should see his misdeed in terms of its contradiction of the Christian's duty to love his neighbour. True conversion could not be achieved simply by righting the wrong and by recompensing the injured party; the sinner himself would have to begin to see others as 'neighbour' in the Christian sense and *eo ipso* deserving of his love.

The duty to restore the violated property rights of another had, of course, long been recognised. The ruling of the penitentials is, by virtue of its severity, reminiscent of some of the legal prescriptions of the Decalogue which provide for two-, four- and also five-fold restitution for thefts and other breaches of trust (Ex 22:1–15). It is not beyond possibility either that Finnian draws his inspiration from the episode of Zacchaeus, the penitent tax-collector, who vows to restore four-fold what he had unjustly taken (Lk 19:8). In any case, we may say that the penitentials sanction those property rights which have now come to be recognised in the threefold principle. '*Res clamat domino, res fructifat domino et res perit domino.*'

Finnian also mitigates the penances for those who are deemed to be habitual thieves (Vi.26).[49] He makes no mention of enforced exile and is also careful to distinguish between those who steal once or twice (*semel vel bis*) and those who do so, on the other hand, out of long habit (*in consuetudine longa*). The contrast between the description of these two degrees of sinfulness suggests that there is also a substantial middle-ground where the confessor may, at his own discretion, prescribe a suitable penance.

Finnian's more severe penances are reserved for those who collect money under false pretences—usually with the excuse of wishing to redeem captives. They are to be firstly reprimanded and then enjoined to do penance for a year. Furthermore, the goods are to be given to the poor and the penitent must, as in the case of simple theft, abstain from wine and meat for a further two years (Vi.30).

The penance is interesting because even in the case where a person has admitted to having despoiled churches and monasteries, the ill-gotten goods must still be distributed to the poor and not returned, as one might expect, to the original owners. Evidently, the penitentials' concern here is to bring about good even out of a situation which was originally evil. The aim is not solely to restore the equilibrium after the sin had been committed, not simply to undo the wrong which had been brought about, but, instead, to also seize upon the opportunity in order that the virtue of the injured party, as well as that of the thief, might be increased. It is almost as though the penitential authors wish to use these instances to remind Christians that all must continuously seek conversion and not alone those who are confessing in a more particular way.

In the case of the unrepentant thief, however, the penitentials deliver a very severe verdict. He is to be excommunicated and branded as anathema to all Christians. Furthermore, he is to be beaten until he is 'converted' (Vi.31). It should be remembered here, all the same, that in this case what is being meted out is not so much a penance as a punishment for one who refuses to acknowledge that what he has done is evil.[50]

Further refinement of the evaluation of theft is to be found in *Columbanus*, who concurs with Finnian's categories of occasional and habitual theft as well as with the penitential fasts, abstentions and principle of restitution. As regards habitual theft, however, Columbanus gives more comprehensive advice. Directives are thus given that the penitent should not communicate again until the Easter of his second year under penance; further, he must give an undertaking not to repeat his sin and he is obliged to give alms to the poor out of the fruits of his own labour (Co.B.19).[51]

The emphasis on almsgiving here is typical of the penitential literature as a whole. The various texts all see the individual Christian as gravely obliged to assist the poor, out of the superfluity of his own wealth.

As usual, Cummean provides the most detailed analysis of all the penitential authors on this subject and he introduces many new categories of sin which are deemed to fall under the heading of avarice. More specifically, on the question of theft he agrees with the foregoing authors but adds that the offender's penance is to be decided according to his age or state of knowledge (Cu.III.2).[52]

This allowance for the penitent's *qualitas eruditionis* is worthy of note since it is a proviso which is frequently referred to in penitential literature.[53] It demonstrates the writer's awareness that not all penitents were equally capable of discerning and understanding what was demanded of them by Church teaching. Clauses therefore, such as '*ut es qualitas eruditionis*' afforded the confessor some considerable freedom in judging for himself the intellectual and penitential capabilities of particular penitents. At a later juncture, Cummean goes on to outline the categories of age more fully. Thus, he distinguishes a small boy from a youth in his twentieth year, the latter being in turn distinguished from one who has arrived at manhood.[54]

In the text known as the *Canons of Adamnan* the faithful are warned not to purchase nor to accept into their possession goods which may have been stolen. The author argues that the 'soldier of Christ' must reject what Christ before him would have rejected because of the dishonest manner of its acquisition (Ad.15). He adds, quite logically, that the suffering endured by the injured party also renders null and void any apparently good intention that a thief may have had, in the event that he subsequently donates his cache to the poor.[55]

Unfortunately, because the text is not a strictly penitential one it merely lays down the precept and gives no further indication of the penance which a 'possessor in bad faith' must carry out, for his sin to be remitted. Neither, for that matter, does it make any provision for the 'possessor in good faith', that is, one who unknowingly and without any malicious intent of his own comes into possession of misappropriated property.

False oaths The earliest mention of false oath-taking and perjury in the Irish penitential material is to be found in the document relating to the *Synod of the Grove of Victory*.[56] One canon here makes provision for those who swear false oaths, lead others to perjury, unknowingly commits perjury and, finally, suspect they may be being led into perjury but swear, nevertheless, in order to honour an agreement (Lu.5). The penances given here are four, seven, one and two years respectively. They reflect an attempt to distinguish between levels of sinfulness.

The last-named scenario, the more interesting one, introduces the notion of the moral dilemma or conflict situation. The sinner is aware that he may be about to commit perjury, yet he must do so in order to honour a previous promise. The author gives no guidelines as to how the individual is to act in such situations. The relatively lenient penance, however, bears testimony to his awareness of the moral complexity of such situations.

In his treatment of the same subject, Finnian points out the gravity of the subject-matter. In typically Celtic, enigmatic style he describes the offence as so great that it can hardly be expiated at all (Vi.22)—clearly giving way to more than a little hyperbole here, for he immediately proceeds to explain precisely how penance is to be done in such cases. Firstly, he stipulates that the sinner must never again take an oath. He supports this directive with excerpts from the following verse drawn from the Book of Sirach: 'A man who swears many oaths will be filled with iniquity and the scourge will not leave his house; if he offends his sin remains on him and if he disregards it he sins doubly' (Sir 23:11). Finnian sees this passage as a stern rebuff to the oath-taker, but he concedes that 'by the medicine of immediate penance' the sinner can hope to avoid 'perpetual pains in the future'.[57] Accordingly, he prescribes a life free of further oath-taking, seven years of penitential fasting and the setting free of a servant or maidservant, or else the donation of their equivalent value to the poor.[58]

Whilst drawing his biblical citations from the Old Testament, Finnian's teaching seems more closely allied with New Testament doctrine. His prohibition on oath-taking echoes Jesus' directive to his followers: 'Do not swear at all . . . Let what you say be simply "Yes" or "No"; anything more than this comes from evil.' (Mt 5:34–7). The monastic authors are, therefore, aiming at a situation where oath-taking becomes less and less important as a result of the increasing honesty among the Christian community.

The subject is carried a stage further still by Columbanus. As well as concurring with the severe tones of Finnian, he also outlines a specific penance for lay people who confess their guilt. Their penance is very severe; they are to sell all their property, take the tonsure, enter a monastery and leave the world for good. However, this applies only where the perjury was committed because of the sinner's own greed (*per cupiditatem*: Co.B.20).

Where the motive, was not one of greed but of fear, the penitent is enjoined to a three-year penitential fast in unarmed exile and a further two-year abstinence from wine and meat; finally, for a further two years he must strive to free slaves, give much alms and continue to abstain from meat. Only after the seventh year is the penitent to be allowed communicate again.[59]

The Bigotian author's analysis of this subject draw's heavily on the doctrine both of Columbanus and Theodore. The latter had attempted to distinguish in some way between the various levels of oath-taking. Hence, oaths which are sworn in a church or on the hand of a bishop, priest or deacon are, he believes, to be regarded very differently from those sworn on the hand of an 'ordinary' man. In the latter case Theodore deems that there is really no oath at all (*nihil est*: Bi.III:3,2–3).[60]

Clearly, the later authors are here trying to make a distinction between valid oaths and doubtful expressions and commitments which are evidently not to be regarded as oaths at all. The penitentials are here presuming in favour of the sinner and surmising that the handshake was not the sign of an intention to swear, but rather more the expression of a traditional gesture which may have been carried out without sufficient aforethought.

False witness The more usual term to describe dishonest speech of a non-oath character is 'false witness'. This term is to be found much more frequently than *mendacio*, which only appears in the later documents.[61] Penitents guilty of this sin are given a mandatory penance of two years fasting, 'together with loss or restitution of the object in dispute'.[62] Presumably, the penitentialists are referring here to a case where one dishonestly claims ownership of an item. For the penance to be efficacious the principle of restitution must be honoured and the sinner must learn to surrender what he had originally sought to seize for his own private gain.

The term 'false witness' assumes its more usual meaning in Cummean's manual; namely, wrongly accusing or imputing something of another. His response is interesting and twofold. First, peace must be made with the injured party and then the offender must undertake to do penance for the very same charge with which he had originally accused the other. In other words, the sinner is seen to be guilty of the fault which in malice he had sought to attribute to his brother (Cu.III.12). The penitential thus logically concludes that since the sin is indeed a product of the offender's imagination he must do penance for it as though he had committed it in fact.[63]

The Bigotian author, in turn, repeats this canon in its entirety. He also goes on to deal with the related topic of lying. He prefaces his brief treatment of the subject by recalling the following words of Solomon in the Book of Wisdom 'a lying mouth destroys the soul' (Wis 1:11). He links the sin also with the vice of greed and affirms that anyone who lies for this reason (*pro cupiditate*) must make satisfaction to the person he has cheated (Bi.III:5,1–2).

Here again, it seems that the penitential considers the principal cause of the sin to be the underlying greed. The lie misleads the other person into pursuing actions, or adopting dispositions, which may be prejudicial to him but favourable to the offender. Hence, the lie offends against the injured party's dignity and for this reason the penitential directs that satisfaction be made to him. Ultimately, the victim has been robbed of a part of his human dignity because of the greed of the offender who sought personal gain at the expense of his brother.

On the other hand, the penitential literature does not attempt to demonstrate that lying is of itself grievously sinful. The emphasis, instead, always seems to rest on the underlying avaricious motive rather than the breach of truth in itself. Accordingly, in two subsequent canons where there is no mention of greed as the ulterior motive, penances are surprisingly lenient—an hour of silence for the person who lies out of ignorance and three days of silence or thirty psalms where the lie was intentional (Bi.III:5,3).

Inhumanity The term 'inhumanity' has a very particular meaning in the penitential texts. It is introduced in the *Bigotian Penitential* and is used to describe the person who fails to show fraternal love through, what moralists of a later age would have called, the corporal works of charity. (Bi.III.pr.tit.6). The exact phrase used by the Bigotian author and Cummean is: 'He who fails to fulfil any of those things for which the Lord will say: "Come ye blessed of my father, etc.", for whatever time he has continued thus he shall do penance'.[64]

The text referred to here is taken from the Gospel of Matthew where Jesus speaks of the end time:

> Then the king will say to those at his right hand, 'Come O blessed of my father, inherit the kingdom prepared for you from the foundation of the world; for I was hungry and you gave me food, I was thirsty and you gave me drink, I was a stranger and you welcomed me, I was naked and you clothed me, I was sick and you visited me, I was in prison and you came to me' (Matt 25:34–5).

This passage is a summary of what has come to be described as the corporate works of charity. It demonstrates the fundamental Christian calling to reach out in love to others in need or who lack the facilities, resources or support to lead a truly human life.

The thrust of Christian charity has, through the ages, been recognised as one which consoles the poor with eager care and relief. It is, therefore, a truly humanising force and it is perhaps for this reason that the monastic author describes actions which lack this virtue as works of inhumanity. This fault is also clearly rooted in avarice and selfishness. It translates itself into an inhuman disregard for the welfare of others. For this reason, the penitentials seek to correct it with the proviso that in the future the penitent shall become a 'liberal donor'.[65] Moreover, should he fail in this matter he is to be cut off from the community irrespective of whether he be lay or cleric.[66]

The texts, however, do not give any indication as to just what is to be considered necessary and what superfluous, but it is probable that this judgement was left to the confessor. The penitential author is evidently concerned though to bring about a total conversion or *metanoia* in the heart of the sinner. It is not sufficient for the penitent merely to do penance, even arduous penance: he must make profound changes in his whole outlook upon life; he must be prepared to give to the poor and to be of a generous disposition for the rest of his life.

Usury In common with much early and medieval theology, there is some evidence that the penitentials considered the taking of interest for loaned money or merchandise to be unjust and hence to be regarded as usury.[67] We have already noted how the penitentials display a keen awareness of Old Testament precepts where the practice of interest taking is also frequently denounced.[68] Nevertheless, the practice is not deemed to be sufficiently grave or widespread as to warrant a mention by most of the penitential authors. The only place where it is expressly referred to, in fact, is the *Excerpts from a Book of David* where it is forbidden and a penance imposed whereby money earned in this way must be surrendered (Da.13).[69]

Avarice: the Penitential Remedy

In seeking to counter the vice of avarice the penitentials most frequently resort to the imposition of periods of fasting or abstinence. We have already discussed why such manner of penance was favoured by monastic confessors. Nonetheless, it has been clear from our analysis of this topic, that here too the penitential authors strive hard to implement the doctrine of Cassian. So, just as there are many different symptoms of spiritual disease and just as there are various ways in which the vice may manifest itself, so too there are a variety of means by which avarice may be overcome.

Remedial penances The treatment of this subject is in complete accord with Columbanus' axiom that a 'diversity of offences causes a diversity of penances'.[70] Accordingly, in addition to fasting and abstinence, the penitentials also have recourse to many other measures in their efforts to offset the various expressions of avarice. Among these measures are: restitution, almsgiving, donation of possessions, chastisement, confinement, imposition of silence, enforced exile, liberation of servants and in extreme cases even excommunication.[71]

The nature and severity of the penances set forth here concur with their authors' claims that avarice is the root of other vices. The remedial measures all seek to turn the sinner away from a selfish preoccupation with his own needs and to urge him instead to reach out to others whose need may be greater. The penitential authors are keenly aware that the sin of the avaricious person represents most typically what happens in all sinful activity. In turning toward himself and his possessions, the sinner turns away from his neighbour and ultimately from God. In seeking to hoard what he considers to be of great value the sinner abandons and loses the only value which is ultimately worth seeking. Columbanus explains:

> Wretched man . . . do not prefer your possessions to yourself. Love your person more than your property, your soul more than your wealth . . . For what is your own except your soul? Then do not lose your one possession for the sake of naught. (Co.Inst.III)[72]

He exhorts the sinner, in this vein, to come to his senses, lest in caring only for material wealth and possessions he becomes ever more deeply ensnared in the web of sin. For, as with all forms of sin, avarice is a disease: either the sinner by penance and fasting begins to cure himself, or the vice strengthens its stranglehold upon him and eventually corrupts his whole spiritual life.

> . . . (monks) should be satisfied with small possessions of utter need, knowing that greed is a leprosy for monks who copy the sons of the prophets, and for the disciple of Christ it is revolt and ruin, for the uncertain followers of the apostles also it is death. (Co.Reg.Mon.IV)[73]

Penances focussing upon others Many of the penances prescribed in this way by the penitentials have as their principal focus other people and especially the poor. There can be no half way measures in the cure of avarice which is rooted in selfishness. Either the sinner learns to avert his gaze away from self and towards God again, or he remains a victim of vice. Thus, in conformity with Cassian's doctrine of cure by contraries the penitentials seek not only to eradicate the vice of avarice but at the same time to replace it with a spirit of generosity, kindness and concern for others.

The fact is that for the penitential authors there can be no middle ground, no neutral state where one is cured of greed but not yet committed to a spirit of generosity.[74] In combating greed one must employ generosity because the two are but different poles of one continuum. In diagnosing the cause of the penitent's malady, the confessor has the task of eliminating the sinner's illness and also leading him toward the corresponding virtuous state.[75]

Avarice: the Wholesome Antidote, Generosity

Although the penitential texts, by their very nature, tend not to contain much 'positive' teaching, this is not entirely the case in their analysis of avarice.

Generosity and the individual Finnian avails himself of the opportunity to point out some of the duties of the Christian with regard to his material possessions. He ordains that money be spent on the redemption of captives and also on fruitful help to the poor and needy. In another canon he reminds his followers that they are obliged to show generosity to all who are in need; specifically mentioned here are pilgrims, the sick and prisoners (Vi.32–33).[76]

His teaching is based loosely on Chapter 25 of Matthew's Gospel and in particular on those verses where Christ reminds his followers that in feeding the hungry, clothing the naked, curing the sick, and visiting prisoners they render, in effect, the same service onto him. Finnian describes this as a teaching of the Church, and the importance he attaches to it is witnessed by the fact that this is the only time he devotes canons of 'positive' teaching without reference to penance of any form.

Generosity and the Christian community Finnian's aim is to describe the attitude and outlook upon life which is to be adopted by all who seek to embrace the Christian message. For the saint, these things are not a matter of option but rather of obligation and he refers to the Letter to the Hebrews where it is written: 'For all shall know me from the least unto the greatest' (Heb 8:11). Evidently, Finnian has in mind a situation where the poor and weak are cared for by the stronger members of the Christian community. In such a state of affairs self-love would be replaced by other-centredness and avaricious behaviour would give way to a spirit of generosity.

Columbanus shares this vision and describes 'nakedness and disdain for riches' as the 'first perfection of monks'. In his *Rule* and *Penitential* he urges his followers to be hospitable and to serve others with all diligence. Monks are to display a generosity toward guests and pilgrims despite the austerity of their own lives (Co.Reg.Coen.VIII).[77]

Generosity and charity Moreover, they are to be at all times 'unwearying in charity'. This charity must be born out of discernment. It must be a humble love which reaches out to the lowly, *amator mediocrium*. His vision is one of a unified Christian attitude where all will be one in spirit and where, he wishes, 'all men's wills to be in agreement, as also their way of life so that they may have true peace and unbroken charity' (Co.Inst.VI).

Similarly, the *Old Irish Penitential* is sure of the goal which must be striven towards. It urges Christians to be generous, taking the Gospel message to heart and freeing oneself from one's possessions. 'As for him who desires to reach the pitch of perfection he distributes all he has to the poor and needy and goes on pilgrimage or lives in destitution in a communal church 'till he goes to heaven' (OIP.III.6).[78]

Generosity and the religious life Likewise, those who have already committed themselves to the religious life are asked to continually examine their habits and lifestyles, lest their initial enthusiasm wane and they begin to become ensnared again by the vice of avarice. They too must seek a more perfect expression of their commitment to the Gospel message: 'A cleric or nun who lives in a communal church and has somewhat more than suffices him/her, let him/her give it to the poor and needy of the Church where he lives' (OIP.III.10).[79]

It should be pointed out, here, that the Irish monasteries of the earliest period would have been quite poor and should not be equated in terms of the amount of wealth and property with later Irish and European establishments which benefited from donations by kings, princes and other rulers.[80]

Despite the emphasis on the poverty, the Irish monk was not permitted to beg since this was deemed to offend his human dignity. This was an ancient rule of Irish monasticism and one which underlines the more humane and discerning side of their spirituality. Evidently, the vision of a truly Christian society espoused by the early Irish monastic fathers was one in which the dignity of all should be preserved and none should be forced to beg for their livelihood.[81]

III. THE SINFUL DISEASE: ANGER

Anger embraces a wide range of sub-divisions within the penitential literature; among these are included parricide, murder, suicide, abortion, physical injury, hatred, strife, curses, insults and clamour.[82] The *Old Irish Penitential* uses the image of a weapon which pierces a human body to describe how anger swiftly penetrates the soul, thereby corrupting it and leading eventually to spiritual death (OIP.V:1a).[83]

In similar fashion, Gildas describes the person who harbours anger in his heart as being in a state of death (Gi.17–18). For this reason, he requires that the behaviour of any monk under the influence of wrath be reported to the abbot by his brothers 'not indeed in the spirit of an accuser, but of a physician'.[84] Anger is seen as a malaise which seizes upon the individual, leading ultimately to a violent expression of his feelings and even, at times to murder.

Finnian agrees with Gildas on this point (Vi.29). He describes wrathfulness as a capital sin and one of several which 'slay the soul and cast it down to the depth of hell'.[85] It must be cured by the practice of the 'contrary virtues' which are, according to him, patience, gentleness and mercifulness. He cites from the Letter of St James to illustrate his point:

> Know this my beloved brethren. Let every man be quick to hear, slow to speak, slow to anger, for the anger of man does not work the

righteousness of God. Therefore put away all filthiness and rank growth of wickedness and receive with meekness the implanted word which is able to save your souls. (Jas 1:19–21.)[86]

This text, in common with the penitential literature, juxtaposes anger with meekness. The former is to be resisted, the latter cultivated. Meekness is not seen as a sign of moral timidity nor is it equated with weakness or shyness in the sense that modern usage of the term sometimes connotes. In fact, the opposite is true: the person who is given to anger is to patiently learn how to dominate and control his emotions so that he is capable of responding with gentleness and reason to a situation which might otherwise have provoked an irrational and violent outburst.

This teaching is also advocated by Cummean, who describes anyone allowing hatred to foster within them as a murderer (Cu.IV.4).[87] Here he draws on the theology of St John who reasons thus:

We know that we have passed out of death into life because we love the brethren. He who does not love his brother is a murderer and you know that no murderer has eternal life abiding in him. (1 Jn 3:14–15)

Again, this passage places the emphasis on the contrast of opposing moral states—the state of hatred, to be countered by love; that of death, which is opposed to eternal life. And again, the thrust of the exhortation is clear: the Christian is to make a choice either to live in hatred and die in sin, or to live in love and win eternal life.

Anger: the Symptoms

For the true Christian, of course, there can be only one option, namely to seek to grow out of a negative hatred and resentment and toward a positive, life-giving love. This is the context in which the penitential texts choose to place their discussion of the various sins which arise out of anger and of the penances which are to remedy them.

Murder Murder is the greatest crime arising out of a wrathful disposition.[88] The earliest reference to it is to be found in the text known as the *Synod of the Grove of Victory*. This document distinguishes between murder which has been carried out with malice aforethought (*ex odii meditatione*) and that which was born of sudden anger (*iracondia subita*: Lu.2).[89] For the first category we are given no indication of what penance is to be undertaken; for the second the penitent must undertake a penitential fast lasting three years.

Unlawful killing is also referred to briefly in the *David* text, where the author uses it to demonstrate the various degrees of penitential censure which can apply according to the office and status of the murderer (Da.7,11). The Irish manuals beginning with *Finnian* afford a more detailed analysis of the subject. Finnian adopts the earlier Welsh distinction regarding foreknowledge and passionate outbursts (Vi.23).

The most serious type of premeditated murder is deemed to warrant a ten-year period of exile coupled with various degrees of fasting. This must be accomplished to the satisfaction of the priest or abbot. Even then the expiation is still not complete: upon his return to his own community he must seek out his victim's parents or family and offer himself by way of compensation for the son or brother that was lost. He must then undertake whatever tasks the family should ask of him.

The latter requirement was known as the *pietatis obsequia* and had a parallel in Irish law.[90] There was also another custom in early Irish society whereby a youth who was about to enter the monastery had first to honour, as it were, his filial debts and responsibilities to his parents before he could freely engage in the monastic life.

Here, however, Finnian seems to be adapting this ancient usage for a new purpose. The repentant killer, having already repented for having taken another's life, is now asked to offer his own life in a form of practical repayment or atonement for his sin. Thus, he must carry out the tasks and duties which his victim would otherwise have done had he still been alive. His willingness to surrender control of his own life in this manner to his victim's parents is evidence of his true conversion. The selfish and malicious motives which had formerly dominated his behaviour now give way to a more other-centered, altruistic attitude.

Hence, in 'becoming' in some sense the person he has killed, the sinner has turned full circle and begins to undo the evil he committed (Vi.23). The words with which he is to place himself at the disposition of his victim's parents are equally telling: 'Lo, I am in the place of your son; I will do for you whatever you tell me.'[91] These words testify to an openness to obedience and to a humility which would not have been possible for the sinner when he killed his victim.

Further, the penance is also of interest insofar as it challenges the victim's parents to overcome their grief and resentment. To receive their son's killer into their service they must overcome the hatred and vengefulness which might otherwise be their attitude toward him. Here again, the penitential author is striving to bring about the greatest possible good from a situation where evil is done. We shall see in fact that the idea or principle of maximising good is a measure which these texts invoke with great frequency.

Instead of allowing hatred to be fostered, leading to anger and possible further bloodshed, efforts are made to break the cycle of sin and to foment real reconciliation. The disposition toward malicious behaviour is cured by concrete virtuous action, blind hatred is turned into a Christian expression of love which learns to see things from the other's perspective, and the desire for revenge gives way to reciprocal forgiveness and acceptance.

By contrast, killings which were not born out of long-fostered hatred receive a much more lenient penance. Finnian distinguishes carefully here between various putative scenarios (Vi.24). He refers to the situation where two people were friends but because of a sudden burst of anger or diabolical temptation (*instincto diaboli obreptione*) one kills the other.[92] The penance prescribed by Finnian here amounts to six years exile, three years of which must be spent fasting and the other half abstaining from wine and meat.

Finnian also refers to the hypothetical case where a monk begets a child and then, for one reason or another, subsequently kills it (Vi.12–13). He considers this situation to be doubly sinful since it involves both fornication and homicide (Magnum est crimen fornicatio et homicidium). Accordingly, he enjoins a nine-year period involving various degrees of fasting, seven of which must be spent in exile. At the end of this term it falls to the abbot or bishop to decide whether the sinner should be restored to his former status. Great emphasis is placed on the need for a genuine attitude of remorse and contrition throughout the penitential period as well as constant prayer and supplication for divine mercy.[93]

Finnian's teaching is repeated by Columbanus in its entirety. He does, however, add the rider that if the sinner refuses to place himself in the service of his victim's parents he is not to be allowed return to his native land but instead must 'like Cain . . . be a wanderer and fugitive upon the earth'[94] (Co.B.1). The 'sentence' is however mitigated by a later canon in the same text which reduces the number of years, but retains the notion of mandatory exile and compensation for the injured party's family through filial piety (Co.B.13).

The practice is not, however, continued by Cummean, who instead introduces a further category of unlawful killing (Cu.IV.5–8). This now brings the number of such categories to three. The first refers to the scenario where the killer nurses hatred in his heart and eventually kills his victim. The second describes the act which is carried out in a sudden passionate outburst. The third is one of accidental killing where the killer had no intention of harming his victim and the death was brought about accidentally. Cummean acknowledges the absence of a malicious motive by prescribing the lenient penance of a year's penitential fasting. Whilst discarding the obligation to render compensation to the victim's parents, he nonetheless adds some new penitential requirements of his own, namely almsgiving and forfeiture of arms.

The moral evaluation of unlawful killing is expanded still further by the Bigotian author. He distinguishes first between parricide and other forms of murder and prescribes a heavier penalty for this (Bi.IV.1). In his discussion of the other kinds of unlawful killing he repeats the teaching of Theodore, who had enjoined a seven- to ten-year penance for vengeful killing. The notion of compensation to a victim's family is also re-introduced. It now takes the form of a monetary repayment rather than the penitent offering his own services. Whilst such payment may reduce the sinner's penitential burden it cannot eliminate it altogether.[95]

The killing of clergy is given special attention. Thus, someone guilty of murdering a monk or cleric is ordered to lay down his arms and to spend the rest of his life serving God, or else undertake a seven-year penitential fast. Whichever of these penances is opted for, they must be carried out 'according to the spirit of forgiveness of the New Testament' (Bi.IV:1,2).[96] It is not immediately clear whether the author has a particular text in mind here. New Testament doctrine considers unbounded, sincere and authentic forgiveness to be a distinctive and primary duty of Christian fraternal love. This duty is referred to in the 'Our Father' text (Mt 6:12–15), which affirms that we must be as ready to forgive others as we are to receive forgiveness for our own offences. In the parable of the unforgiving servant (Mt 18:23–5) we are given an allegorical interpretation of the same teaching. And Paul reiterates the point when he teaches: 'Let all bitterness and wrath and anger and slander be put away from you, with all malice, and be kind to one another, as God in Christ forgave you' (Eph 4:31–2).

Evidently, the ideal is that Christians should forgive each other, thus bearing witness to divine mercy. And it is this ideal which the Bigotian author has in mind when he advises that the killer of a monk or cleric should serve out his days in the 'service of God'. The sinner is being challenged to do a *volte-face* and to embrace with generosity and commitment that which had previously provoked him to hatred, anger and violence. Similarly, the monastic community, by having the reformed evil-doer in their midst, are challenged to overcome their natural hostility toward him and to accept him with forgiveness and mercy.

The same penitential also makes brief mention of the murder of priests or bishops (Bi.IV:1,3). The text points out that these crimes by law come under the jurisdiction of the king (*regis iudicium deco est*) and gives no further ruling on the matter. One can surmise, though, that the crime would automatically be punished with considerable severity by the civil power so that the confessor could then, at his own discretion, decide what further penitential activity would be required in order to effect a spiritual cure.

Finally, the same manual also rules that killing in the course of warfare warrants a penance of forty days. The leniency of the penalty here suggests that the author is aware of the conflict of values which are at issue in a time of war, namely those of respect for human life and defence of the common welfare. The point, however, is not elaborated upon by any of the penitential authors.

Suicide Suicide is recognised as a separate section to be classified under the general heading of sins of anger.[97] Not much is written on the matter for the very obvious reason that there was no possibility of it being confessed. The question does arise, however, as to what the faithful's attitude should be toward those who have taken their own lives.

The Bigotian author, once again referring to Theodore, distinguishes suicide brought about because the individual was 'vexed by the devil' and suicide as a result of despair (Bi.IV:2,1). He deems that the souls of those pertaining to the first category may be prayed for, whilst those belonging to the second may not. Further, those who intentionally take their own life are not to have mass offered on their behalf, but prayers and alms may be offered nevertheless for the repose of their souls.[98] No mention is made of putative instances where the Christian may have to lay down his life for the sake of a greater good. Instead, all the scenarios referred to involve the direct taking of one's own life, on one's own authority.

Despair is deemed to be the root cause of this sin. However, since most of the texts devote a separate section to the study of despair under the heading *Tristitia* the subject is not explored in any great depth at this juncture.

Abortion Abortion, of a sort, is referred to by the Bigotian text (Bi.IV:2,2–3). The term *abortio* is never used; instead, phrases which suggest the destruction or expulsion of the foetus from the womb are preferred.[99] Penances prescribed for the sin range from three years in one instance to fourteen years in another.

The *Penitential of Finnian* goes some way toward explaining the huge discrepancy in terms of length of penance. This text refers to the hypothetical case of a woman who 'by her magic destroys the child she has conceived' and prescribes a half year's penitential fast plus various other requirements (Vi.20).[100] In terms of Finnian's other pronouncements on wilful murder, however, the penance prescribed here is remarkably lenient. The only reasonable conclusion to be made here is that Finnian did not accord to the foetus the same status as a human being after the moment of birth.

This theory also helps shed light on the later Bigotian text which prescribes, as we have said, three years' penance 'for the destruction of the embryo of a child in the mother's womb' and fourteen years' 'for the destruction of flesh and spirit in the womb' (Bi.IV:2,2–3).[101] The variation in the terms employed here to describe the unborn child is quite telling. The implication is that in the first instance the author wishes to denote an early phase of the foetus' development where he believes it has not yet attained the status of a normal human being. In the second instance, by contrast, the use of the terms 'flesh and spirit' seems to describe a subsequent stage of development by which time human life is now deemed to be present. The text, however, gives us no indication as to the limits of each of these phases.

For a clarification of this issue we must turn to the English *Penitential of Theodore*, which explains: 'A woman who conceives and slays her child in the womb within forty days shall do penance for one year; but if later than forty days she shall do penance as a murderess' (Te.XIV.27). Another canon points out even more explicitly: 'Women who commit abortion before (the foetus) has life, shall do penance for one year . . .; more than forty days after conception they shall do penances as murderesses . . .' (Te.XIV.24).

It is evident then that in the later penitential literature authors are already beginning to grapple with the issues as to when the precise beginning of human life is to be set and consequently from which time the foetus may be considered a human being in the strict sense. Their contention is that the fortieth day marks the limit between an inanimate human foetus and the presence of a live human being. In view of this distinction, they cannot speak of abortion in the strict sense before forty days have elapsed; hence, the extraordinary variation in the corresponding penances to be assigned. After the forty-day period, however, all abortions seem to be treated as wilful murder and there is no attempt by any of the authors to allow for mitigating circumstances.[102]

Strife The problem of contention and strife leading ultimately to physical injury is dealt with at length by many texts.[103]

Finnian rules that any cleric who harbours ill-will toward his neighbour or strikes him is in fact a murderer of sorts (Vi.8).[104] He bases his judgement on the words of St John: 'Anyone who hates his brother is a murderer, and you know that no murderer has eternal life abiding in him' (1 Jn 3:15). As well as doing the prescribed penitential fast—one year for clerics, forty days for laity—the penitent is exhorted to 'pray in weeping and tears' that he might attain God's mercy.[105]

If a layman goes so far as to strike someone he must, in addition to his fast, also offer some financial compensation to the victim.[106] A cleric is not permitted to do this but is to be deprived of his office for a year.

These penances are subsequently increased and made more specific by Columbanus, who prescribes three years penance for the monk who causes bloodshed (*sanguinem fuderit*). He also reiterates the principle of payment of compensation, discussing this in greater depth than Finnian and ruling that the offender must restore to his victim the value of all damage which he has caused. Where the penitent does not have the wherewithal to offer financial recompense, he must undertake to do the injured party's work and to ensure he receives adequate medical attention until such time as he is recovered (Co.B.21).[107]

Thus, where a Christian has caused physical injury and harm it is not sufficient for him to perform a merely symbolic gesture of repentance. This approach is repeated and developed by Cummean who enjoins payment of medical expenses as well (Cu.IV.9–10). Only in the event that a penitent is deemed physically incapable of carrying out these tasks, is he to be allowed to do the alternative penance of a year's fasting.[108]

Cursing and quarrel-making Less serious expressions of anger such as cursing, quarrelling and raised temper are also censured by the penitential texts.[109] Cummean admonishes those who curse or use injurious language. In all such cases, the need for making satisfaction to one's opponent is constantly stressed. Penances range from one day to seven days' fasting, but the more onerous task is that of making peace with the erstwhile enemy. The text rules that even those who merely feel incensed must make satisfaction to those who have annoyed them.

Thus, while it is true that these texts often deal with gruesome and indeed macabre offences, on this occasion, they prove to be equally adroit at detecting and remedying sinful behaviour in its most subtle of forms (Cu.IV.15).[110] Cummean lays great store on the necessity of admitting one's guilt to the other party. He sees this as an indication that the penitent has the strength to overcome his weaknesses and his personal likes and dislikes. By the same token, refusal to make such an admission is considered to be a recipe for more sinful activity.

It is as if the resentment fostered by the sinner wounds his moral life and continues to foment and breed new forms of corruption both in himself and in those who come into contact with him. No penance, affirms Cummean, can effect a cure in one who remains so recalcitrant (Cu.IV.3). Until he is capable of overcoming his hatred and reaching out to the other person in love, he will remain incurable, becoming progressively more contagious, a source of sin and spiritual disease to his community. For this reason, he is to be cut off from his community: 'He however who will not confess to him who has incensed him, that pestilential person shall be cut off from the company of the saints.'[111]

The Bigotian text adopts, in large measure, Cummean's provisions; it stops short but of imposing exile on the recalcitrant quarreller, ruling instead that he should fast on bread and water for as long as he remains implacable (Bi.IV.4). The text also foresees a situation whereby, despite the best intentions and efforts of the penitent, the other party may refuse his reconciliatory overtures. In this event, it rules that that the penitent be allowed to undertake an alternative penance according to the judgement of a priest. It further rules that the other must also do penance now because of his stubborn refusal to make peace.

This is further evidence of the typical Celtic penitential strategy to challenge the injured party as well as the repentant sinner. The expiation of the sinful act is exploited to the full so that the good is maximised, yielding rich dividends in the lives both of the penitent and of his opponent and taking them both to a new degree of spiritual health.

Clamour The Bigotian text identifies clamour as a further off-spring of anger.[112] In essence, the description of the offence does not differ greatly from that of sins belonging to the previous section. It does seem, however, that the emphasis is being placed here on the disruptive aspect and the excessive rowdiness of the angry person as opposed to the particular content of his words.

In any case, it is left to the confessor's own discretion to decide what type and degree of penance is appropriate here. The text avails of the occasion to remind him that clamour is but the external symptom of an underlying spiritual malady which must be healed by silence and fasting (Bi.IV:6,1).

Anger: the Penitential Remedy

The treatment of the sins of anger, in the penitentials, is perhaps one of the best examples of their application of Cassian's 'cure by contraries'. Almost all expressions of anger, from the very violent to the extremely subtle forms, are to be countered with a sincere effort on the part of the penitent not alone to do penance but also to attempt to undo the harm he has done.

Anger cured by its contraries Thus, he must try to replace quarrelsomeness with understanding, noisiness with silence, destructive activity with compensation, injury with medical attention, angry words with words of forgiveness, threats with forfeiture of arms and murder with an offer of one's own time and effort in lieu of the victim's. Penances such as exile, prayer, almsgiving, fasting, abstinence and deprivation of clerical office are also prescribed, but the underlying emphasis remains one which moves away from merely symbolic acts and towards constructive activity to repair the damage caused by uncontrolled passion.

A resolute determination is shown, on the part of the penitential authors, not alone to correct the penitents sinful activity but also to break the cycle of destruction and strife this normally begets. They are keenly aware that the seed of anger must be quelled in both penitent and opponent, for if it is allowed to fester and develop a whole community can become infected.

Given the clan structure of early Irish society, it was essential that the monastic brethren, who saw themselves as moral guardians, should take some steps toward reducing the possibility of revenge, recriminations and bitter vendettas.[113] All of these forms of rivalry were at one time commonplace in Irish society and, indeed, much folklore is based around inter-clan fighting and feuding for the sake of family honour.

Penance as a true change of heart However, the penances prescribed in the penitential texts are far from being mere measures of political expedience. The sinner is, instead, challenged to swallow his pride and his anger and admit his sin to his opponent. He must be prepared moreover to give proof of his personal change of heart by his actions and personal sacrifices. In offering himself as the breadwinner for his opponent's family the penitent not only suffers the ignominy and embarrassment of being the servant of his one-time enemy, but must also sacrifice the earnings which would rightly have been his were he free to carry out his own work. This provision for sick maintenance was long a feature of brehon law and the transition to penitential literature would, therefore, have been a relatively easy one.

The various expressions of anger, whatever their form, all display an inability on the sinner's part to control his emotion's. Therefore, by enjoining a penance which entailed regular contact with his opponent, the confessor challenged the solidity of his conversion and gave him a means by which he could grow in personal control and maturity.

In this context, the more usual penances of fasts and abstinence would also play an important role since they constituted a useful aid in teaching the penitent how to overcome and dominate his bodily appetites and desires. This would seem to be precisely the reasoning of the Bigotian author when he declares: 'And that murderer who hates his brother shall go on bread and water as long as he does not overcome his hatred and he shall be joined to him whom he hates in sincere [*non ficta*] charity' (Bi.IV.4).[114] The choice of the term *non ficta* here to describe the charitable disposition augurs against a false or feigned conciliation. The apology and admission of guilt must not be a merely mechanical ritual. Otherwise, the penitential cure cannot be effective and penance must be continued until the penitent has an authentic change of heart. None of the reconciliatory activities prescribed by the various manuals are to be taken as token or symbolic gestures but as real expressions of a true conversion. Without such a profound conversion, the spiritual life is moribund and no amount of external gestures will suffice to save it:

> Then let each beware, lest for an angry criticism his root be exterminated from the land of the living. For no one ever criticises him whom he loves; for criticism is the first-born of anger and thus the son of such a father ought justly to be exterminated. It is a dangerous dwelling . . . in which these things are not shunned . . . For if he who loves not is in death, where shall he be who criticises? (Co.Inst.XI.)[115]

In this way, Columbanus underlines in striking terms the necessity for a sincere contrition and conversion. There is no room for ambiguity; either the penitent determines to root out the vice of anger from his heart and grows toward a maturer Christian disposition or he remains a prisoner of his passion and faces certain spiritual death.

Anger: the Wholesome Antidote, Meekness

The *Old Irish Penitential* affirms that meekness and gentleness are the virtues which have been appointed to combat the sins of anger (OIP.V:1,c). It goes on to list various other expressions of these virtues such as patience, zeal, benevolence and docility.[116] Cummean advocates an attitude of mercifulness and describes this as one of the means by which sins may be remitted (Cu.III.10). He cites from Christ's teaching in the Sermon on the Mount and, in particular, the verse: 'Blessed are the merciful for they shall obtain mercy' (Mt 5:7).

Meekness and forgiveness He goes on (Cu.III.12) to urge a spirit of pardon and forgiveness, this time drawing on Luke: 'Judge not, and you will not be judged, condemn not and you will not be condemned, forgive and you will be forgiven' (Lk 6:37). Cummean is anxious that a spirit of mercifulness should prevail amongst his monastic brethren. He sees these as Gospel values which are capable of healing the baser, uncontrolled instincts and passions which lead us into sin. Mercifulness and forgiveness are the contraries with which anger and stubborness of heart must be overcome.

The Bigotian text reinforces Cummean's teaching with an excerpt from Corinthians where Paul reminds his brothers that: 'Love is kind and not provoked by anger' (Bi.pr.60–61). He also draws upon the

Rule of Benedict to point out what this concretely means for the monk and what sort of behaviour will be expected of him:

> . . . to put nothing before the love of Christ, not to do according to one's anger, to bear no falsehood in one's heart, not to give a false peace . . . , not to return evil for evil, not to do wrong and to suffer the wrong incurred . . . , not to love quarrel, not to hate anyone, to turn away from thinking oneself important.[117]

The message here is, clearly, a résumé of all that the penitentials have sought to put into practice in combating anger.

Meekness and peace Peace, too, is the term chosen by Columbanus in his homiletical material on this topic. He sees peace as a dynamic concept and not something which can be brought about by passivity on the part of the Christian (Co.Inst.XI): one must strive to create peace; the monks, says Columbanus, must be living images of peace in the manner that Christ himself once exemplified peace. It is a difficult task, he believes, to create a situation where such peace reigns, because it can be so easily destroyed by a thoughtless word or gesture: 'The most valuable things require the most care and the surer keeping.'[118] And yet the challenge remains a clear one; it does not suffice that a penitent should put away his sinfulness: he must strive to grow into a living image of Christ. For everyone espouses a particular image, whether good or bad, and he who does not choose to put on Christ may very well end up showing forth the image of a despot:

> Then lest perhaps we should import into ourselves despotic images, let Christ paint his image in us, as he docs by saying, My peace I give to you, my peace I leave to you. But what advantage is it for us to know that peace is good, if it is not well preserved? For each best gift is usually the frailest, and the most valuable things require the most care and surer keeping; for a thing is over-frail that is lost by light talk and perishes with the slightest injury of a brother.[119]

IV. THE SINFUL DISEASE: DEJECTION

Tristitia, or dejection, fits very snugly into the theory of virtues and vices as opposite poles of a single reality. The Bigotian text affirms that there are, in fact, two different kinds of dejection, one which brings salvation and the other which is the cause of rancour, small-mindedness, malice, indifference and ultimately despair (Bi.V:1,1).[120]

To support this argument, he recalls Christ's words in the Sermon on the Mount: 'Blessed are they who mourn, for they shall be comforted.' The text explains that what is entailed here is a legitimate form of grief which expresses sorrow 'for our sins and for our neighbour's ignorance' and for the shortcomings in one's personal relationship with God.[121] By contrast, there is also another form of dejection which ultimately leads to death. More akin to a form of despair, it is born of the sorrow which is caused when 'we are deprived of friends or have suffered damage or loss of bodily goods'.[122] This is described as a dejection which corrupts and one which is brought about by the devil. It consists in a loss of trust in the goodness and mercy of God and is, at the same time, representative of a selfish disposition insofar as the sinner is increasingly given to self-pity.

Ultimately, argues the same text, it is a question of the will, for whilst hardships, difficulties and sufferings can and do befall all Christians from time to time, these must not be allowed to provoke a state of permanent dejection, instead the Christian must decide to rise above such trials (Bi.V:3,2). Further reference is made to Christ's beatitudes and in particular to the statement: 'Blessed are you when men revile and persecute you and utter all kinds of evil against you falsely on my account. Rejoice and be glad, for your reward is great in heaven, for so men persecuted the prophets who were before you' (Mt 5:11–12).

Just as Christ teaches that pain, affliction and suffering can be converted to spiritual joy, the penitentials argue that the Christian who undergoes emotional trauma must conquer this difficulty and use it to strengthen his relationship with God.

The *Old Irish Penitential* describes moments of personal grief and sorrow as occasions when the Christian is being 'mocked by the devil'.[123] He must, therefore, counter this attack with fervency of prayer and openness of mind toward God (OIP.IV.2). Episodes of suffering and distress must never be allowed to drive a wedge between the Christian and his God.

Dejection: the Symptoms

Comparatively few canons are devoted to the sins of dejection and this is not entirely surprising, since, given the nature of the vice, its detection would have been difficult. Moreover, some related areas of sinfulness, due in large measure to an underlying sentiment of despair, are dealt with under various other headings: for instance, suicide is treated as a sin of anger, even though it might very well have its origins in a deep-seated spiritual dejection. Nonetheless, almost all the major texts make at least some reference to the problem of loss of hope and trust in God.

Bitterness of heart Finnian says that dejection must be combated with spiritual joy, for 'gloom certainly devours or consumes the soul'.[124] However, he does not provide any more specific advice. By contrast, Cummean believes that despair will manifest itself in an attitude of 'bitterness of heart'. His choice of vocabulary suggests that it is not so much the sentiment in itself which is sinful as the reasons for which it is espoused and the manner in which the individual deals with it.

Thus, someone who 'harbours bitterness in his heart' (*qui diu amaritudinem in corde retinet*) is to be healed with a joyful countenance and a glad heart (Cu.VI.1). The use of the verb *retinere* suggests a deliberate holding on to the bitter sentiment such that the sinner becomes more and more embittered. A second canon reinforces this interpretation; it ordains that if the unwholesome attitude is not 'quickly laid aside' there will be need for fasting (Cu.VI.2).

A final canon holds that in the instance where one who is cured of his despair relapses into bitterness of heart, he must be cut off from the community and must fast on bread and water until he 'willingly and gladly' acknowledges his fault (Cu.VI.3). Again, the author's choice of language is significant. The admission of guilt by the sinner must be genuine and sincere (*alacer laetusque*). His confession must arise out of an authentic gladness at having seen his fault for what it really is, namely, a lack of trust in God, or even a feeling of resentment toward him. The penitent cannot rejoin his community until he has been able to admit this to himself because only then can a cure be effected.

Once again, Cummean resorts to the imagery of cure and healing to illustrate the confessor's task. The penitent must be brought to an awareness of the spiritual illness which is afflicting him; if not, he is to be cut off from the community lest the disease should spread. As soon as the sinner, however, is capable of acknowledging the nature and extent of his ailment he may be readmitted to the community and the rest of the cure effected there.

Cummean's remedy is later echoed in the Bigotian text but the latter also contains some new suggestions (Bi.V:3,2).[125] For instance, it advises the chanting of psalms as an alternative measure to fasting and it quotes St Paul's exhortation to Timothy: 'Take heed to yourself and to your teaching; hold to that for by so doing you will save both yourself and your hearers' (1 Tim 4). The emphasis is being placed here on prayer as a means for re-discovering God's love. By re-doubling his efforts at prayer and the psalms, the penitent demonstrates his willingness to restore the bond which had been damaged by sin and despair and in this way he is open to a return to spiritual wholeness.

Keening The practice of keening is severely censured throughout the penitential literature. Keening was carried out over a number of days at wakes and funerals, generally by women, by way of a lament or dirge. During these days the mourners raised their voices when weeping like the Egyptians, Jews and Greeks of old. This wailing was called *cái* in the native tongue and the verbal form *caoineadh* was thence anglicised to 'keening'.[126]

Although this custom was quite prevalent in early Christian Ireland (and indeed is not unknown even today) its origins belong to a much earlier pagan period. The Bigotian text takes a dim view of the practice and censures it with a fifty-day fast. This fast, however, is considerably lessened where the deceased is a relative of the penitent, or a cleric or civil or religious leader (Bi.IV:6,1–6).

What is being discouraged is not so much the legitimate expression of grief at the death of a loved one, but rather the ancient pagan practice of raising a mournful lament irrespective of whether or not one knew the deceased. The former is seen as a valid expression of sorrow, whereas the latter bears testimony only to despair and lack of hope.[127]

The author explains the distinction being made here with the aid of some scriptural illustration. He points out that Jacob and Issac both lamented for forty days in Egypt and for a week in Canaan, and likewise the women of Jerusalem wept for Christ during the agony of his Passion. He explains that this form of mourning may be considered the result of a worthy motive (*pro bono merito*), but that keening on the other hand must be seen as quite the opposite (*pro malo merito*: Bi.IV:6,7).

Keening, because it is a contrived and inauthentic expression of sorrow, runs contrary to Christian hope on behalf of all the faithful departed.

Dejection: the Penitential Remedy

We have noted that the principal forms of penitential cure prescribed in this section are the cultivation of a 'joyful countenance and a glad heart', fasting, temporary exile, fervent prayer and the chanting of psalms. The order in which these measures are to be imposed is important.

Inculcation of joy Cummean's usual remedy for the dejected penitent is an exhortation to joyfulness, and it is only in the event that this measure should fail that fasting is to be resorted to. He explains this with the phrase '*si autem non cito eam deponet*', that is, if the penitent does not lay aside his dejection (Cu.V.2). There is the suggestion that, in such a case, the individual has become so immersed in his grief that he prefers to remain in a state of self-pity.

At this point fasting is to be introduced in order to wrest him away from these selfish motives and towards a concern for his brothers. And again, it is only in the event of fasting failing to break the vicious circle of sinfulness that exile is to be imposed (Cu.V.3).[128] The reasoning seems to be that the sinner has become so consumed with his own cares that he has in effect already cut himself off from that Christian witness of generosity and sharing which might otherwise be reasonably expected of him. Exile, then, is a final attempt to bring him to his senses and to give him a true sense of perspective as to where his sin is leading him.

Prayer and spiritual exercises The Bigotian author's approach is more influenced by his theory of the two forms of dejection, that is, one which edifies and one which corrupts. For this reason, he enjoins fervent prayer and the chanting of psalms, by way of a penitential cure. By re-discovering prayer the penitent should be able to see more clearly whether his sadness springs from a worthy motive, namely, sorrow for one's sins and shortcomings; or whether it is a spiritual malaise which fosters an excessive sense of self-pity and lack of hope in God's love and mercy.

The Bigotian author attributes the origins of this approach to St Syncletica and absorbs it entirely into his own teaching (Bi.V:3,2). He adds that the penitent ought also to rejoice daily in the commandments of God and reiterates Paul's exhortation to the Philippians:

> Rejoice in the Lord always; again I say rejoice. Let all men know your forbearance. The Lord is at hand. Have no anxiety about any-

> thing, but in everything by prayer and supplication with thanksgiving let your requests be made known to God. And the peace of God, which passes all understanding will keep your hearts and your minds in Christ Jesus. (Phil 4:4).

The inference here is quite clear: if the penitent can square his behaviour with the commandments then he can be sure that any sadness he may feel is not in discord with the Gospel message. If his sorrowful mood cannot be reconciled with these divine precepts, then he must repent and do penance until true joy and peace reign in his heart once more.

We may conclude, then, that the exhortations to a state of contentment and joy and to fervent prayer are solid evidence that the texts have attempted to base their penitential methodology on Cassian's doctrine. From a state of despair and lack of hope the penitent is to be roused to a new spiritual wholeness. He must transform his erstwhile dejection into a spiritual happiness or else into a worthy form of sorrow, namely, one which stems from an awareness of his own moral weakness and need of divine mercy. Thus, he must seek to rid himself of his vice and cultivate virtue in its place.

Dejection: the Wholesome Antidote, Spiritual Joy

Spiritual joy, faith and love of God are the principal virtues to be striven after by the penitent who is seeking to cast off spiritual dejection (OIP.VI.1,e).

Spiritual joy and suffering The process, however, can be helped by fostering a legitimate form of remorse which laments one's own personal sinfulness as well as the sinfulness of the world: 'For he who deplores his own sins and his neighbour's sins shall be joyful with God in heaven.'[129]

Columbanus develops a similar theme in his *Instructiones*. He points out that young people who are preparing themselves for the various trades and professions such as craftsmen, builders, musicians, doctors, philosophers and politicians must, first of all, be willing to put up with some hardship during their time of training, in order that they may eventually do their work with great skill (Co.Inst.IV). There is, he suggests, a suffering or sorrow which all Christians must learn to bear with during their earthly pilgrimage so that they might one day attain true spiritual joy. He explains: 'This is in fact the training of all trainings, and at the price of present sorrow it prepares the pleasure of unending time and the delight of unending joy.'[130]

But it is important for the Christian to remember that the joys and sorrows of this world are transient. Therefore, while they are to patiently bear with difficulties and trials when they arise, they are not to give way to them. They are not to fall victim to either excessive remorse or excessive rejoicing: to do so would be to abandon the ultimate goal and to put oneself at the mercy of one's emotional states.

Spiritual joy and faith Instead, the Christian must remind himself that the Master has already conquered these things once and for all and that, with faith and spiritual strength, he too may follow in the Master's footsteps:

> We should yield to no joys or sorrows, no blandishment, or bitterness; for the world is full of both and both have been conquered by the Captain of our war . . . For though we are filled with the sorrows of our present woes, though we are saddened by the repetition of our sins yet victory over both is free rejoicing and a sterling joy; and though for a time we are on pilgrimage from the Lord . . . we ought not to be over-sad knowing that we shall soon go to him and with him dwell forever.

The challenge, then, facing the follower of Christ is to not allow the difficulties with which life may present them, harden their hearts thus losing trust in God and despairing of his goodness. Doing this, they would gradually neglect their daily Christian duties and become ever more ensnared in the quagmire of sin and self-pity. They would sever the bond between themselves and God as well as the ties which unite them to their fellow Christians.

But fear of God, repentance and the cultivation of regular prayer will lead the penitent eventually to a strengthened faith and spiritual joy in the sure hope that one day he will see his God as he truly is.

CHAPTER THREE

TEXTUAL ANALYSIS: THE SINS OF LUST, LANGUOR, VAINGLORY AND PRIDE

I. THE SINFUL DISEASE: LUST

Much more attention is given to the sins of lust than to any other category in the Irish penitential literature.[1] None of the early Latin texts, however, has much to say about the nature of the underlying vice. The Bigotian document repeats Paul's teaching to the Corinthians: 'Do not be deceived; neither the immoral, nor idolaters, nor adulterers, nor homosexuals will inherit the kingdom of God' (1 Cor 6:9–10) and then goes on, like the earlier texts, to outline penances for various kinds of sexual sin (Bi.pr.38).[2]

The *Old Irish Penitential* attempts to analyse at greater length the nature of the vice which is responsible for the sinful behaviour. It affirms that the lustful vice is doubly damaging since it 'does violence' to 'both the will of God and the will of man'. The victim of such a vice, it affirms, is eventually rendered useless and incapable of exercising his own will 'because the man who is constantly under its power and dominion has no thought of learning or piety or wisdom' (OIP.II:1a).[3] The author likens it to fire because it eventually burns up all the other virtues which the person may have, such that he becomes totally preoccupied with worldly desires and needs and loses sight of his spiritual goal. The Old Irish text agrees with the *Bigotian Penitential* that the principal areas of sinfulness born of this vice are inconstancy, rude discourse, concupiscence, fickleness and preoccupation with the affairs of the world.

The earliest documents have as their concerns sexual sins committed by monastic brethren, whereas the later texts broaden the scope and treat of matters pertaining to marriage and family life.

Lust: the Symptoms

The Irish penitentials provide a broad range of canons concerning a wide variety of sexual transgressions. The following divisions are largely our own, but cover the most important material.

'Natural' fornication This is the first sin to be analysed by Gildas and he prescribes three years of penitential fasting for it (Gi.1).[4] The

offence, however, is grouped along with sodomy suggesting that the author did not see either one as being more serious than the other. The other Welsh text, namely that of David, provides some more detail on the subject. Thus, penances vary in the first instance according to the clerical status of the sinner and, in the second, according to the marital status of the sexual partner. Hence, David distinguishes between consecrated virgins, married women, virgins and widows (Da.5).[5] In the event that the partner is betrothed the sinner is enjoined to pay the bride-price.

This requirement, in fact, draws upon what was already a pre-existing custom in Celtic society whereby the bridegroom always was obliged to pay a sum of money to the bride's parents.[6] The violation of one who is vowed to Christ or to a husband is seen as much more serious than illicit sexual intercourse with an unbetrothed woman, and the respective penances reflect this difference.[7]

Fornication involving clerics These teachings are echoed by Finnian who enjoins penances for clerics who 'lose their crown' (that is, their virginity) through fornication and also for those who are in the habit of sinning thus (*in consuetudine peccati*: Vi.10–11). In each case the penance entails penitential fasting and abstinence; the habitual sinner, however, also loses his clerical office as part of his punishment.

Finnian also makes provision for the case of a cleric who formerly as a layman had a wife and family but who subsequently took monastic vows (Vi.27). Should such a person go back to his wife and have sexual intercourse with her, this must be seen as a sin of fornication just as though 'he had been a cleric from his youth and sinned with a strange girl'.[8] The sin here, explains Finnian, is against religious vows and consecration of a person to God. Similarly, a lay person who seeks forgiveness for fornication is to live apart from his wife throughout his three-year penitential period. Only after completing a three-year abstinence, giving alms in the form of a feast for the needy and being restored to communion, may he resume sexual relations with his wife (Vi.35).

Fornication involving the married A very similar, though less severe penance, is enjoined for the married man who has sexual relations with a virgin; again he is directed to abstain from sexual relations with his wife, to give alms and never again to have extra-marital sexual intercourse 'so long as he is in this body' (Vi.36). This latter phrase, in fact, is repeated several times throughout Finnian's teaching on sexuality. It is drawn from the Second Letter of Saint Peter where the apostle states: 'I think it is right so long as I am in the body to arouse you by way of reminder since I know that the putting off of my body will be soon as our Lord Jesus Christ showed me' (2 Pet 1:13–14).

In this way, Finnian gives the sinner a timely reminder of the transitory nature of human existence, so that he might convert to a life of virtuous activity and thus prepare for the life to come.[9] Finnian does not mention the 'bride-price', but instead enjoins payment of alms to the poor and of the 'fruit of one's penance' to a priest. This *fructum penitentiae* is an interesting concept, for it suggests that not only was fasting to be undertaken but that the value of what was thus saved was also to be put to good use.

Sexual relationships between married men and their female slaves are also forbidden by Finnian. For the sinner this offence carries a mandatory penance of a year's fasting and prohibition from sexual intercourse with one's spouse (Vi.39–40). Further, the female slave is to be sold unless she has borne a child, in which case she must be set free and may not be sold.

Married partners who have become separated from each other, for whatever reason, either through force or of their own volition, are enjoined to remain faithful and to await the return of their spouse in patience and charity. Even where the other partner has committed fornication and is co-habiting with a third party, the deserted spouse must still remain faithful 'in the hope that God may perchance put penance in the heart of the spouse'.[10] Further, if conversion does eventually come about and the unfaithful partner returns to be reconciled, there is to be no immediate resumption of sexual relations. Instead, the faithful partner is to see to it that the other carries out a year's penitential fasting, by way of expiation, and only when this is completed are normal sexual relations to be restored (Vi.51).

Fornication involving virgins To a large extent, Columbanus echoes these provisions of Finnian, although in some instances the penances are more severe. He does not mention the 'bride-price' either, but he does introduce the related notion of the 'price of chastity' or 'virginity price' (*praetium puditItiae*) which was to be paid, by the offender, to parents of whom a virgin daughter had been violated. The only exception to be made here is where the sinner is himself a virgin. In this event, affirms Columbanus, both parties may, with the parents' consent, become man and wife after carrying out a year's penance (Co.B.16).

Fornication. Other penitentialists A more systematic approach is adopted by Cummean toward the sin of natural fornication. He determines the severity of the penance according to status or rank. Hence, penances range from twelve years' fasting plus loss of office for a bishop, to three years' penance for a monk not in orders (Cu.II:1–4). Laymen guilty of fornication and the shedding of blood are to be remedied with a fourfold privation; thus, they are to do penance 'without wine, without meat, without arms and without their wives' (*sine vino, sine carne, sine armis, sine uxore*: Cu.II:22).

These provisions, together with those of the aforementioned earlier texts, are also echoed in the Bigotian document. At one point, however, the author, quoting Theodore, warns against penances which are too harsh. For instance, he declares the penance of seven years' fasting to be altogether too severe and replaces it with two days' fast each week plus the forty days of Lent (Bi.II:5,2).[11]

Unnatural fornication There are several forms of unnatural fornication listed in the penitential literature; among these are what we might nowadays describe a; homosexual activity, bestiality, masturbation and incest.[12]

Homosexual acts The document pertaining to the *Synod of the Grove of Victory* condemns homosexual activity in its various forms and prescribes penances ranging from four two to years depending on the nature of the offence (Lu.8).[13] The severity of the penance is, however, sharply increased by Finnian, who prescribes a seven-year penance for habitual offenders and a two or three-year term for non-habitual offenders depending on whether they are boys or men (Vi.pr.2).[14]

The penance is further increased by Columbanus who gives a mandatory penance of ten years' fasting for clerical offenders in this regard as well as the instruction that they are never to live again with the other party (Co.A.3). A later canon also enjoins a seven-year period of penance for laymen guilty of homosexual activity (Co.B.3.).[15] As well as employing the term 'sodomy', Columbanus introduces the notion of 'effeminate intercourse with a male' (Co.B.15). Both expressions, however, appear to be co-terminous here.[16]

The same is not true, however, of Cummean, who distinguishes between sodomy '*scelus virile ut Sodomite*' (Cu.II:9) and femoral intercourse '*in femoribus*' (Cu.II:10). Whereas the first is to be corrected with a seven-year fast the second merely incurs a two-year penance. Clearly, two different acts are being referred to here: the first presumably refers to homosexual anal intercourse, whereas the second refers to non-anal homosexual intercourse.[17] The penance for femoral intercourse is reduced to one hundred days where the sinner is a 'boy of twenty years' (Cu.X:8) and that of sodomy may be mitigated to two years for penitents also belonging to this age group (Cu.X:15).

There seems, then, to be a recognition (though not acceptance) of a certain tendency toward homosexual activity among adolescent youths and even children. This is spelt out more clearly again in the Bigotian text which, drawing on Theodore, states that boys between the ages of twelve and twenty are to be punished by half the normal penance and that 'younger ones are to be punished even more lightly' (Bi.II:2,5). In all instances, however, what is being penalised is overt homosexual activity rather than an inner homosexual tendency.

Masturbation The sin which is today referred to as masturbation is given extensive coverage in the Irish penitential texts. Although this term is never employed by the penitential authors, they do, nevertheless, use phrases which describe sexual pollution and which suggest masturbatory activity.[18]

Most authors strive to make a distinction as to whether an act of sexual pollution was voluntary or involuntary. Thus, Gildas prescribes a standing vigil or the chanting of psalms for one who has been 'willingly defiled' in his sleep (Gi.22).[19] The *Synod of North Britain* outlines a graded penance for this sin, the severity depending on whether the sinner is a boy, youth, adult, deacon or priest (Aq.2). Confinement is a feature of all such penances. Finnian and Columbanus reiterate this teaching in a less systematic way.

More attention, however, is devoted to this topic by Cummean. He makes more distinctions between the various forms of sexual pollution. Thus, a penitent who harbours a desire to fornicate and, as a result, has a seminal emission is more severely censured than he who does so because of the 'violent onslaught of a thought' (Cu.II:11–12).[20] The language here is again reminiscent of that used for the sins of anger. The penitential author is seeking to distinguish between acts which are carried out because of an overwhelming urge and those which require a greater degree of forethought. In a later set of canons he enjoins markedly different penances for voluntary and involuntary pollution (Cu.II:15–16).

The topic of auto-eroticism is again raised in the tenth section of the same penitential which deals with the sinful playing of boys. Here

Cummean decides that young boys who kiss each other licentiously and thus prompt a seminal emission are to be corrected with ten special fasts (Cu.X:2). Adults, on the other hand, are to be cut off from the Christian community and enjoined to live on bread and water (Cu.X:3).[21] Youths (up to the age of twenty) who practise mutual masturbation are to do penance for twenty to forty days, for one hundred days if the offence is repeated, and for a year if it becomes a habit (Cu.X:6–7).[22]

As usual, the Bigotian text gives the most detailed treatment of the subject, as well as distinguishing between voluntary and involuntary pollution, it also introduces two new terms namely, touching the genitals (*tangit manu*) and stimulation of same (*excitat ipse*: Bi.II:1,1–4). Judging, however, by the the similarity of penance accorded for each offence the latter distinction does not appear to be crucial.

Bestiality Fornication with a beast is condemned by almost all the penitential texts. Gildas prescribes a year's fasting for sins of this nature (Gi.11), whilst the *Synod of the Grove of Victory* increases this to two and a half years, and David to three years.[23] All the aforementioned penances, however, apply only to those who have already taken vows and Finnian further explains that boys guilty of this sin should only be held to a penance of one hundred days (Vi.pr.1).[24]

Columbanus only mentions bestiality among sins of the laity.[25] He prescribes a year's penance for the sinner if he is married and half this if he is single (Co.B:17). Thus, there would seem to have been some concessions toward those who did not have the possibility of legitimate sexual intercourse with a partner (Co.B:17). The same principle, affirms Columbanus, may also be applied to masturbation. Those who are married and who resort to masturbation are to undertake double the penance of the single person. These provisions are largely echoed by both Cummean and the Bigotian text, which enjoin one- and two-year penances respectively depending on whether the sin is an isolated or habitual act.[26]

Fellatio The sinful act described, in contemporary parlance, by the term *fellatio* (i.e. oral fornication) is referred to at several junctures throughout the penitential literature. Those who befoul their lips are denounced by Cummean (*moechantes in labiis*) and he enjoins a four year penance, which is to be increased to seven years where the failing is habitual (Cu.II.8). This same activity is later described as 'satisfying desire with the lips' (*desideria labiis complentes*) and an identical penance is enjoined (Cu.X:16). The Bigotian text agrees with Cummean's provisions but describes the sin differently as 'fornication of the lips' (*fornicantes labiis*). The author also adds, with some temerity, that such a sin is a 'crime even to mention' (Bi.II:2,4).[27]

Incest Sexual intercourse between persons who are closely related by blood or affinity is deemed to be sinful behaviour by several penitentials. The *Synod of the Grove of Victory* enjoins a three-year penance with perpetual pilgrimage for the individual who has sexually defiled his mother (Lu.6).[28] David concurs with this view and puts incest on a par with murder, adultery and bestiality in terms of gravity (Da.11).

By contrast, Columbanus does not refer to incest in the generic sense, but rather to a more particular expression of it which we today might describe as 'child abuse' (Co.B.18).[29] The Latin term here is vague (*infantem suum oppraesserit*); however, the verb remains the same as that used by Cummean in reference to the 'sinful playing of boys' where the offence is clearly of a sexual nature (Cu.X:9). Moreover, the penance of one year's fast and two years' abstinence as well as the exhortation that the husband must in future 'use his bed lawfully' leave us in no doubt as to the nature of the sin. Further, sexual abstinence, says Columbanus, is to be observed throughout the period of penance.

These provisions are, in turn, echoed both by Cummean (Cu.II.7) and the Bigotian text (Bi.II:3,1–2), the latter, however, also offers a more severe alternative, namely penances ranging from seven to fifteen years. A similar penance is also enjoined for homosexual incest.

Prostitution Prostitution is not referred to in any of the major penitentials but, it does receive an oblique mention in two of the lesser known texts. The document containing the *Canons of Adamnan* forbids a husband who has deserted his wife to marry again (Ad.16).[30] It is clear, though, that the author is here branding the unfaithful wife with the term 'harlot' (*meretrice*) in an attempt to underline the seriousness of her sin. Consequently, he is not making any suggestion that sexual intercourse is being offered for money in the way that the terms harlotry and prostitution would normally connote.

The *Second Synod of St Patrick* (Pa.II:XXVI) cites from *Corinthians* where the apostle teaches: '"Do you not know that he who joins himself to a prostitute becomes one body with her? For, as it is written 'the two shall become one' " (1 Cor 6:16). In the next phrase, however, the penitential author goes on to apply this teaching again to the case of an adulterous wife (*adultera*). There is no reliable evidence then that the term prostitute is being used in its usual sense; it seems to be more indicative of the author's strong disapproval of infidelity in marriage.[31]

Non-coital sins of lust By this term, of course, we mean sins not involving full sexual intercourse. We shall discuss the more important of these.

Kissing Many of the penitential texts provide penances for monks and clerics who confess to having kissed virgins. David enjoins a three-day penitential fast for this sin (Da.15). More serious still is the view of Finnian in the case of the cleric who has 'given himself to their lascivious embraces' (*oscolis inlecebrosis*: Vi.14–15). This sin is deemed to warrant a half-year's penitential fast provided that the penitent has 'preserved himself from ruin', by which phrase we may assume the author means that he has stopped short of sexual intercourse.[32]

The penance is increased to a year by Cummean, who also censures any monk who has even had a few conversations with a particular woman (Cu.II:18–19). As we have already noted, Cummean also gives detailed instructions regarding the penances to be imposed for 'homosexual kissing' among young boys.[33] The Bigotian author repeats Cummean's penance of one year's fasting for the monk who has kissed and embraced (*osculatis et amplectans*) a woman with whom he is in love (Bi.II:1,9), but mitigates this to twenty days when this is done because of an overwhelming desire (Bi.II:1,1).

Impure thoughts The texts are quite unanimous in their opposition to the deliberate enjoyment of sexual fantasies and impure thoughts. The Bigotian text (Bi.II:1,5) reminds us of Christ's words in his Sermon on the Mount: 'But I say to you that everyone who looks at a woman lustfully has already committed adultery with her in his heart' (Mt 5:28). Thus, the serious desire to commit sinful actions of a sexual nature is itself deemed to be sinful. There is, then, already a recognition in the penitentials that the wish to commit unchaste actions constitutes an interior sin against Christian morality in the same way that the various illicit forms of sexual behaviour are external sins.

Finnian says that the individual who feels the stirrings of evil thoughts is to beat his breast and to seek help from God by day and by night.[34] He is to continue thus whether he has mastered the lustful feelings or indeed has been mastered by them '*aut victor aut victus*' (Vi.2). The struggle then, is precisely one for control; either the individual succeeds in overcoming his sinful urge and emerges as the *victor* or he succumbs to temptation, surrenders his self-control and becomes a slave or a *victim* to sin. The task for the confessor, then, is to establish whether the penitent has allowed himself to be carried along by his sexual impulses or whether he has striven to control them and to accept responsibility for his actions.

Finnian affirms, also, that the sinner who sought to do evil or to fornicate, but who was unable to do so through lack of opportunity, is guilty of the same sin as would be the case had he fulfilled his sinful desire (Vi.3).[35] He has, by intention, reasons the penitentialist, already committed the sin in his heart (*in corde suo*) even though it was not completed in deed (*effectus*). Nevertheless, the fact that the sinful effect was not brought about in reality means the penance may be mitigated, even though the sin remains the same (Vi.3). This scenario, explains Finnian, differs greatly to that where a person sins through inadvertence (*per inreptionem*). Such a sinner may be corrected with one simple fast and a caution to be on his guard (*cavere se*) in the future (Vi.4). These provisions are retained by Columbanus, who advises a sincere confession and fasts ranging from fifty days to half a year in cases where fornication or adultery was contemplated (Co.B.11,23).

Cummean develops the teaching on this matter still further and examines the way in which individuals eventually succumb to sin. He explains that a person may be almost, as it were, lured or taunted by an evil idea (*inluditur*) until his defences are gradually breached (Cu.II:14).[36] He believes that the sinner's fault here may be one of having resisted too half-heartedly and having entertained the temptation up to the point where it eventually was able to overpower him.

In any case, the general principle applies that the penitent is to do penance for as long as the evil thought endures. Again this situation is sharply distinguished from that where an individual gives way to sin after the violent assault (*inpugnatione*) of an evil thought. In a similar way, a monk who cultivates an exclusive affection for a particular woman is to undertake a fast of seven days. The penance would, of course, increase were the monk to bring his desires to a physical conclusion.[37]

Thus, there is a graded scale of categories from simple desire to conversation, amorous advances, embracing, sexual intercourse, and begetting a child. Each of the stages therein carries with it a mandatory penance and the confessor could readily ascertain the correct penance by determining the degree of attachment in any given relationship (Cu.II.18–21).

Immodest words or actions Other sins which are classified under the general heading of sins of lust include general verbal and physical expressions of immodesty. For instance, Columbanus censures those who, when bathing, wash themselves in the standing position. This is deemed to be immodest and is to be punished with twenty-four strokes. However, adds Columbanus, the sinner may be excused if he acted with the intention of 'cleansing dirt more fully' (Co.B.27).[38] Those guilty of uncovering their knees or their arms are to be corrected with a prohibition on further bathing for six days. Columbanus does point out, however, that rules of modesty may be relaxed in the case of *seniores* or elderly monks who may require assistance; and may therefore be washed by another with impunity (Co.B.28).[39]

In similar fashion, Cummean also speaks of the possibility of sexual pollution occurring as a result of an evil word or glance (*turpiloquium vel aspectu*). Therefore, the Christian is to be always on his guard against even these lesser infringements of morality lest they lead him into graver sin (Cu.II:12). The term *turpiloquium* itself suggests a form of speech which is already impure, fouled, or dishonoured and in need of purification. By indulging in this practice the individual himself becomes defiled or befouled (*coinquinatus*).

Whilst the term is evidently a reference to seminal emission or sexual pollution it is also representative of the effects of sin in a more general way. Impurity of speech leads to impurity of action, sinful temptation once yielded to becomes progressively stronger and sin continues to beget sin until the sinner is eventually overwhelmed by his own passions and bodily appetites (Bi.II.1,6).

Love potions A final area of sex-related activity, which receives a mention in the penitentials and to which we have already alluded, is that of the use and fabrication of aphrodisiacs. These are censured by both Finnian and Columbanus. Finnian enjoins a year's fasting to the sinner who has given someone a potion for the 'sake of wanton love' (*pro inlecebroso amore*: Vi.19). Whilst Colombanus accepts this judgement, he does allow for more lenient penances where the offender is a lay person (Co.B.6). Nonetheless, the penances here are quite severe in comparison with other instances of sexual desire and lust.

We may conclude, then, that the penitential authors see instances of potion or aphrodisiac making as evidence of much malicious forethought as well as a general intention to deceive the other party. Here again, we find ourselves at the boundary of various categories of sin.

Not merely one vice but even two or more vices may be at work here in producing the sinful effect.

Lust: the Penitential Cure

In correcting the sins of lust, a variety of measures are employed. Among these fasting is, as usual, foremost. The penitentials, however, do also enjoin sexual abstinence, corporal punishment, loss of rank, exile, chanting of psalms, payment of compensation, lying upon stone, almsgiving to the poor, separation from spouse, and increased prayer.[40] There is a marked emphasis on penances which are designed to subdue and counter bodily appetites and physical comfort.

Corporal punishment and fasting The *David* text, for example, as well as prescribing a three year fast also enjoins the unusual measure of sleeping upon the ground for one year, upon stone for another and upon a board for a third (Da.11). Similarly, Columbanus' choice of penance entails, as we have seen, corporal punishment (Co.B.27–8). Cummean's penance for laymen guilty of fornication entails a fourfold privation from wine, meat, arms and marital relations (Cu.II.22). Again, the Bigotian text in assigning a penance for voluntary seminal emission rules that the penitent should sing thirty psalms, taking care to bend the knee at the end of each.[41]

Although it does not receive universal application, there is a general recognition among the penitential authors that sins of lust may best be corrected and eliminated through activities which involve mastering and subduing other bodily appetites and cravings. Hence, the penitentials prescribe measures which are aimed at quelling the body's desire for physical comfort, food, drink, cleanliness, protection and rest, as well as the sexual appetite. The reasoning seems to be that, in learning how to deny the body other forms of physical gratification, the individual will gradually learn also to master his sexual urge.

In this way, using the language of Finnian, the cycle of sin can be broken and the sinner is no longer the *victus* but instead the *victor* over his physical appetites. Thus, genuine penance involves a process of self-discipline and self-conquest. In and through penance the penitent acquires the possibility of ordering and forming a basic physical urge without seeking to destroy it altogether.

Exercises in self-mastery Thus, for example, Columbanus advises that after having carried out the requisite penance for incest the sinner must in future learn to 'use his bed lawfully' (Co.B.18).[42] Likewise, where a man has had illicit sexual intercourse with a young woman and where they have 'lain as virgin with virgin', then the two are advised to marry after completing the requisite penance (Co.B.16). In both instances penance is seen as a measure which orders the sexual appetite rather thas one which is designed to quench it entirely.[43] In this way, the individual is able to keep all his drives in check and to overcome tendencies toward excessive or deviant sexual behaviour. He thus fosters a constant discipline which demands effort and sacrifice but which, at the same time, safeguards him from the excesses of self-indulgence.

Similarly, where the sexual drive has become disordered, that is to say, not oriented toward heterosexual union, penances tend to be more absolute and seem geared toward a total change in the penitent's behaviour. And so, one guilty of homosexual intercourse is not only enjoined to carry out a severe penance but also to refrain in future from living with the other party: '*et non maneat cum alio in aeternum*' (Co.B.3).

Likewise, where a cleric has become emotionally involved with a woman but where the relationship has not progressed to full sexual union, the penitential advises that he withdraw from communion of the altar, by way of penance, and at the same time tear out of his heart his fellowship with the woman: '*de corde suo abscederit*' (Vi.14). The point at issue here is that the exclusive nature of the cleric's relationship is at odds with his vowed way of life. He must, therefore, be prepared to take decisive action or else his vocation will perish.

While penances, here, often fall short of fully implementing Cassian's doctrine of 'cure by contraries', there is, nonetheless, quite frequently an attempt on the part of the penitential authors to provide some practical measure which will help the penitent to overcome his sin. Thus, for example, the penance for one who is prone to sexual pollution during sleep is to arise frequently and to sing psalms in a kneeling position. The measure prescribed here is one designed to rid the individual of his unwholesome thoughts by replacing them with the words of the psalms and with some physical discomfort, in order to subdue the physical stirrings of the body (Bi.II:1,7). Again, where a penitent is struggling with the temptation of impure thoughts, he is advised to do penance according to the 'duration of the thought' (Cu.II:4).[44] In this way, penance provides him with a means of 'doing battle' with sinful temptation and of eventually learning to control his natural drives and to channel them into non-sinful activity.

(iii) *Sexual Abstinence* Sexual abstinence is a measure frequently adopted by the penitentials in their efforts to inculcate self-discipline and self-control. The texts tend to agree that laymen repenting of adultery should abstain from normal marital relations with their spouses throughout the period of their penance.[45] As soon as the penance is completed they are then free to resume intercourse.

Whilst this penance may at first seem quite severe, its strength lies in its degree of coherence with the sinner's action. Having committed adultery, a man ruptures the relationship with his wife. To resume full sexual relations immediately afterwards would be a dishonest and inconsistent gesture. Instead, the penitent must undergo a lengthy time of penance. During this period he will have the opportunity to discover his error and the harm which this has done to his marital relationship. He will then be better disposed toward making a 'journey of repentance', as it were, to the day where he can once more with honesty and sincerity express his love for his partner in full sexual union (Vi.35).

Assessment of penitential measures There is evidence, then, that the penances prescribed for the sins of lust as for the other categories of sin, were designed to foment a real change in the penitent's behaviour. Finnian says that one who is guilty of adultery must take care never to be guilty of the same sin again as long as he lives.

Moreover, his repentance is to be sincere and he is to give alms to the poor and the fruits of his penance to a priest. In other words, the penance must be purposeful; it must be expressive of a real change of heart and of a new sensitivity toward other people, especially the poor (Vi.36). The emphasis must be shifted away from an instinct of self-gratification through which the sinner first seeks illicit sexual intercourse and toward a new attitude of Christian compassion which focuses upon the needs of others. Furthermore, if the conversion is to be sincere, the sinner must 'at all times deplore his guilt from his inmost heart' so that his new self-effacing outlook will be reflected by 'an attitude of the readiest obedience' (Cu.II:2).[46]

Finally, just as in conversion from other sinful activities care is to be taken that the penitent is not over zealous in his penance. The penitential activity must not become an end in itself, so that a penitent might lose sight of his broader Christian vocation, instead: 'After a year and a half he shall take the Eucharist and come for the kiss of peace and sing the psalms with his brethren, lest his soul perish utterly through lacking so long a time the celestial medicine' (Cu.II:2).[47]

Lust: the Wholesome Antidote, Continence

Among the virtues identified by the *Old Irish Penitential* as antidotes to lust are perseverance in chastity, steadfastness, modesty, faith, hatred of the present world and love of the world to come (OIP.II:1,d).[48]

Continence in marriage Finnian too devotes six lengthy canons to the right ordering of sexual behaviour. He sees the marital relationship as the only lawful context for sexual activity. Furthermore, even within this context, there must be, he says, a responsible and controlled attitude on the part of the spouses toward their sexual activity: 'We prescribe and exhort that there be continence in marriage since marriage, without continence is not lawful but sin' (Vi.46). The marital act cannot, therefore, become merely a means of sexual gratification for one or both parties. Instead marriage 'by the authority of God is permitted not for lust but for the sake of the children'.[49]

Continence and procreation The pleasurable gratification of the sexual urge must be seen as subordinate to the procreation of children and the propagation of humankind. Finnian cites from Genesis: 'Therefore a man leaves his wife and they become one flesh' (Gen 2:24.). He adds that this union of flesh is intended for the generation of children and not for 'lustful concupiscence'. By way of demonstrating their appreciation of the ends of marriage, Finnian also advocates that married couples should abstain from sexual intercourse at various times. Among these are the three *quadragesimae* as well as one night a week (either Saturday or Sunday) and during a pregnancy. In carrying out this recommendation, they will, Finnian believes, demonstrate that they are worthy of the 'Lord's Body' (Vi.46).

Continence and virtuous behaviour However, abstinence in itself is not sufficient to ensure a good marriage. The married couple must also undertake good works, give alms, fulfil the commands of God and expel their faults if they truly wish to fulfil their matrimony (*explere matrimonium*: Vi.46). And it is clearly to this end that Finnian would have all married people aspire, because, he says, those who do 'fulfil matrimony' will reign with Christ in the life to come along with 'holy Abraham, Isaac, Jacob, Job, Noah, and all the saints'.[50] For Finnian the procreation of children is the naturally ordained end of sexuality and for that reason is only to be realised within matrimony.

Matrimony, in itself, is not to be regarded as a simple union of partners; instead, it is to be seen as a school of virtue where both partners must now strive together to live out their response to Christ's message more fully and more authentically. Married couples who do fully espouse this teaching will, says Finnian, 'receive the thirtyfold fruit which in the Gospel Christ has set aside for married people' (Vi.46).[51] Marital fidelity is also a virtue by which Finnian sets great store. Spouses are to do their utmost to remain faithful to each other even when great hardships are involved. Thus, for example, where a wife is infertile (*sterilem*) the couple are to remain together and to dwell in continence (Vi.41). Moreover, says Finnian, they will be greatly blessed if they live out a life of chastity.

He points to the biblical examples of this response and cites the unions of Abraham and Sarah (Gen 16:1.), Isaac and Rebecca (Gen 25:21.), Anna, the mother of Samuel (Sam 1:6) and Elisabeth, the mother of John (Lk 1:7.). He affirms that what is important is to remain faithful to Christ's teaching whether in times of hardship or plenty (*sive prosperum sive contrarium*). And he cites too from Paul's advice, namely 'that those who have wives live as if they had none . . . For the form of the world is passing away' (1 Cor 29–31).

Continence and marital problems The same degree of fidelity is required in situations where one partner has been deserted by the other. The abandoned partner is exhorted to remain faithful and chaste even when the other spouse does not do so. Finnian declares, from the outset, that such manner of separation is wrong: 'We declare that a wife must not leave her husband' and, in the event that she does, 'that she remain unmarried or be reconciled to him' (Vi.42).[52] He acknowledges that the teaching in turn comes from St Paul. On the other hand, where one or other spouse has been unfaithful and has committed adultery, Finnian teaches that the faithful partner should remain so and 'wait in all patience and chastity in the hope that God may perchance put penance' in the heart of the other (Vi.45).[53]

For Finnian, then, the marriage bond is indissoluble and the truly Christian spouse is to bear witness to this indissolubility even at the cost of great personal sacrifice and suffering. Where two spouses have become estranged, there can be no valid sacramental marriage involving a third partner during the lifetime of the other spouse.[54] Further, where a partner has been co-habiting with another and has had sexual intercourse with the other, he, or she, may still be welcomed back by the spouse providing the will to return is sincere and that is what is fully desired (*si satis ac libenter expetere*). Nor is the deserted spouse to make any payment to the other in order to entice him to return.

Finally, if and when two estranged partners do decide to be reconciled, they must first undertake a year's penitential fasting on bread and water. Moreover, during this time of penance the couple are to sleep in separate beds until the penance is completed, whereupon they may then resume married life as before the sinful episode (Vi.44).

In this way, penance is seen to be a practical, pastoral policy which enables the couple to overcome the division between them, to put their guilt behind them in a real and concrete manner; and finally to rediscover their love for one another and to nurse that love back to a state of health.

Some of the other penitential writers echo Finnian's strict teaching on the prohibition of divorce for whatever reason. But the document known as the Second Synod of Saint Patrick seems to mark a departure from this position. This document appears to advocate exceptions in difficult cases. Citing the fornication clause in Matthew in support of its opinion, it teaches: 'It is not permitted for a man to put away his wife except because of fornication' (Pa.II:XXVI).[55]

Similarly, whilst the Bigotian text provides very severe penances for those who divorce their spouses, there is no direction as to whether they are to return to their former partners or not (Bi.II:6,1). As a general rule, however, the penitential literature does support the indissolubility of the marriage bond and it extols the virtue of fidelity as a means of safeguarding the married couple from sin and division.

Continence and the consecrated life Chastity is the name given to the virtue which Columbanus seeks to cultivate as a response to the sins of lust, especially within the bounds of the monastery. In his *Regulae* he calls to mind Christ's teaching in the Sermon on the Mount: 'I say to you that every one who looks at a woman lustfully has already committed adultery with her in his heart' (Mt 5:28). He affirms that the words of Christ demonstrate that a monk's chastity is to be 'judged in his thoughts' (Co.Reg.Mon.VI).

The good monk, therefore, must be circumspect; it is not sufficient for him merely to be chaste as regards his external activity. Rather, his chastity must spring from within and so he must critically examine his internal dispositions and thoughts. Columbanus calls to mind: '. . . those who indulge in the lust of defiling passion . . . They have eyes full of adultery, insatiable for sin. They entice steady souls' (2 Pet 2:10–14).[56]

Virginity should, Columbanus affirms, be as much a feature of the mind as it is of the body. Echoing Paul's words that God dwells in the human body which is a 'temple of his Holy Spirit', Columbanus reminds his followers that they must, therefore, keep their minds undefiled in order that there may be 'no adulterous thought, no stain of a spirit polluted and no spot of sin'.[57]

Continence: conclusion Continence, as described by the penitenialists, is thus seen as being a 'moderating virtue'. In the unmarried and religious Christian it seeks to exclude all voluntary impurity in body and mind, whilst in the married it strives to regulate and control the sexual urge. As Columbanus understands it, the perfect chastity and continence of the Christian must embrace abstinence from all sexual sin, not alone in the external act, but also in internal thought, desire and complacency.

II. THE SINFUL DISEASE: LANGUOR

Languor or sloth, says the *Bigotian Penitential*, is the cause of many other vices among which are idleness, drowsiness, unseasonableness, restlessness, wandering and instability.[58] Not surprisingly, then, the same penitential seeks to cure sinners of this vice by means of work, vigils and increased prayer and thus steer them toward a renewed zeal in mind and body, as well as inculcating the virtues of constancy, perseverance and stability (Bi.VI passim).

Languor: the Symptoms

Among the principal subdivisions of languor we may count the following:

Laziness Cummean recommends that the idle person should be given 'extraordinary' work. Gildas, on the other hand, enjoins a fast from one meal or from half the daily allowance. However, he is quick to point out that tasks may be left undone for a variety of reasons. Thus, the confessor is to establish whether the motive was one of contempt (*contemptus*) or whether it was a simple case of oversight (*vero oblivione*).[59]

Here again, we are at a point of intersection between the influences of various vices. A monk's slothfulness may be deemed to be symptomatic of a sinful pride resulting in recalcitrance and unwillingness to carry out his duties. On the other hand, it may be just an expression of a more general negative disposition toward physical labour from which he will therefore need to be corrected by hard work and greater application to his monastic responsibilities.

The Bigotian author spells out in clearer terms precisely what the term 'extraordinary work' is to be taken to mean: the idle person must be given more work than all the others (Bi.VI:1–3). This stance is, in turn, justified by a citation from St Paul, who advises: 'Let the thief no longer steal, but rather let him labour, doing honest work with his hands, so that he may be able to give to those in need' (Eph 4:28). To tailor this Pauline teaching to the present argument, the author omits the first part of the phrase, referring to the thief, and directs the exhortation toward the idler instead.

On the other hand, it is not improbable that the Bigotian author also sees idleness as a form of dishonesty insofar as the lazy individual fails to fulfil what might be reasonably and justly expected of him. And he retains Paul's line of reasoning that the fruits of extraordinary labour should be given to those who suffer need.[60] He then proceeds to take an image from the Lives of the Fathers and in particular from Abbot Pastor, who teaches that just 'as bees are expelled by smoke so that their sweet labour may be taken from them, so rest of the body expels from the soul the fear of God and will take away from it every good work' (Bi.VI:1,2).[61]

The most profound motive for work, then, is the service which is rendered on to God. Work is seen as a way of ordering daily Christian life, whereas idleness is precisely the negation of this and a disorderly form of living. In returning to disorder and chaos in his daily life the sinner loses sight of God and of his bothers and sisters who are in need and thus plunges into selfishness and sin.

Drowsiness The drowsy or sleepy person (*somnolentus*) is, according to Cummean, to be given a penance of a lengthy vigil and is to busy himself by chanting psalms. Columbanus, on the other hand, believes the sleepy person should be corrected by watching which we may again interpret as some form of vigil (Cu.VI:1). In his *Regulae*, however, he also prescribes the chanting of psalms: those who are frequently sleepy are to chant twelve psalms, whilst the occasional doser is to be corrected with six. Similar penances are to be given to those who, because of heavy sleep, do not hear the call to prayer and to those who arrive hurriedly for the celebration of the eucharist clad only in their night shirt or night girdle (Co.Reg.Coen.XII).

The Bigotian author, as usual, attempts a more systematic analysis of the subject. He draws upon the lives of the Fathers and cites the phrase which describes 'continuous sleep' as the 'image of death' (Bi.VI:2,1). Later, he cites another learned patristic source as instructing that 'If it so happens that sleep has befallen me and the hour of my ministry has gone by, my soul in shame no longer wants to carry out its work.'[62]

Inordinate sleep, then, is the cause of missed opportunities to minister to one's brothers; moreover, it begets shame resulting in reluctance to carry out further work and so the sinner becomes caught up in the cycle of sloth and sin. For this reason, the Bigotian author reminds his readers that the best remedy for the slothful person is to rise from his bed, immediately upon waking, and to begin his work at once (Bi.VI:2,3). He recalls the words of the psalm: 'Thine is the day, thine also the night' (Ps 74:16), thus demonstrating that God may be praised and glorified at any hour.

What is important, then, is that the penitent should be capable of decisively breaking the vicious circle of sloth and laziness irrespective of what time it may be. By making a conscious decision to put an end to his torpor and to take up his work again, the sinner is able to cure himself of his sloth and re-open the lines of communication with God through his work and activity.

The whole episode is interesting, in that it demonstrates that the penitentials did not restrict their understanding of man's relationship with God to the moments, of formal prayer and liturgy; instead, all daily work and activity was looked upon as a continuous act of praise and worship to God (Bi.VI:2,3).[63]

Instability Instability, or the tendency to wander off either physically or mentally, is also seen as a sin of languor.[64] This, however, is to be distinguished from the notion of desertion which would generally have been caused by some other motive, such as pride or disobedience, rather than simply a general tendency towards idleness and sloth.[65]

The early document known as the *First Synod of Saint Patrick* prohibits the monastic community from having vagrant clerics (Pa.I.3).

Cummean, on the other hand, says that the wandering and unstable person is to be 'healed' by 'permanent residence in one place and by application to work' (Cu.VI.2).[66] This teaching is, in turn, reiterated by the Bigotian author who adds that languor and instability are to be overcome by steadiness or constancy of body, heart and thought. Again, he has recourse to the lives of the early Fathers and repeats Moyses of Sycthes' teaching, 'Go and sit down in thy cell and thy cell will teach thee all things.'[67]

Great store is laid on the ability of the monk to be alone in his cell. This is seen to be the means by which he will develop constancy and grow ever stronger in his relationship with God. A further image is taken from the teachings of Anthony: 'As fish die if they tarry on dry land, so also monks staying for long away from their cells or conversing with men of the world, lapse from their vocation for a retired life' (Bi.VI:3,4).[68]

The wandering monk is like a fish which is stranded out of water; his spiritual training is not adapted for an itinerant lifestyle but rather for one of religious life in community. Cut off from his community for too long, he is deprived of the oxygen of prayer and penance and his spiritual life is choked to the point of death. The Bigotian text is here placing in juxtaposition the terms *vagus* and *in cella*, which do not admit of reconciliation. Either the monk renounces his wish to live in his monastic cell and takes to an itinerant lifestyle, or else he should redouble his efforts to remain faithful to the ideal of stability, thus dedicating himself totally to the praise of God.

The Bigotian author draws upon one final image from ancient authors, this time Syncletica. According to this view the wandering monk or virgin is like the brooding hen that deserts her eggs robbing them of the chance to hatch into chicks and eventually dies herself 'by wandering from one place to another'. Again, the emphasis here is on spiritual death, which is brought about by neglect and instability (Bi.VI:3,5). The unstable monk not alone occasions his own spiritual death through lack of commitment and application; he also robs his brethren of the support and solidarity which would normally be their due.[69]

Distraction at prayer Distraction at prayer, or wandering of the mind, is also regarded by the Bigotian author as a sin of sloth. Yet again, the imagery used to describe the sin is drawn from the early Fathers.

> A brother asked an elder saying 'My thoughts stray and I am worried' and he says 'Thou sit down in thy cell and thy thoughts will come again. For as it is with the mother ass: if she is tied to the plug, her foal moves hither and thither, but wherever it is it always returns to its mother, so it will be with the thoughts of him who, for the sake of God sits patiently in his cell; even though they stray a little they return again to him. (Bi.VI:3,6)[70]

Physical stability, then, is the key to mental and spiritual constancy. The monk who remains committed to spending time alone in his cell with God will continue to strengthen his spiritual life despite the momentary distractions which may come his way. Indeed, the penitential author here accepts a certain amount of distraction at prayer as normal and not a cause of great alarm.

He explains, too, that just as food which is chewed upon (*ruminare*) gives nutrition to the body, so too do prayers and psalms nourish the spiritual life, even if the mind sometimes wanders or wanes in concentration (Bi.VI:3,7). Prayer must be seen then, as food for the soul which, if chewed upon, will yield great spiritual nourishment, and will be best achieved, according to the same author, when allied to a spirit of constancy, steadiness, perseverance and stability.

Carelessness Various forms of carelessness and negligence are accounted for throughout Celtic penitential literature. Finnian, for example, censures with a penance of seven days those who lose a consecrated object (Vi.52). Similarly, Columbanus prescribes a special fast for the monk who is so remiss as to leave open the gate of the enclosure during the night, and a punishment of twenty-four blows is enjoined should it be left open during the day (Co.B.26).

Any layman whose child dies without baptism, through negligence on his part, is to do penance for three years, according to Cummean, and is to abstain from sexual intercourse throughout that period. And he enjoins penances of three special fasts for priests who change or omit words of the mass, and of fifty strokes for priests who stammer over the words of the consecration (Cu.II.32).

By our standards, these penances may all seem somewhat harsh. For the penitentialists the various acts of carelessness are all seen to be indicative of a lack of concentration and of application to the Christian way of life. Throughout the penitentials there is a keen awareness that individuals who fall victim to serious sin are first led astray in little matters.[71] For this reason, Columbanus devotes a subsection of his work to 'minor sanctions for monks', whilst each of the other penitentials are also careful to provide guidance and penances for sins of greater and lesser importance alike.

Languor: the Penitential Remedy

A variety of measures are to be employed in tackling the problem of languor.[72]

Work Both Gildas and Cummean place emphasis on the value of work. Gildas urges monks to be willing to undertake the tasks of others (Gi.16); this must be done in a spirit of modesty so that the monk lets only his abbot know of his extra activity. Similarly, if the abbot should request that a monk do extra work, it should be carried out without question. Evidently, the penitentialists regard the undertaking of manual work as intrinsically linked to all the other forms of serious and purposeful activity which form a part of the active Christian life.

In this context, work is seen as a universal duty and as a demand of fraternal charity. Further, Gildas' observations on the spirit with which work is to be undertaken shows that he believes that, through his work, the good Christian places himself at the service of his brothers. There is, therefore, a strong communitarian dimension to physical labour. In applying himself with renewed vigour to his appointed tasks the sinner will eventually raise himself out of the snare of languor and lethargy and through his work will further not alone his own personal development, but also the well-being and welfare of his community.

Prayer vigils The imposition of lengthy vigils, accompanied by the praying of the psalms, is also prescribed as a remedy for laziness. Whilst at first sight this form of penance may seem somewhat punitive, the ultimate goal remains therapeutic and oriented toward personal development. A strong juxtaposition is made in the penitential texts between sleep, which is seen to be the 'image of death', and wakeful activity, which represents the Christian's true imitation of his creator. Where sleep and rest are conceded too great an amount of time, the individual becomes weak-willed and lazy, and his life is in danger of regressing toward an image of death rather than progressing toward new life.

The monastic authors believe that disciplined, arduous and often repetitive activity must be imposed in such cases if the sinner is to re-assert control over his life and continue to grow and develop for the glorification of God.[73] Prayer is also prescribed in this context because discipline (and the lack of it) and languor and laziness are all seen to apply to every facet of the individual's life.

Thus, for the monk, the effects of languor will be observable in his spiritual life as well as in his working, academic and community life. A vice which thus manifests itself in a variety of ways must, if it is to be effectively cured, be countered by a penance which is equally wide-ranging. Renewed vigour and effort at prayer, work, early-rising and stability are all recommended, simultaneously, to provide a comprehensive response to the problem of sloth. Laziness cannot be overcome by mere words alone. A confessor or soul-friend will not succeed in healing the disease of sloth unless he is able to instil a new spirit of zeal, toil and diligence within the penitent:

> Will a man by talk alone cleanse his house from some disfigurement or move the dusty piles of squalid rubble by mere speech? . . . Therefore while we cleanse the house of the inner man, we need patience and application and toil and unwearied zeal, that we may show patience in injuries, application in religion, toil in business, zeal in progress . . . (Co.Inst.II.3)[74]

Good intentions and new resolutions must, then, always be allied to firm and decisive action on the part of the penitent. The slothful person will only overcome his sinful malaise by hard work, prayer, commitment and application.

Sloth: the Wholesome Antidote, Zeal

The healthy state, which is to be sought after by the repentant idler, is one which is described principally by terms such as perseverance, constancy, stability, application, zeal and discipline.[75]

Zeal and the Christian life This is an attitude, therefore, which should pervade every facet of the good Christian's life—not just his duties regarding work and physical service. For this reason, a holistic approach is to be adopted by the confessor, with the aim of a renewed balance and commitment in the penitent's mental, physical and spiritual activity: 'Languor may be overcome by steadiness of body, heart and thought' (Bi.VI:3,2).[76]

Zeal and moderation The notions of balance, stability and 'finding the mean' are, as we have already noted, cherished by the penitentialists and in particular by Columbanus. We have seen how the latter developed this notion and how he recommended that it be always held up as a guideline in order that the individual Christian should not stray, on the one hand, into a lax minimalism, nor, on the, other into the dangerous regions of excessive penitential activity (Co.Reg.Mon.VII). We have also noted, at a later juncture, how Columbanus set great store on the Christian attitude of remaining patient and steadfast throughout the time of training (*disciplina*) in order that one might be the better prepared for the vicissitudes of life (Co.Inst.IV).[77]

Zeal and self-discipline The penitential teaching on sloth and its remedy is, then, in direct continuity with these thoughts of Columbanus. Training (*disciplina*) is never completed for the true Christian; instead, he must learn to internalise it showing forth discipline in his daily life. In exercising discipline the Christian becomes most truly a disciple and he learns to assert control over his bodily passions and instincts. In short, he assumes control and responsibility for his moral life. Conversely, if idleness gains the upper hand and the individual succumbs to the physical dictates of his body, his creative energy is dissipated and stultified and the opportunity for ministry is lost (Bi.VI:1,1).

Interestingly, the term *disipare* is predicated here of the effects of idleness and sloth in precisely the same fashion as it had been previously employed with regard to the sinful effects of excessive eating and drinking. The end result is the same; in both instances the creative energies of the individual are diverted away from the service of God and others and toward a selfish service of self. The practice of discipline, steadfastness and constancy, whilst most usefully employed in the remedying of sloth, are also essential prerequisites for an authentic living out of the Christian life in all its spheres.

Any attempt then, to avoid the responsibility of self-discipline is to be seen as an inauthentic response to the Christian calling. There are no short cuts to sanctity and one may not seek to avoid effort and responsibility if one is truly to attain the ultimate goal of union with Christ. Columbanus explains: 'Let us not seek upon the way what shall be in our homeland. Therefore, we must be aware, lest perhaps we be careless on the way and fail to reach our true home' (Co.Inst.V).[78]

Zeal and spiritual development The thrust of the Christian life, must be seen as developmental and progressive in the best sense of these two terms. As the Christian matures in years, his life should become more stable and steady and less of his energies should, thus, be dissipated in sinful and futile activity. The Christian must gradually seek to wean himself away from purely physical instincts, so that he may the better concentrate on the higher goal he has set himself. He must constantly set himself new targets and aim for new heights of spiritual growth. To fail to do this means spiritual death, for, as soon as the Christian loses his ardour for personal growth his spiritual life will turn lukewarm and eventually die (*frigescit et mortificatur*: Bi.VI:3,5).

The truly moral life is, then, for Columbanus and his fellow penitentialists a life-long project. As in the natural world, so too in the spiritual domain, each new day must be a day of new growth and another step along the life-long path toward eventual union with Christ: 'let the mind in its progress press onward, even as life presses on its course and let ripeness of the mind increase with fulness of age; and as the spans of life grow shorter, so let the number of our vices lessen' (Co.Inst.VI.2)[79]

III. THE SINFUL DISEASE: VAINGLORY

The vices of pride and vainglory, although seen to be closely related areas of sinfulness, are each accorded separate categories by the later penitentialists. Whereas pride is seen to be a sin opposed, primarily, to the obedience of faith and resulting in blasphemy, disobedience and murmuring, vainglory is described more in terms of an offence against the true nature of worship. Thus, heresy, preoccupation with novelties and contentious behaviour are listed among the offspring of this sinful condition.[80] And whereas, true worship would be centred upon God's honour and glory, vainglory, on the other hand, is seen as sequestering religious activity for less noble ends and indeed for man's own utility.

Vainglory: the Symptoms

Vainglory is also seen to be operative outside of the strictly religious sphere and may be detected in other basically sinful attitudes and activities such as boasting, promoting discord and animosity (Bi.pr.46) In this case, the focus is upon an inordinate striving after praise and esteem. What is being sought by the vainglorious individual is recognition and praise from others, even where such praise is not worth having. Vainglory is, then, so called because the pursuit of 'glory', whilst itself a legitimate and even praiseworthy goal, in this instance is not referred to its proper end. The individual instead of seeking to grow, develop and dedicate his life to the glory of God adopts a sinful and selfish stance whereby he seeks to live and act for his own glory alone.

Contention Contentious behaviour is seen by both Cummean and the Bigotian text as one of the most frequent expressions of vainglory.[81] Whereas disobedience (classified under sins of pride) represents a direct refusal to implement the wishes of a superior, contentiousness seems to be more of a general recalcitrant attitude and a lack of docility. This in turn also distinguishes it from 'murmuring' (a sin of pride) since murmuring, as understood by the penitentialists, implies not alone a spirit of recalcitrance but also a desire to incite and entice others toward the sinful attitude.

Cummean views contentious behaviour as severely reprehensible; he strongly condemns it and rules that the contentious person should 'submit himself to the decision of another: otherwise he shall be anathematized since he is among the strangers to the kingdom of God.'[82] The Christian, in giving way to selfish motives and in seeking always to have his own way, has effectively estranged himself from the Gospel message and has become an *alienus*. The notion that contention is to be seen in terms of a deep-seated sinful attitude, rather than simply isolated instances of disagreement, is further sustained in Columbanus. He makes the distinction between simple contradiction (*contra verbum semplicitur*) and contradiction because of contention (*ex contentione*), and the latter is, evidently, adjudged to be the more serious offence (Co.A.9).

The Bigotian author, in turn, carries this line of reasoning a stage further. He sees the attitude of contention as being quasi synonymous with, or equivalent to, vainglory itself. Thus, it is described as a vice from which many different areas of sinfulness can issue forth, among these being; untruthfulness (*inveritate*), quarrelsomeness (*inquitate*) and heresy. The author attributes the root cause of contention to the replacement of the Christian, oblative, other-centred worldview by a greedy, self-centred and worldly disposition (*facultate saeculi*: Bi.VII.4).

Heresy Very similar language is used with regard to the sinner who intentionally follows a doctrine which is 'other than the Scriptures or a heresy'.[83] Again, the offender here is deemed to have estranged himself from the Church (*alienatur ab ecclesia*). Heresy is understood as a wilful rejection by the sinner of the gift of faith or at least a part of his faith. If a person's religious views do not concur with, or run contrary to, the Scriptures and he continues to persist in these views, then he is to be deemed a heretic. However, just as the heretic falls from grace initially by a wilful decision on his part, so too may he return to grace and renounce his heresy by publicly repenting and condemning his prior opinion (*suam sententiam damnet*: Bi.VII:2).

As we have already seen, Columbanus echoes this teaching. He draws the distinction between sinners who enter into unsound communion with the followers of Bonosus and other heretics either for reasons of ignorance (*per ignorantiam*) or for reasons of contempt (*per contemptum*). Whilst sinners belonging to the first category are to rank among the catechumens and be separated from other Christians for forty days, those belonging to the second category are to undertake the more severe penance of penitential fasting for one year together with periods of abstention from wine and meat (Co.B.25).

The language used by both authors reinforces the close connection between heresy and contention. For Colombanus, the contentious sinner is basically showing forth an attitude of contempt or scorn or disdain; in other words, a stubborn conviction that his own view is superior to the truth and to the will of God. Similarly, the Bigotian text describes the heretic's intention as being above all one of deceiving (*decipere*) or cheating or beguiling (Bi.VII:2). The sinner in his *vain* search for *glory* convinces himself that things are other than they are and seeks to gain esteem and recognition because of his erroneous views.

Boasting The term *iactantia* is employed by the Bigotian author to describe an attitude of boastfulness which he lists among the offspring of vainglory (Bi.VII.tit.). Cummean, however, uses the same term to describe vainglory itself (Cu.VII.tit.). What is being criticised by both authors is basically the same sinful disposition, namely, a tendency toward excessive ostentation and making oneself unnecessarily conspicuous. By drawing attention to his good deeds, the sinner undoes all the merit of his actions. Human glory is juxtaposed to the glory of God (Cu.VII:2).

The boastful or vainglorious person sins because, in seeking human glory, he has directed his activity away from the good and true end, which is God, and has settled instead for human praise. The penitential authors however, are not advocating that personal gifts and talents be hidden; rather, precisely because these are God-given gifts, the merit and praise which they engender should properly be directed to God, the creator rather than to man, the creature.

In this context, then, it is easy to see why the Bigotian author also includes the sins of presumption and hypocrisy as further expressions of vainglory.[84] For, just as boasting represents an inordinate extolling of one's own good qualities or gifts, presumption, in like manner, is seen as the inclination or wish to undertake what is above and beyond one's own God-given capacity, and hypocrisy, in turn, is the feigning of virtues and qualities which, in reality, one does not possess.

Whilst some of these terms may seem rather archaic or even outmoded to the modern ear, the penitentialists are referring to a facet of human nature which is universal and may be applied with equal accuracy to people from whatever era. In today's language we would probably speak of the area at issue here as being that of 'inordinate ambition', that is, an excessive striving after recognition or reward. The quest for such goals, though not sinful in itself, becomes sinful when the sinner has no just claim to the goals in question or when he has adopted unlawful means to attain them.

Perhaps, the most clear account, however, of why such behaviour is out of harmony with the Gospel message is given in the *Old Irish Penitential*. It states clearly: '. . . whatever we do for the sake of pomp or praise from men is called vainglory, and the only reward we gain from it is the praise we have from men, as Christ himself says, "*Amen dico vobis perceperunt mercedam suam*".'[85]

This is evidently a reference to Chapter 6 of St Matthew where Christ condemns hypocrisy. The context of the verse is one where Jesus points out that hypocrites disfigure their faces in order to show others that they have been fasting. These, he affirms, have already received their reward and therefore can expect no other. The true Christian, on the other hand, is to put oil on his head and to wash his face, so that it will not be obvious that he has been fasting. Instead, only his Father in heaven will be aware of the extent of his sacrifice and he in turn will reward him.[86]

This, then, is taken by the penitentialist as being a *modus operandi* for all Christian behaviour. The good Christian will be content that his heavenly Father is aware of his virtuous activity and that he will eventually reward him accordingly. In acting thus, the individual not alone acts charitably and justly toward his fellow men, but he also makes out of this activity an act of faith.

In not seeking public recognition for his Christian service he demonstrates his belief in a God who sees all things and whose love and care far exceeds that of men. Hence, just as in the words of Jesus, the true disciple has no need of 'disfiguring' himself or his activity in order to gain worldly recognition; instead he responds spontaneously and sincerely in fraternal love, secure in the knowledge that he will be rewarded ten-fold by the all-caring father.

Vainglory: the Penitential Cure

Among the measures employed to overcome the spiritual sickness of vainglory are fasting, silence, corporal punishment, exclusion from the Christian community, subjection to another, acts of humility, condemnation of heresy, conversion of others, and restraint in talk.[87]

Whilst Columbanus seeks to remedy the complainer with the more usual monastic methods of imposed silence and fasting, and even physical punishment (Co.B;25), Cummean (Cu.VIII.1) and the Bigotian author (Bi.VII:1) devise other forms of penance which are more specifically geared toward tackling the precise areas of weakness in the vainglorious penitent and helping him overcome these flaws.

Subjection to another Cummean, for instance, instructs the contentious person not only to mend his ways 'but even to subject himself to the decision of another'.[88] The strength of this penitential remedy is reflected in the verb *subdere* which Cummean employs here: the penitent must subject his will to another person; he must exercise precisely that form of control which was heretofore missing in his conduct.

Moreover, in subjecting himself to another person he is, at one and the same time, carrying out an act of great humility as well as one of trust. Humility, because the penitent is called upon in this moment to renounce the dictates of his own will and accept those of another, and trust, because having placed himself in subjection to the other he has rendered himself open and vulnerable. It is this same attitude of openness and vulnerability which will allow God's grace to enter the sinner's heart once more and lead him back to spiritual health.[89]

As well as being a remedy for vainglory, we may point out at this juncture that the attitude of subjecting oneself to another person's judgement is also, in a sense, a description of what the monastic authors saw as the necessary disposition for the confession of sins. Each time a penitent approaches his confessor he too subjects himself to the other's will, and it is this great act of personal humility which disposes the penitent to hearing the voice of God's spirit in his heart. The penitent's own thoughts, opinions and wishes are momentarily suspended and subdued as he places himself before his confessor as one ready to listen and to hear the will of God.[90]

Acts of humility In addition to this form of subjection, Cummean and the Bigotian author both prescribe that the boastful person should humble himself. No more specific instruction is given here, the thrust of the directive, however, remains consistent: the sinner must not allow himself an exaggerated portion of praise or recognition. Instead, he must seek to highlight the fact that he is but a creature and, as such, has received whatever gifts and talents may be his, from his creator (Cu.VII:2).

Conversion of others The penance prescribed for heretics is, interestingly, more specific. Not alone are they to undo the personal harm they have caused themselves by repenting of their erroneous view and publicly condemning it; they are also 'to convert back to the faith those whom they have deceived'.[91] Again, the emphasis is clearly on humility. The sinner has the humbling, even humiliating experience, of pointing out his error to the very persons whom he originally led astray and, in so doing, he has to explain to them the selfish and sinful motives which were a a part of his action. This penance represents a painful, but powerful, journey toward true Christian humility. The penance is not merely a personal exercise which punishes the penitent for his sinfulness; it is a measure specifically designed at once to undo the harm which was done and to restore the sinner to spiritual health.

Restraint Finally, drawing on the lives of the early Fathers, the Bigotian author points out that vainglory will not find a place in the heart of the ordinary, humble, monk, but that it may be strong in priests and kings and those who are in positions of responsibility. In other words, those who have been entrusted with offices of great responsibility must be constantly on their guard, lest they misconstrue their position as being one of power rather than one of service (Bi.VII:4).

If the vice of vainglory does gain entry, it is to be healed 'by restraint in talk and food and by stripping ourselves of the things of the world and by humility'.[92] Thus, the tendency toward vainglory is a subtle and difficult one to overcome, for, instead of decreasing as the individual progresses in years and responsibility, the converse is true, and the more responsibility an individual is given the more possibilities he has for dominating others for selfish ends. Such domination is sinful, for, as the verb suggests, it usurps the role of the master (*Dominus*), to whom alone belongs the power to lead his people.

By continually cultivating a spirit of humility, the person in authority will remind himself of his true position and will be able to fulfil his role in the service of the master and of his fellow men.

Vainglory: the Wholesome Antidote, Docility

We have already pointed out that in countering the vice of vainglory the penitential authors seek to inculcate the virtue of humility and that a great deal of the penitential measures which they prescribe are also designed to cultivate this virtue. One might argue that if humility is to be the antidote sought after here, then surely vainglory and pride collapse into one and the same notion, since humility would more usually be seen as the opposite of pride.

While it is true that the dividing line between vainglory and pride in the penitentials is rather thin and that the subject matter of both these cases is inter-related, nevertheless, the emphasis in each instance is different. The sinful offspring of vainglory, as described here, is above all concerned with recalcitrance and stubbornness in the face of authority. The vainglorious person seeks recognition and reward rather than be led humbly by the spirit.

Docility and conversion For this reason, we may say that if we were to adopt a modern term to describe the virtue in question here, we would most probably use 'docility'. That is to say, it is not humility in its most general form which is being promoted here but more specifically that humble disposition which both Cummean (Cu.VII:1) and the Bigotian text (Bi.VII:I) describe as 'subjecting oneself to the knowledge of another'. This docility demonstrates an openness to the spirit which is usually absent in the vainglorious person.

We have already remarked how this attitude of docility is also paralleled in the moment and act of confession of one's sins. It is, therefore, central to the conversion experience as understood by the Irish penitentialists, a *conditio sine qua non* for true repentance and reconciliation.

Docility and wisdom This juxtaposition of vainglory, on the one hand, and docility, on the other, is strikingly evident in the *Regulae* of Columbanus (Co.Reg.Mon.V), where the latter calls to mind the parable of the Pharisee and the tax-collector (Lk18:9–14). The Pharisee, who is not like other men (robbers, evildoers, adulterers and tax-collectors) personifies the vainglorious person; the tax collector, who stands at a distance and beats his breast and says, 'God have mercy on me a sinner', represents the authentic penitent. Columbanus sums up the moral of the parable thus: 'By these and by that most notorious case of the Pharisee who excused himself, we gather that vanity and proud self-esteem are the destroyer of all good things, when the Pharisee's vainly extolled goods perished and the publican's self-confessed sins vanished away. Then let no large word proceed from a monk's mouth lest his own large labour vanish'.[93]

The humility at issue here, however, is not simply self-abasement. Humbling oneself, according to Columbanus, is but the first step toward opening oneself to wisdom, whence his directive to 'Do nothing without counsel.' And he continues, adding that, whilst it may seem 'hard-hearted that on should always hang upon the lips of another', yet this form of docility is essential, if the good monk is to truly serve Christ and not merely himself (Co.Reg.Mon.IX).

Docility and the life pilgrimage Further, this understanding of docility gels very neatly with Columbanus' 'pilgrim theology'.[94] Docility safeguards the Christian from abandoning his earthly pilgrimage toward Christ or from futilely cultivating some 'human argument or skill, or any vainglorious philosophy, which is unsound' (Co.Inst.II).

Vainglory, on the other hand, ensnares the individual enticing him to 'love the roadway rather than the homeland' (Co.Inst.VIII). So, the Christian must strive to continuously remind himself that his earthly life is but a journey. If he succeeds in doing this, he will be capable of seeing the temptations to vainglory and earthly ambition for precisely what they are, namely spurious and empty attractions.

In the same way, the sinner who repents of this area of sinfulness must realise that repentance means continuing the pilgrim journey. As a slave to vainglory, the sinner has ceased to travel and to grow and instead compromises his call, preferring to settle for temporal glory. As a repentant sinner, he must once again respond to his calling and resume his journey: 'Therefore let this principle abide with us, that on the road we so live as travellers, as pilgrims, as guests of the world, entangled by no lusts . . . but let us fill our minds with heavenly and spiritual images.'[95]

IV. THE SINFUL DISEASE: PRIDE

Whereas the Irish penitentialists considered vainglory to involve an undue exalting of personal gifts or talents, especially with regard to matters of doctrine or discipline, pride, whilst overlapping to some degree, tends to focus more upon interpersonal relationships. For this reason, contempt and envy are cited as foremost among the offspring of this vice. Columbanus describes pride as a disease by which an individual may be infected (*quia superbiae morbo detenetur*: Co.A.11).

Pride: the Symptoms

Other areas of sinfulness which are deemed to issue forth from pride, according to the Bigotian text, include disobedience, blasphemy, murmuring and detraction (Bi.VII:tit.). Pride is portrayed as arising from that self-love which is innate in human nature. This, in turn, is magnified out of due proportion so that the individual develops an exaggerated spirit of independence which is impatient of subjection to any authority, whether human or divine, and also to a deprecation, contempt or jealousy of others.

Envy In a brief reference to the problem of envious behaviour, Finnian instructs that it is to be countered by a spirit of 'kindliness or love of God and of one's neighbour'.[96] He understands envy as striking at the root of the Christian's primary obligations of reverence for God and charity toward one's neighbour. It is, therefore, opposed to the truth because it seeks to magnify one's own gifts and talents and, at the same time, to diminish and deprecate those of others.

A more concrete remedy is prescribed by Cummean, who recommends that the envious person should make amends or satisfaction to whomsoever he may have wronged. And, if he has gone so far as to cause them harm in any way, then he must undo this by giving his 'victim' gifts. Where the harm has been more a case of verbal criticism, due to envy, the sinner is to be set apart from the assembly for four days, during which time he must also fast (Cu.VIII:7–8). These prescriptions are, in turn, echoed and reproduced in full by the Bigotian author (Bi.VIII2:1–2).

The best analysis of envy, however, is perhaps that given in the *Old Irish Penitential* (*c*.800). Here, the author compares envy to a fire which 'burns indifferently what is below and above and about it' and therefore 'envy assails indifferently him that is lower and him that is higher and him that is equal so that it is an enemy to every man whether good or bad, near or far'.[97]

Thus, is envy seen to be a sinful attitude into which the Christian may slip at any time, if he does not exercise due caution. The penitentialist asserts that, just as the envious person has 'no dwelling for God in his heart', so too shall there be 'no dwelling for him with God in heaven' in the next life.[98]

The sinner who succumbs to envy estranges himself from God. In his relations with other people and in his assessment of them he has chosen to ignore the fact that they are God's creatures. In this way, the envious person gains a false perspective upon life and upon human nature. Because of his own sinful pride, he exalts his own merits and strengths, while at the same time considering other people's talents and abilities as prejudicial, detrimental and ultimately a threat to himself.

In his jealousy the envious person has subtracted God from the equation of human relationships. His interaction with other people becomes primarily hostile; he no longer sees them as representative of the glory of God's creation but, instead, a threat to his own ego and standing.

The same penitentialist identifies envy as the vice which 'caused Cain to kill Abel son of Adam, and the Jews to kill Christ'. The author concludes that envy is to be shunned because it can enter even the most intimate of relationships including those of parent-child, husband-wife, monk-abbot and disciple-master. It is, moreover, an especially pernicious vice, he affirms, in that it makes an enemy out of someone precisely because of 'the good that is in him' (OIP.IV:11). In short, it is a vice which seizes upon what is good and wholesome and turns it into an object of malice and corruption instead.

Detraction Detraction is the second of the sinful areas which results from pride. In a passing reference to the problem, Finnian (Vi.29) advises that restraint of heart and tongue (*continentia cordis et lingue*) is the most efficacious remedy here and he cites variously from the apostle James who teaches 'Do not speak evil against one another brethren' (Jas 4:11) and from the psalms: 'Him who slanders his neighbour secretly I will destroy, The man of haughty looks and proud heart I will not endure' (Ps 101:5).

The slanderer and he who willingly listens to a slander are to be punished equally according to Columbanus (Co.A.10). This teaching is also repeated by Cummean, but he takes special care to define the terms in question here (Cu.VIII.10). He points out that if a monk is reporting another's faults for his own good, then this cannot be deemed either detraction or slander. He reasons that to speak the truth can never be seen as defamation (*non est detrahere vera dicere*) and suggests that the matter is best resolved by meditation upon Christ's words where he advises: 'If your brother sins against you, go and tell him his fault, between you and him alone' and later 'If he refuses to listen, tell it to the Church' (Mt. 18:15–17).

'The blasphemy of detraction' is denounced by the Bigotian penitentialist (Bi.VIII:3). He recalls the words of Hyperichius who taught that 'It is better for a monk to eat meat and to drink wine than to eat the flesh of his brethren by defamation'.[99] Here again, the penitentialist is giving his readers a salutary reminder that ascetical activity has its place in the individual quest for holiness, but this place must not be exaggerated beyond reason. Severe and heroic acts of penance are of no use if the penitent does not strive to align his behaviour and attitude with the spirit of the Gospel.

The Bigotian text goes on to recall how the same patristic source traces the biblical origins of defamation to the Genesis creation account and in particular to the words of the serpent to Eve in the garden. He argues, then, that just as the serpent's spurious words to Eve 'caused her to be ejected from Paradise, so too it is with he who speaks against his neighbour because he destroys the soul of him who listens and does not save his own'.[100]

The penitentialist thus sees defamation as an offence against justice, truth and love. An offence against justice, because of the affliction to the injured person's honour, which is, in a sense, stolen from him; one against truth, because, as Cummean has pointed out, defamation is by definition a falsehood or at best a mixture of truth and falsehood. Finally, it is also an offence against love because the Christian is called upon to love his neighbour rather than judge him.

Detraction is seen by Cummean as a sin in which one may participate by cooperation. That is to say, the person who hears a defamatory statement has a duty and responsibility to refute it otherwise he too will share the guilt. Indeed, Cummean makes no distinction between the penances to be imposed on the defamer and upon his cooperator, since both are found to be equally at fault (Cu.VIII:8).

The crucial phrase here, however, is that the cooperator must have 'willingly listened' (*libenter audire*) to the other. The use of the term *libenter* suggests a space, or a possibility to choose another course of action, had the listener so wished. Conversely, by failing to exercise his moral judgement the listener allows himself to be controlled, as it were, by the sinful party and ultimately has an equal share in his sin.

The *Old Irish Penitential* takes up this theme afresh and seeks to clarify it further. The penitentialist argues that there are four instances in which fault-finding may be deemed as legitimate. These are:

(a) To prevent another person from cooperating in the evil.

(b) To correct the evil itself.

(c) To confirm the good.

(d) Out of compassion for the sinner.[101]

Thus, where the correcting party is genuinely concerned for the moral welfare of the sinner and where he sincerely believes that he may be able to halt the spread of evil, he is entitled, and indeed duty bound, to indicate to the sinner his weakness.

This is an important point in the context of our general thesis, for, as we have already observed, it forms an important part of the confessor or *anamchara*'s role. The good confessor must be able to insert himself into that complex problematic of another's sinfulness with the goal of pointing out his error and areas of weakness and leading him back toward spiritual growth and wholeness. If not inspired, however, by the sincerest of motives, the soul-friend risks becoming merely a negative voice, a detractor and judge who, instead of breaking the cycle of sin merely adds to it all the more (Cu.VIII:16).

Murmuring Murmuring (*murmorare*) is considered another expression of sinful pride by many of the penitentialists. It is, moreover, above all a sin of the cloister. Columbanus, for example, imposes a penance of three special fasts for the murmurer (Co.A.9). He gives no direct explanation, however, as to what precisely is meant by this term; the implication is clear, that he is describing the behaviour of monks who complain about the tasks they have been set or about other facets of their lives about which they must follow the decisions of their superiors.

This sin is distinguished from that of disobedience in that the sinner here does not actually refuse to carry out what he has been directed to do, but rather does it begrudgingly or in bad faith. In so doing, he is not truly giving himself to his work but is instead holding back, or placing limits upon his Christian response. For this reason, Cummean orders that the murmurer be set apart (*separetur*) and that his work be rejected (*abiectiatur*: Cu.VIII:6).

Here, in fact, it would seem that penance is recognising in a public manner what has already taken place privately in the sinner's heart. In giving only a half-hearted unwilling commitment the recalcitrant monk has already set himself apart from his brothers and is no longer sharing honestly in their common way of life.

An elaborate, biblical meditation is once again introduced here by the *Old Irish Penitential*. The penitentialist advises monastic superiors that care must be taken to check and to quell 'murmuring about food'. For, he affirms, it was precisely this failing which, on the one hand, allowed the Devil to tempt our first parents into sin 'and on this account, they were driven out of Paradise to hunger and poverty and thirst and death and hell henceforth'.[102]

Secondly, it was this same evil which overtook the Israelites in the desert 'so that only two of them reached the land of promise, Joshua and Caleb'. And it was the same sin which was 'prompted in Judas Iscariot whereby Christ was afterwards crucified' (OIP.IV:9–10). The penitentialist concludes that wherever there has been murmuring and recalcitrance and resentment there has also been a cycle of evil which foments and begets still more evil.

Here again, we have an instance, in the penitential literature, where great attention and analysis is being accorded to an apparently minor transgression; in harmony with our general thesis that the penitentialists were anxious to get to the root cause of evil and to the underlying vice from which a variety of sinful deeds spring. It is for precisely this reason that the penitentialists devote much time and thought to such apparently paltry notions as murmuring and contention.

As they saw it, these more subtle expressions of sin often tell us more about the true roots of sin than its more striking manifestations such as murder, theft or sexual misconduct. Whereas the sinful nature of such acts are readily acknowledged and may be countered by a severe penance, they do not tell us much about the underlying psychology or patterns of sinful behaviour. Those sinful dispositions, however, which remain at the level of attitude or mental disposition can often be more insidious and harder to detect and, for this very reason, the ancient, Celtic monks were all the more determined to 'do battle' here in order that sin might be lured forth from its lair and overcome.

Contempt We mentioned, at the beginning of this section, how contempt (*contemptus*) was also regarded by the penitentialists as among the foremost of the sinful fruits of pride. What is at issue here is that attitude which in modern ethical parlance one might also refer to as 'contumely'. In other words, this attitude differs from detraction and envy in that it is expressed in the presence of the 'victim'. Once again, though, it is basically a sin against the honour of the other person. It represents an attempt to deprive another of that honour which is his due whether positively (by means of words or gestures) or negatively (by omissions).

There is agreement between Cummean and the Bigotian author that the individual who 'proudly censures others' for reasons of contempt should make satisfaction to the injured party. This is clearly a case of 'positive' contempt where another individual is wilfully dishonoured by the sinner.[103] Some examples of 'negative' contempt are also given in these texts. One such instance is the case where a monk, out of contempt, 'disdains to bow to a senior'. Here, we note that the gravity of the offence depends, to some extent, on the dignity of the person who is dishonoured. Whilst the omission of a particular form of greeting may not, on the face of it, seem to be particularly offensive among lay people, for instance, inside the monastery this omission takes on a new significance for it suggests a lack of respect for one's superiors (Cu.VIII:18).

Similarly, a monk may also be disobedient out of an attitude of contempt and this is seen as more serious still. Here, not alone does pride dishonour the superior, but it also leads the individual to contravene his expressed wishes, thus placing him effectively at odds with the rule of his community. For this reason, the penitentialist suggests that such sinners 'shall remain outside the assembly without food' until they are healed, whence they shall 'humbly knock until they are received'.[104]

Informing and complicity According to the teaching of Cummean, informing and complicity are two sides of the same sinful coin. Thus, both the informer and he who fails to correct his brother's sin are to be penalised. In both cases, what is called for is fraternal correction in the best sense. The informer lacks charity and loyalty; he is concerned only to see his brother censured for his sin, rather than healed and restored to spiritual health. Therefore, Cummean affirms that he who is informed upon and the informer are of the same sinful status (*dilatus et dilator consimili persona*: Cu.VIII:11). The former would not have been informed upon were he not guilty of some sinful transgression, and the latter is equally culpable since he did not strive to help the other but, instead, sought only to have him censured.

By extension, this teaching of Cummean affords us some further insight into his views on penance. For the confessor it is not permissible to have as one's end the punishing of the sinner. Instead, concern for true penance will lead toward his conversion and eventual restoration to a wholesome spiritual life.

Just as the informer is to be reprimanded, so too must he who is silent about another's sin. Cummean believes that the truly Christian attitude before another's transgression is not silence or a tacit compliance, rather, one is to 'rebuke the sinner with confidence' (*arguere eum cum fiducia*).[105]

Again, the penitentialist is here disclosing, to some extent, his views on what the approach of the confessor or soul-friend must be. That is, he cannot remain silent about areas of behaviour or thought which he knows to be sinful; he must rebuke the sinner in a fraternal way in order to point out the right course of action to him.

Cummean is, however, careful to emphasise the crucial difference between reprimanding another in trust (*arguere cum fiducia*) on the one hand, and excessive, ill-mannered correction (*arguere proterue*) on the other. This pert or impudent type of censure is not compatible with Christian charity and is itself deemed to be reprehensible, so that the person guilty of this type of attitude is humbly invited to do penance and to enlighten the burden (*lenire primo eos*) which he has imposed on the other (Cu.VIII:21).

Pride: the Penitential Cure

Among the measures listed, by way of a penitential remedy, for pride are condemnation of false views, conversion of others, exclusion from the assembly, rejection of work done, making satisfaction, silence, acts of humility, conciliation of others as well as the more usual practices of fasting, abstinence and chanting of psalms (Cu.VIII:1–27.passim).

We can see here that these penances fall broadly into two distinct categories. There are those penances, which are designed to eradicate the root of pride from the sinner's heart, such as acts of humility, silence, fasting and prayer; and those more specifically designed at making good the damage caused to others by the sinner's attitude and actions, such as making satisfaction, together with conversion and conciliation of others and a public avowal of the erroneous nature of one's previously held ideas. Hence, the penitentials have a keen awareness of the communitarian dimensions of sinful behaviour.

Concern for others Just as sin does not limit itself to the individual sinner but instead extends its sphere of influence begetting further sin and infecting more and more people, like a disease; so too conversion, if it is to be sincere, must seek to heal both the sinner and those who have been harmed by him. Indeed the order in which these measures are to be adopted is also quite clear and consistent.

The former heretic, for instance, is first to condemn his opinion and convert others and only afterwards does he do private penance. Similarly, the proud person who censures others must first make satisfaction to them and later undertake a fast. The envious person must first make satisfaction with gifts and later shall do private penance. And again, he who rebukes others shall first conciliate them and then sing psalms.[106] The priority is, then, always to seek to undo the harm which has been done as a first step toward genuine conversion.

The logic here is incontrovertible; if a penitent's desire for conversion is sincere and authentic, he will be able to prove this by undoing the evil which he has caused. Further, by acting quickly, the damage caused by his sinful pride may be contained and the vicious circle of sin which begets further sin may be broken. Moreover, since the conversion is, of its nature, a lengthy often life-long path, it would be most impractical, not to say impossible, to await a full cure before setting about undoing the results of one's sinful activity.

Undoing the effects of sin Instead, the penitentialists deem that the initial desire for repentance is sufficient evidence to suggest that the penitent may now begin to remedy the sinful effects of his pride among others. Indeed, in this public admission of guilt the penitent will also strengthen his private conversion since what is being dealt with here are not two separate elements but rather two sides of the same reality.

The practical wisdom of this penitential practice is as impressive as is its logical consistency. The reformed sinner knows better than any other the weaknesses and failings in his nature which first led him into sin. He, then, more than any teacher, is best disposed to highlighting the dangers of pride and selfishness. He can teach others with a voice of experience as one who had once succumbed to the temptation of egoism or contempt or envy or whatever other form of pride but who has now turned from sinful behaviour and begun to walk the path of repentance instead.

Paradoxically, through this manner of penitential praxis the sinner actually employs what formerly was an area of weakness to strengthen his own faith as well as that of others. In so doing, the sinner has begun at last to act selflessly and he can now truly be 'proud' in the best sense of the word, of his activity since he now renders glory to God rather than to himself alone.

Pride: the Wholesome Antidote, Compassion

According to the Old Irish penitentialist, the virtues which are to be sought after as a spiritual antidote to pride include 'kindliness of heart without malice, . . . brotherly love, helpfulness to one's neighbour, speaking well of others, hatred of reviling, rejection of murmuring, magnifying the good, rebuking the evil and a compassionate mind'.[107]

Compassion and others The penitent, in other words, must be able to see others in a new light; he must no longer look upon them as rivals, opponents or adversaries, but instead must recognise them for what they are, his brothers and sisters in Christ. He must acknowledge their talents and indeed seek to 'magnify' these, whilst at the same time 'rebuking' any unworthy sentiment of envy or jealousy on his own part. In this way, he will show forth a 'compassionate' spirit rather than a competitive one. He will learn to suffer and rejoice with others rather than be scornful or critical of their good fortune.

This, then, is the attitude which should characterise both the penitent and the monk, according to the Bigotian author. Both in the course of their ascetic activity and penance run the risk of succumbing to pride on account of their penitential activity. The penitentialist explains:

> We should beware of this vice which sometimes thrives on virtuous exercises, that is on fasting, vigils and abstinence, which however by lowly and ignoble service and above all by humility and pure prayer, fades away so that we may say from the inmost heart with the Psalmist: 'From my secret sins cleanse me, O Lord'. (Bi.VIII.6)

There is, thus, a keen awareness on the part of the penitentialist that the very activity which is employed in the sinner's rehabilitation may become the eventual Achilles' heel of his spiritual renewal. There is always the danger that the penitential exercises and ascetic activities would come to be regarded as ends in themselves. In that event, the whole penitential and therapeutic project would fail and the penitent would fall victim to one of the most pernicious and insidious of vices, pride.

Compassion and service For this reason, he is anxious to underline that all penitential activity must be carried out in a spirit of 'lowly and ignoble service' (*ministratione vero indigna et servile*: Bi.VIII:6). The term *ministratione* suggests a sense of direction; that is, penance cannot be undertaken simply for its own sake; it must be an activity which is ultimately at the service of God and of others. This spirit of service must be allied to 'pure prayer' and the 'greatest humility' (*maxima humilitate*), and the whole attitude must be born of a sincerity which comes from the inmost heart (*intimo corde*). Thus, repentance and conversion must spring from an authentic desire to change oneself and to purge oneself of all sinful motives.

Compassion and contrition Therefore, the penitentialist evokes the psalmist's plea: 'Clear thou from me hidden faults. Keep back thy servant also from presumptuous sins let them not have dominion over me. Then I shall be blameless and innocent of great transgression' (Ps 19:12–13). Here, at the level of his most intimate motivation, the penitent must wage his battle with sin. At stake is the sincerity and veracity of his whole penitential project. For, unless the penitent can purify his intention and motivation from all stain of pride, he will merely have escaped from one form of sin to fall into another which is more subtle and, ultimately, more dangerous.

The conviction that pride must be purged from the heart of the disciple is shared by Columbanus. In the first of his *Regulae* (Co.Reg.

Mon.I), he reminds his monk's of Paul's great christological hymn which recalls how Christ 'humbled himself and became obedient onto death even death on a cross' (Phil 2:8).

Compassion and obedience The humility and obedience of Christ, therefore, must become the archetype of all truly Christian behaviour. Columbanus argues that the obedience of the disciple must be so solid and resolute as to never refuse whatever challenge comes his way, 'however hard and difficult it may be'. Instead, the Christian's life must be characterised by a 'zeal and gladness' (*fervore et laetitia*) to be obedient to the divine will. And he recalls the words of Jesus in the Gospels where he reminds his followers: 'he who does not take his cross and follow me is not worthy of me' (Mt 10:38).[108]

Compassion and suffering For Columbanus, then, the road to true discipleship and, by extension, the road of authentic conversion and repentance necessarily implies some hardship and suffering. The penitent, or disciple, must have as his model the suffering Christ so that joining himself to his passion and death he will also eventually rise with him and be exalted with him. The way of humility and obedience and penance is precisely that—a way—and, like all ways, if followed faithfully will eventually lead to the ultimate goal which is union with Christ.

Concluding observations

We can see that, in the vice of pride, the penitentialists believe they have arrived at the ultimate and most subtle expression of sin. Whereas other areas of vice produce obvious sinful effects, pride is regarded as more subtle and pernicious. Precisely because of its elusive nature there is always the risk of it not being fully eradicated by penitential activity, thus leaving it free to produce further patterns of sin. For this reason, Columbanus considers pride and its opposite humility as the two primary poles from which most other expressions of good and evil are produced: 'But what departs from its established goodness and innocence is the first evil, which is the pride of primal wickedness; the opposite of which is the lowly esteem of a righteous goodness that acknowledges and glorifies its Creator and this is a rational creature's first good'.[109]

Thus, the penitentialists, in placing pride last among the vices to be dealt with in their survey of human sinfulness, have, as it were, peeled away the various layers of sinfulness which afflict the human condition and at last arrived at the most subtle, and yet most profound, expression of the human rejection of God.

The proud attitude represents a refusal, on the part of the human subject, to recognise his creatureliness and consequently a refusal to recognise God as creator. The true disciple, on the other hand, will always bear in mind his Christian lowliness (*Christianae humilitati*: Co.Reg.Mon.VIII). Lowliness will thus be his strength, affirms Columbanus, for, in acting out of obedience and humility, the Christian will 'according to the Lord's word feel the yoke of Christ pleasant an his burden light' (Mt 11:30). And, he continues, 'lowliness of heart is the repose of the soul when wearied with vices and toils and its only refuge from so many evils'.[110]

This lowliness, then, must equally be the goal of the penitent as of the disciple or monk. For, only in a lowly and humble attitude will the penitent find refuge from the sin which burdens him and open his heart to the healing, forgiving and restoring power of God.

CHAPTER FOUR

CELTIC PENANCE AND THE CATEGORIES OF THE *ORDO PAENITENTIAE*

In the foregoing two chapters our efforts have been largely exegetical; we have sought to gain a clearer concept of the Celtic understanding of sin, penance and conversion by tracing the penitential process through each of the eight categories of vice, remedy and virtue. This material is what the canonist might refer to as the remote material of penance, the sins or vices or moral weaknesses which the penitent must acknowledge and confess as part of his conversion process.

Another question now automatically presents itself for consideration: what do the penitentials and Celtic penitential discipline have to say about the proximate material of penance? In other words, do these texts recognise the traditional elements of contrition, confession and satisfaction and, if so, what insights do they offer to the modern student and pastor?

At this juncture, it is also timely to recall the original terms of our study—to relate the fruits of our current labours to the practice of the sacrament of penance today. With this in mind, we have modelled this chapter largely upon the categories set forth upon sections two and three of the new *Ordo Paenitentiae* (1973) which deal with the 'Reconciliation of Penitents in the Church's life' and the 'Offices and Ministries in the Reconciliation of Penitents'.[1] The *Ordo* itself was introduced not solely in order to offer new formulae for penitential celebrations, but also as a contribution toward a renewal of the very concept of Christian penance and of favouring the progressive construction of an integral, organic and articulate penitential system.[2] The introduction to the *Ordo* gives us, then, an idea of the theological framework in which the Church's teaching on this aspect of the sacrament of penance is to be discussed.

Evidently, if our present study is to bear fruit for present-day penitential practice and theology it must be available and accessible to analysis and discussion in the terms and categories of this kind of theological framework.

Consequently, there now follows an analysis of the sacrament of penance and its parts passed through the filter, as it were, of Celtic penitential theology.

I. CONTRITION: PIERCING THE HEART[3]

As with current understanding of the sacrament of penance, so too in the penitentials there was an awareness that true conversion could not take place without purposeful sorrow, confession of sin and the making of satisfaction. Furthermore, the process of conversion began at the first moment of compunction when the penitent began to turn back to God in sorrow and from here continued through the moment of confession, through the time of reparation, the granting of absolution and beyond, until it was intimately woven into the daily life of the penitent.

A Purposeful Sorrow

Finnian at the beginning of his penitential explains the conversion process thus:

> In the name of the Father and of the Son and of the Holy Ghost. If anyone has sinned by thought in his heart and immediately repents, he shall beat his breast and seek pardon from God and make satisfaction and so be whole.[4]

Thus, the first stage of conversion is compunction or purposeful sorrow for sin. Sin has it roots in the heart and therefore from the heart it must be excised. Finnian goes on to urge that the repentant sinner should be in a state of 'weeping and tears by day and night' (*in fletu et lacrimis*), as long as he remains in a state of sin. This state, however, is not to be confused with one of a morbid gloom, for such a disposition is in itself sinful and serves only to further erode the penitent's moral strength (Vi.29).

The Bigotian author, as we have already seen, takes up and develops this idea. For him, sorrow can be either a source of life (*salutiferum*) or a source of death (*mortiferum*).[5] Obviously, the first of these is to be the authentic response of the sinner. There is an awareness, here, on the part of the penitentialist, that heartfelt sorrow and aversion to sin are not quite the same thing. For this reason, he points out that no other sorrow, not even the sorrow caused by the death of parents or dear ones or any other calamity, is to be equated with the sorrow which we have for our sinfulness (Bi.V.13).

In fact, he claims, even the sorrow of bereavement or loss will eventually lead only to death if it is over-indulged in. True contrition involves a purposeful sorrow which arises from a genuine Christian aversion to sin, this aversion being the pain we feel on account of the presence of evil or the absence of the good. The penitentialist explains:

> The one (sorrow) that brings salvation (is found in us) when we are sorry for our sins and for the sins of others and (these sins) moves us to an abundance of tears with due penance.[6]

A Decisive Act

This aversion to sin, moreover, is a key element in contrition, as the penitentialists perceive it. It implies a willingness to turn away from the sins of the past, to make reparation for them here and now, and to so modify one's behaviour that one remains free of sin in the future. Thus, sorrow does not remain at the level of sensible feeling but leads to an act of the will so that the individual penitent decides to modify his personal behaviour.

The penitentialist seeks to further reinforce this notion with a citation from the writings of Saint Syncletica who reasons: 'Sorrow for our good means that we should sigh for our sins and for our neighbour's ignorance and that we should not fall short of our vocation and that we should attain to the goal of perfect goodness.'[7]

Consequently, contrition is ineluctably bound up with the notion of one's Christian calling or vocation. Thus, a more emotional type of sorrow for sin merely because of the loss it has incurred does not suffice. The sinner who is sorry because sin has ruined his good name, or his health, or his fortunes is responding solely to natural motivations. In order to find true conversion, the motive of his sorrow must have reference to God. Cummean states clearly that true penance must involve turning to penance, correction of the error, and spiritual rehabilitation of the sinner (Cu.ps.4). There is, then, a logic in authentic conversion which necessarily draws the penitent to a true inner change or *metanoia* and eventually to a closer relationship with God.

An Inner Conversion

The later penitential texts seek to shed more light on the place of contrition and remorse within the penitential framework. Cummean, for instance, lists twelve ways in which sins may be remitted.[8] These are:

1. Baptism
2. Charitable activity
3. Almsgiving
4. Shedding of tears
5. Confession of sin
6. Affliction of heart and body
7. Amendment of one's ways
8. Intercession of the Church
9. Showing of mercy
10. Conversion of sinners
11. Showing of forgiveness
12. Martyrdom

The order of this list is most important. Therefore, baptism is the first sacrament by which sin is remitted, enabling the Christian, to lead a Christian life. Once sin, however, begins to erode his Christian testimony he must 'shed tears' and confess his sin, 'afflict his heart and body' and mend his ways. Then, once he has begun to master his own sinfulness he is able once more to give Christian witness in the form of forgiveness, 'conversion of sinners' and ultimately martyrdom in the typically Celtic sense, namely a life of heroic witness.

Cummean cites from the biblical example of Ahab's acts of penance (1 Kings 21:29) where the Lord says: 'Because (Ahab) has humbled himself before me, I will not bring this evil in his days.' Ahab's conversion was not merely a superficial one, for, we are told, 'he rent his clothes, and put on sackcloth upon his flesh, and fasted and lay in sackcloth and went about dejectedly.'[9]

In the same way, for Cummean, the penitent must not merely desire to change at a superficial level but must seek a complete change of heart. The Bigotian text echoes this sentiment with an excerpt from the writings of Gregory which recalls the contrition or compunction of St Paul.[10] The text argues here that Paul's contrition arose out of the discrepancy which he perceived between his status as one who is called by God and his present sinful state; this gives rise to the admission: 'For I am the least of the apostles, unfit to be called an apostle because I persecuted the church of God' (1 Cor 15:9).

Similarly, the penitentialist observes, Paul was often moved to a heartfelt sorrow when he recognised that he was torn between two laws so that he had to confess: 'I see in my members another law at war with the law of my mind and making me captive to the law of sin which dwells in my members' (Rom 7:23). Yet the Apostle's sorrow is never a self-pitying gloom but is at all times linked to a purpose of amendment and a desire to draw ever closer to Christ; this is to be seen in another of the Pauline texts chosen by Gregory: 'I do not run aimlessly, I do not box as one beating the air, but I chastise my body and subdue it lest after preaching to others I myself should be disqualified' (1 Cor 9:26–27)

A Christocentric Activity

Contrition, as described here, therefore, is not a self-indulgent sorrow but a sorrow which has a definite direction and purpose. The same passage recalls that a recurring theme in the writings of St Paul is his *Sehnsucht* for the light of Christ. The penitentialist emphasises how the apostle sees earthly life as a pilgrimage to God: 'Now we see in a mirror dimly, but then face to face. Now I know in part; then I shall understand fully' (1Cor 13:12).

Therefore, sorrow for sin must be placed squarely within a Christ-oriented context. Due to our dim sight, our imperfect understanding and our feeble faith we are sinful creatures; but by turning away from our sin and toward Christ we can overcome sin and our spiritual myopia. It therefore makes no sense to separate sorrow for sin from the desire to follow Christ more closely because both are ineluctably a part of the same moment of contrition.

The Pauline view is reflected and developed in the writings of Columbanus. He reinforces the notion that sorrow for sin must be a wholesome sorrow, a sorrow which does not give way to despair, but one which shares, instead, in the death and resurrection of Christ: 'let us be sad even unto death with Christ that our sorrow may be turned into joy.'[11]

Contrition, then, of its very nature must look ahead; always aware of the evils of sin, it must be equally conscious of the joy of Christ's resurrection. The two cannot be separated. Columbanus holds that the moment of considering one's sins implies, for the Christian, a simultaneous awareness of Christ's saving activity.

Consequently, the sinner must not be over-indulgent in his sorrow (*nimium tristes*). Instead, sorrow for sin should be tempered by rejoicing for Christ's saving power, just as rejoicing should also be tempered by an awareness of one's sin: '. . . sorrowing for our sins, rejoicing for the hope of eternal life, sorrowing for Christ's absence, triumphing likewise, because we read, "we shall see him as he is".'

Therefore, both sorrow and joy are part of the moment of contrition. The sinner rejects his sin, decides to renounce it and to follow Christ instead, and, in so doing, he anticipates the joy which true union with Christ entails. He is not the prisoner of some guilt-ridden, anguished state out of which there is no passage. Rather, his contrition, by its very nature, orients him toward the joyful experience of a God who saves.

For Columbanus, as for the Bigotian penitentialist, contrition entails a God-oriented or life-oriented sorrow. It is for this reason, too, that Columbanus links the penitent's sorrow with that of Christ. Thus, contrition becomes a true participation in the sorrow of Christ and not a self-centred, self-reproaching remorse.

On the contrary, it is precisely this selfish component which must be purified and transformed within the conversion process: 'Therefore let us die, let us die for the sake of life, since Life dies for the dead, so that we may be able to say with Paul, "I live, yet no longer I, but Christ lives in me."'[13] In this manner, Columbanus emphasises the need for contrition to be true and internal—not mere words and signs but, instead, a genuine, inner piercing of the heart. At the centre of the conversion experience is this desire to turn away from an orientation to sin and to turn toward an orientation to Christ and his message.

Likewise, when the new *Ordo* speaks of 'heartfelt contrition' in terms of a conversion which 'affects a person from within so that it progressively enlightens him and renders him continually more like Christ', the concept of contrition advocated here is broadly similar to that proffered by the penitentialists and Celtic penitential theology.[14] Contrition, Columbanus would say, is precisely that act of the will in which the individual turns away from a situation where he is painting in his moral life a despot's image (*pingere tyrannicae imaginis*) and resolves to allow Christ to paint his image there instead (*Christus suam imaginem pingere*: Co.Inst.IX).[15]

A Component of Conversion

The three moments of conversion, namely, renouncement of sin, adherence to Christ and following his message are already present in the act which is called contrition. For while the sinner has not yet attained the desired end, already in his contrite state he is able to look forward to it. Thus, we can say that there is a continuous interaction between these elements of conversion so that there is no break between the moment of contrition, the moment of conversion and the moment of following Christ. On the contrary, in deciding to turn away from sin the sinner also decides to turn toward Christ and toward a Christian programme of life.

This relationship between the elements of contrition, conversion and the will to discipleship is not a chronological interaction but rather a dialogical one. All of the elements of conversion are already present, at least by desire, in that act of the will which is contrition, and from this moment is born a true repentance and will to amend one's life.

What is important, however, is that the sinner's first step towards repentance be a free and genuine one. The *Irish Canons* remind us that "The Lord commands a willing victim" (Hi.III.8) and calls to mind Moses' invitation to his people after the episode of the golden calf: "Who is on the Lord's side? Come to me" (Ex 32:36).[16]

Every penitent must, at the outset, respond to this invitation for himself. It is only after having taken this step in his heart that he can enlist the help of a soul-friend to complete the penitential process and effect a true conversion.

II. CONFESSION: OPENING THE HEART

By and large, the notion of confession, as we understand it today, is the same as that of the penitentialists: the penitent makes a confession or self-accusation to the priest with a view to being officially reconciled in the eyes of the Church.

An Act of Self-Disclosure

And this confession, in turn, is seen as a necessary element in the entire conversion process. Columbanus has this to say:

> It is ordained that confessions be made carefully, especially of mental disturbances before going to mass, lest perhaps anyone should approach the altar unworthily, that is if he does not have a clean heart.[17]

Clearly, confession is understood here in terms of a self-accusation or disclosing of the impurities of sin in order to be purified or healed from one's sin. Columbanus goes on, in the same vein, to describe the moment of confession as one of healing. He affirms that it is 'better to wait until the heart is healed than rashly to approach the judgement of the throne'.[18] Therefore, confession is the logical consequence of compunction. Compunction, as we have already seen, evokes the metaphor of healing and medicine. So, just as ulcers are lanced to allow the corrupt matter within to escape, the heart is pierced, as it were, by the lance of contrition in order to enable it to emit the deadly virus of sin. Confession, then, is the inescapable corollary of contrition which allows this outpouring of sin or *catharsis*. Columbanus describes this purgative action in the following manner: '. . . we must refrain and cleanse ourselves from interior vices and the sicknesses of the ailing soul'.[19]

Furthermore, the initiative for this purgative, purificatory and ultimately healing act clearly belongs to the penitent. Just as the genuineness of contrition was seen to depend entirely upon the sincerity of his purpose, with confession the penitent must allow this purgative and cathartic process to take place in a free and unhindered manner.

It is also important that the confession be full and entire. Columbanus stresses that the penitent is to confess capital sins (*peccatis capitalibus*), sensual sins (*peccatis carnalibus*) and even lesser transgressions and distractions of the mind (*commotionibus animi*).

To the modern observer it may seem that these penitential texts ran the risk of reducing the complexities of personal morality to the simplicities of a list of isolated, individual acts of commission or omission.[20] It should be noted, however, that confession under this system had to take place within the framework and practice of the 'cure by contraries' to which we have often referred already. Presumably, Columbanus and his fellow penitentialists would argue that for the physician of souls to make a prudent diagnosis and judgement he would need as much information as possible about the penitent's spiritual ailment.

An Examination of Conscience

For this reason, too, a formula of examination was found to be helpful. Whilst critics of the Celtic penitential system might, again, regard this as an unhealthy kind of interrogation, we should not forget the context in which these early confessions were made. For we are dealing, above all, with a primitive Church where people did not have Scripture readily at their disposal, just as they would not have had access to the teaching of the Fathers, save for the information they could glean from sermons and homilies.

Given, therefore, the paucity of education and of awareness of such matters among ordinary people, it is not really surprising that the early Celtic ministers of penance felt they had to take a more active role in helping the penitent with his examination of conscience. In so doing, they were able to make of the examination of conscience a privileged moment for a pedagogy of struggle against sin and of personal sanctification.

Given, also, that the penitent's confession reflected his living understanding of sin, morality and the moral life, these early ministers of penance would have felt obliged to inculcate their own vision of the moral life, or at least supplement the penitent's existing vision, in order that the moment of confession might be a significant element in a process of conversion to the Gospel message and not just an exchange of words between penitent and priest.

To help him in his task of assessing the penitent's sin, the confessor used an interrogatory formula known as the *Questiuncula*. Such a formula is twice referred to by the Bigotian text; unfortunately, the formula itself has not survived. It is believed, however, to have been similar in form to the formula used in the later penitential texts of *Pseudo Bede* and the *Corrector of Burchard*; that is to say, a set of questions addressed to the penitent by his confessor, each of which when answered in the affirmative was to be followed by the pronouncement of the appropriate penance.[21]

We may surmise, then, that the *questiuncula* would itself have been based upon the the categories of sin and vice which we have explored in Chapters Two and Three and would, thus, have been ultimately derived from whatever knowledge of Scripture and of the doctrine of the Fathers as was available at that time.

The merit of such a situation is obvious. Confession of sins could not be reduced merely to an internal dialogue between the penitent and God. The penitent did not make a self-accusation according 'to his lights' but, instead, was enabled by the confessor to examine his conscience in the light of the Gospel. The ultimate grounding of confession upon precepts taken from Scripture and Church doctrine helped situate it in a more definitively Christian ambiance; one which precluded any sort of obsessive self-accusation and which pointed the penitent instead toward the path of recovery.

An Opening to God

Moreover, this procedure meant that confession of sins was ultimately linked to a parallel confession of God. Cummean explains this notion with the aid of a verse from Psalm 31: '. . . the Psalmist testifies, "I said I will confess against myself my injustice to the Lord and you have forgiven the iniquity of my sin".'[22] Here, in his avowal of his sinfulness, the sinner is also confessing his belief in a God who forgives. It is true that the penitent is primarily involved in an act of avowal, that he is opening his heart, declaring himself, laying bare his soul, but this laying bare is itself an act of praise and trust and hope and faith and openness to a God who is good and forgiving.

The confession of faith and praise to God is, then, an undercurrent and a necessary corollary to the confession of sins. The sinner has no need to hide his guilt, no need to conceal his sinfulness but instead makes an act of faith in opening out his whole life to divine mercy.

There is, then, a sense in which the moment of confession is not alone a question of confessing sin but also a time for confessing one's belief in a merciful God and of praising him for his goodness. Columbanus advises his listeners to 'request and pray for the unspeakable mercy of the righteous and good God from the bottom of our heart through Jesus Christ his son . . .'[23] This little phrase encapsulates perfectly the triple confession of sin, faith and praise which is at the heart of an authentic conversion.

Again, it is evident here that the interaction of the three elements is not chronological but dialogical. The penitent confesses his sin, precisely because he believes in a good, all-merciful God to whom he wishes to render praise. He is confessing his belief in Christ's saving power and his willingness to enter with him into his paschal mystery. And he is also praising a God who allows his creatures the existential space to fail and to fall, but who calls them again and again into a new and stronger relationship with him.

A Component of Conversion

The nature of this renewal and conversion process is graphically described by Columbanus in his second sermon. Using an agricultural metaphor he compares the work of conversion to that of the farmer who must plough his field to break up the ground and render it receptive and fertile to new seed: 'Break up your fallow ground and sow not over thorns; how much more we ought to clean the field of our heart from the harmful notions of the vices.'[24]

Thus, confession and penitential exercises form the first part of conversion, together they constitute that process which renders the individual open again to the words of Christ. There cannot be two crops in the field of the soul; either the penitent continues with the sinful crop and reaps the sinful harvest; or else he takes decisive action and tills the inner soil with the 'sturdy share' of confession and penance.

This, however, remains but the initial phase; the farmer having cleared his field of 'harmful rubble' must next sow the new seed. Otherwise his efforts to rid his land of 'thorns and roots' will have been in vain and these will eventually grow again. In similar fashion, the sinner who has opened his heart and who has undertaken penitential exercises is engaged in a fruitless exercise unless the whole process is oriented toward the word of God and an improvement in his personal morality:

> . . . it is not enough for us to till our body's clay with the toil of fasts and vigils, unless we are anxious above all to correct our vices and form our characters seeing that we believe our hope of harvest is laid up not on earth but in heaven.[25]

Thus does Columbanus link the processes of correcting vice, personal conversion and the forming of character (*vitia corrigere moresque componere*). Confession, therefore, must not lose sight of its overall orientation. The penitent must undergo an inner change of heart, by which he not alone turns away from sin but turns *toward* a new and improved attitude of life: 'For what use is the religion of the outward man, if there is not also shown an improvement of the inner.'[26] Hence, it is precisely the improvement of the 'inner man' which is the crux of the conversion process (*emendatio hominis interioris*) .

This is, in fact, the closest that Celtic penitential theology comes to describing what we might today call a profound inner conversion or *metanoia*. This type of conversion, however, does not signal the end of the penitent's efforts at combating his sin; on the contrary, it strengthens his resolve to make this a daily activity.

An Acknowledgement of Sinfulness

We have already observed how Columbanus advocates a daily confession of faults. Despite the fact that such confessions would have been based upon the confessor's interrogation, Columbanus also advocates a situation whereby the individual would eventually undertake by himself a daily scrutiny of conscience. He explains: '. . . let us know nothing more profitable for ourselves than to examine ourselves daily . . . keeping account of our words and thoughts.'[27]

Clearly, then, confession of sin before being made to the confessor must first, at least in some sense, be made to one's self. Or, better still, the sinner must initially acknowledge his sinfulness before God and within the context of his spiritual life. This preliminary examination and acknowledgement will then, naturally, lead to the moment of confession proper. The examination of conscience or self-scrutiny is the beginning of the penitential path and represents a spiritual stock-taking, on the part of the penitent, carried out as always before the all good and merciful God: 'Let each examine himself, lest he be found free and living instead of bond and crucified and let each remain before God in that state in which he was called.'[28]

All forms of self-scrutiny and self-examination must, therefore, be carried out only within a context of prayer and awareness of the presence of God. To divorce the scrutiny from this context would be to rob it of its significance and purpose, for the ultimate aim here is not a contemplation of one's own sin or sinfulness for its own sake but the fostering of the awareness of one's need for divine mercy and forgiveness.

Thus, the confession of human weakness must, here again, give way to a confession of faith and praise in the all merciful God, so that the penitent having acknowledged his own sin can then pray with Columbanus:

> Inspire our hearts . . . O Jesus with that breath of your Spirit and wound our souls with your love, that the soul of each of us may be able to say in truth, Show me him whom my soul has loved for by love am I wounded.[29]

Confession in Celtic Spirituality

The confession of sin spilling over into a confession of divine praise is typical of Celtic spirituality.

Patrick's own *Confessio* is precisely a confession in this broader and more accurate sense of the word. For, whilst the text does frequently refer to Patrick's very keen sense of weakness, past sinfulness, the troublesome sensual desires of his youth and his awareness that he is a sinner and unlettered, all of this is very much secondary to his own explicit statement of purpose for writing his confession which is primarily 'to reveal and confess the works of God'.[30]

Columbanus shares this dual meaning of the term confession. For, whilst he urges his monks 'to make confession . . . whenever it is opportune, since confession and penance free from death', he prefaces his homiletical material by expressing the hope that the faith which is in the hearts of his listeners should open '. . . the mouths of all Christians to a salutary confession . . .'[31]

Whereas in the first instance the confession in question is evidently an avowal of sin, in the second it is principally an expression of faith, hope and praise. Columbanus has no reservations about employing the same term in these two different contexts, for he has grasped the essential underlying truth, namely, that confession of sin is always matched by a parallel confession of God and his mercy.

Thus, where the introduction to the new *Ordo* states that 'confession of sins comes from the knowledge of self before God and from contrition for those sins . . .',[32] it is re-stating a truth which had long been recognised, namely that the context of the penitent's self-scrutiny is all-important. Confession is, therefore, not merely a verbal recital of one's faults but a revelation of a changed inner attitude to God and to one's fellow men and women. And the fact that this exercise is carried out before God and his minister is itself an act of faith and worship by which God is praised, his justice acknowledged and his mercy proclaimed.

Confession, then, is another stage in that process whereby, as Columbanus would say, Christ is allowed to replace the image of the sinful despot within us with his own holy image. This, in turn, calls the penitent toward a renewed commitment to confess Christ before others in his daily life. Confession brings about an interior freedom in which the repentant sinner becomes capable of living out his Christian response once more. As Columbanus explains in his penitential, by this process 'the heart is healed and becomes a stranger to offence and envy'.[33]

Hence, whereas through sin the individual had become alienated from Christ and his message, through confession the 'tables are turned' and now he becomes a stranger (*alienus*) to sin and vice. The heart which had been filled with corruption and sin and which was lanced by the penitent's compunction is now purged of the evil matter and is on the way to being healed and made spiritually whole once more.

III. SATISFACTION: HEALING THE HEART

The *Ordo* explains that true conversion is completed by acts of penance or satisfaction for sins committed, by amendment of conduct, as well as by the reparation of injury caused.[34]

Satisfaction

Thus the text indicates two different elements within the notion of 'doing penance'. On the one hand, there is the righting of wrongs brought about through the sinful deed; on the other, there is the underlying aim of improving the penitent's personal, moral behaviour. As we have already noted at length in the two preceding chapters this has also been a feature of Celtic penance. We have been anxious to point out that the understanding of penance was not simply one of restoring balance, or returning to an equilibrium, but was primarily concerned with instilling and inculcating new values and ideals into the moral conscience of the penitent: the heart is not only to be opened and purified; it must be healed or made whole.

This is borne out in particular by the terminology employed throughout the penitentials. They recognise both the term 'to do penance' (*poenitere*) as well as that of 'to make satisfaction' (*satis facere*). These terms are, however, not completely interchangeable. For instance, Cummean affirms: 'He who utters in anger harsh but not injurious words shall make satisfaction to his brother and keep a special fast.'[35] Thus, on the one hand, there is the imposition of a penance for correcting the sinner and, on the other, the practical prescription that the sinner will strive to undo the sinful harm that he has caused.

This, in turn, recalls Cummean's dictum concerning penitents, namely, that after being led to repentance they are to be corrected of their error, amended of their vices and rendered such that God is favourable to them. There is then a spiritual progression in Celtic penitential theology and this is in turn reflected in the prescribed acts of penance.

A Holistic Activity

Firstly, there are acts of satisfaction which entail a repayment of what is due. These are characterised by a juridical register of language which, at its worst, tends to reduce the problematic of sin to a logic of commerce, that is to say, a repayment of debts and dues. However, this did have the distinct advantage of consisting of tangible deeds which bore solid testimony to the penitent's sincerity of purpose. Further, at its best, there was here an awareness that one sinful act could unleash a whole chain of harmful and damaging consequences. Moreover, these damaging consequences were not confined to the sinner himself but could serve to wreak havoc upon the lives of others.

Thus, if a family became destitute because someone had killed the breadwinner, that family would remain destitute even though the sinner had repented, unless the sinner was also obliged to take the place and shoulder the responsibilities of his victim (Co.B.13). Similarly, if a man was wounded, his injury, damages and medical expenses were not diminished by the mere fact of the aggressor's repentance. Instead, the penitent had to be brought to an awareness of his responsibilities (Cu.IV.9). There had to be concrete external evidence of the inner change of heart.

It is clear, then, that the penitentialists understood that the personal and social consequences of sin are not necessarily obliterated by the sinner's conversion. They realised that a complete overcoming and vanquishing of sin would require more than a fundamental repentance and reconciliation with God. Such a fundamental repentance belongs properly to the human heart; but the penitentialists saw it as part of their task to find creative ways in which the conversion of heart could become enfleshed in all dimensions of daily human activity.

What is happening here is that the penitentialists are seizing upon the 'inner dynamism of sin' and turning it back upon itself. Hence, just as the individual sinner, through an accumulation of external sinful actions, eventually erodes his Christian core and becomes the image and likeness of a 'sinful despot', so too the penitent who has turned away from sin and decided to allow Christ into his heart will express his new orientation to Christ in his external actions.

The penitentialists are, therefore, proposing what we might describe as an integral or holistic approach to penitential activity. In the same way that the whole person body, mind and soul is involved in the moment of sin, the whole person should participate in the act of penance. In this manner the entire human condition which has been infected and wounded by sin will be integrated, healed and restored in the medicine of penance. Struggle against sin in prayer and in ascetic activity must spill over into concrete action.

For the Celtic penitentialists, (who had a vehement distaste of sorcery and superstitious practices), there could be nothing 'magical' about personal conversion. To be sure, forgiveness is God-given and gratuitous, but the work of overcoming the consequences of sin must be undertaken and come to fruition in daily life. Therefore, just as sin seeps through from the outer layers of the person to infect his heart, the grace of the true conversion would have to seep outward, eventually making itself manifest in concrete other-centred activity.

An Individual Task

It was firmly within this theological framework that the 'principle of contraries' was set. Each penitent required the undivided, professional attention of the confessor in order that the precise kind of penitential activity could be found which would cure him of his sinful ailment. For this reason, Columbanus recommends that 'spiritual doctors treat with diverse kinds of cures the wounds of souls' and that they 'compound their medicines' after the style of 'doctors of the body'.[36] The two foremost factors here are the diversity and composition of the penances. Acts of penance are, therefore, to be individually tailored according to the individual and to their specific needs.

There were several ways in which penances could be thus tailored. We have already alluded, on several occasions, to the grading of acts of penance according to age, health and clerical status. Further, our second and third chapters demonstrate amply how penances for sins might be prescribed using Cassian's 'principle of contraries' as a guide and basis for diagnosing the underlying vices and their corresponding virtues.[37] Placed within Cassian's framework acts of penance could become acts of reparation in that through them the penitent sought to correct his sinful life-patterns.

Despite the oft-repeated criticism that Celtic penance encouraged an unhealthy individualism, the fact remains that those penances which encouraged the penitent to make satisfaction to his 'victim' actually enhanced the social dimensions of reconciliation. It is of course true that the Celtic penitentialists did not exploit to its full potential the riches of this theology of 'cure by contraries'. This, however, need not unduly concern us here, since our aim is to glean what theological wisdom we can from these penitential scriptures rather than catalogue their historical failure to exploit this wisdom to the full. That task is best left to the historian.

Celtic penance did, at least in theory, aim at a rehabilitation or healing of the whole person. Hence, the preponderance of medicinal language. Columbanus sees the confessor as the 'spiritual doctor' who enables cure to take place. Cummean, in turn, is so engrossed in this imagery that he prefaces his text by describing it as a treatise on the 'remedies of wounds' and it is only later that one discovers that the book is in fact a penitential.[38] Even the Bigotian text, which is at times given to the language of judgement, reminds its readers that confessors are 'healers of souls' and as such they will necessarily pay great attention to sinners' age, sex, moral strength, instruction and personal disposition before deciding upon a penance. Moreover, he adds, the confessor's final decision must be reasonable; given neither to an undue laxity, on the one hand, nor to a disproportionate severity, on the other: 'Wise men in regulating penance are to look carefully also to this, not to punish with the rod a crime worthy of the sword nor to smite with the sword a sin worthy of the rod.'[39]

The essence of the good penance, then, according to the Celtic penitentialists is that it be, at once, salutary and suitable. The confessor could not act arbitrarily when assigning penances but would have to make a prudent and just decision. In so doing, he prescribed a healing medicine for the heart. The good penance, after all, was but an incarnation of the principle of contraries. It sought to root out vice and plant virtue in its place. In a preface to his text the Bigotian penitentialist describes 'those virtues which restore the human race to the kingdom of the heavens'[40] and then goes on to prescribe them according to the various putative scenarios.

An Ascetic Approach

Thus, once the importance of the metaphor of healing and of the 'principle of contraries' has been established and demonstrated, one is already dealing with the notion of an exterior aspect of penance. In other words, one is asserting that the interior change of heart has to find real and meaningful expression in external action.

Of course, Celtic ascetic theology, like previous expressions of the ascetic tradition, maintained with equal force that penance had both interior and exterior aspects. Given that penance involved a total change of direction in one's life, relationships and activities it was obviously a very arduous enterprise. So, the Celtic penitentialists, building upon the tradition of the desert fathers and drawing also upon the indigenous, Celtic, pre-Christian culture, lay down rigorous penitential prescriptions in order that practical changes in the penitent's lifestyle might be sustained, nourished and strengthened by an on-going, ascetic regime.

Further, it is no accident that the 'staples' of this regime were prayer, fasting and alms-giving, because these three elements were aimed at a complete programme of repentance. Fasting demonstrated the sinner's sincerity of purpose in his withdrawal from sin; prayer served to deepen his adherence and attachment to Christ; whilst almsgiving and other charitable activities underlined in a more external fashion his fundamental desire to follow the Gospel message and to live a life of service.

Hence, there was no dichotomy between the penitent's interior conversion of heart and his external conversion of life. For, in truth, these were not considered to be two separate conversions but simply two different expressions of the same conversion. Therefore, in order for the penitent to express his conversion in a sincere and authentic manner to others he had to continue to nourish and foster his inner conversion with prayer and fasting. In other words, the penitent had to build into his very life a certain asceticism.

Prayer and fasting became the penitential grammar of his new life in Christ on to which the vocabulary of the various works of charity could be grafted depending on the exigencies of his individual life-situation. For this reason, the penitentialists did not hesitate to prescribe very severe expressions of conversion for their spiritual disciples and penitents. For all their severity, though, these acts of penance were never to be seen as ends in themselves but found their true meaning and grounding in the sacrifice and suffering of Christ, with whom the sinner sought to be united. Columbanus, echoing the words of Christ himself affirms:

> Let him who wishes to make his soul safe lay it down; for he who has laid down his soul for my sake, shall find it. Thus we must gladly lay down whatever we love apart from Christ for Christ's sake.[41]

In a very real sense this form of asceticism and penitential discipline looked forward rather than backward. It concerned itself with a turning toward Christ and his message. We have said that Celtic penitential activity might be seen as a grammar of life and a school of discipline. Both images are useful because they capture the purposefulness of the entire enterprise. Penitents learned the penitential grammar to acquire the language of love and enrolled in the school of discipline to become true disciples. Penance was not simply a matter of self-discipline but rather an undertaking of such sacrifice in order to be cured of sin and cleave ever more closely to Christ: 'But none can die to himself, unless Christ lives in him; but if Christ be in him, he cannot live to himself. Live in Christ that Christ may live in you.'[42]

Throughout the Celtic, penitential literature there is a constant striving and searching for the equilibrium between undoing the evil effects of sin and renewal of the individual's Christian commitment. The Old Irish text states that the aim of the penitential is for the 'annulling and *remedying*' of every sin.[43] It does not therefore suffice merely to remove or anull the negative element; instead this must be replaced by a positive one.

An Orientation Toward Christ

Of course, the fact that monastic practice tended to situate confession of sins within the context of on-going spiritual direction or soul-friendship is significant. This, in itself, made it much easier to focus upon the roots of sin and to see particular sinful acts as expressive of a more pervasive disorientation.

Similarly, where the new *Ordo* states that through his act of penance the sinner 'again becomes part of the mystery of salvation and turns himself toward the future' we can see that this describes the primary thrust of Celtic penance also.[44] Ascetic practices provide but the spiritual and physical context in which the moment of forgiveness and penance must take place.

These practices are, therefore, essentially means rather than ends and they must eventually lead the sinner to God: 'But it is not enough for the contestants to defeat their foes; if you have conquered yourself you shall be found dead to yourself but alive to God.'[45] They are means, moreover, which involve the whole person. For enfleshed human beings it makes sense, after all, that the body should also be involved in conversion. There is a certain irrefutable logic in the argument that sins which were principally 'bodily' in expression should be combated by penances which have an equally marked bodily component.

So long as fasting was seen in its true context it could be a useful sign of the penitent's complete surrender and conversion to God. And its links with prayer and almsgiving were useful correctives to a mistaken attitude which saw fasting merely as a feat of personal endurance and thus, ultimately a source of pride.

The Christian who engaged in ascetic practices was not 'demonstrating what he could do for God', but was instead recalling salvation history and in particular the sacrifice of Christ who shouldered the cross in order to defeat sin and complete the will of the Father:

> For if he (the Christian) had truly taken up the cross of Christ, he would notice that none of these things (sins) is lawful for him, since Christ also gave an example in this that none should seek his own by saying, 'Not as I will but as thou wilt', and 'I came down not to do my will but the will of him who sent me.'[46]

Personal sacrifice, therefore, reminds us of Christ's saving sacrifice and ascetic practices serve to orient us toward our future in God. In this sense too, it is a reminder to the Christian of his pilgrim status; that he 'has here no abiding city' but is hurrying toward his journey's end, where there will be no more fasting, no more hardship but instead union with Christ.

It is, therefore, a wholesome enterprise for the Christian to accept what hardship and suffering come his way in life, in order that he may savour the joy of what will come afterwards: '. . . for toil and weariness are appointed on the journey, but rest and peace are made ready in the homeland.'[47]

A New Vision of Life

This attitude to life, far from being an impoverishing one, serves instead to enrich, liberate and render life more heroic. It is a way of looking at life more honestly and realistically and of not getting enmeshed with the false 'securities' of the world. It gives rise, ultimately, to a vision of life where the individual must live daringly for the Lord, where he casts away his man-made securities and leaves himself open and trusting before Christ.

To the early Celtic Christian, penance was an act of identification with Christ's cross. Penance would have lost all meaning were it used simply as a charm to escape reality. It had to be a daily reminder of one's Christian calling. For instance, Columbanus reminds us that '. . . each ought to live as if he died daily . . .'[48]

Thus did Celtic penance not so much seek to imitate Christ nor to discover him but rather seek to liberate the Christ who was already present in the heart. And therefore just as confession of sin would eventually spill over into an act of praise and worship, so too the genuine act of penance would eventually erupt into an act of love. For, if the Christian truly wished to lead a life of love then no hardship or personal sacrifice could ever be too difficult for him:

> For what has the law of God commanded more carefully or more fully than love? What shall we say for excuse? Can we really say, it is troublesome, it is hard? Love is no trouble, love is more pleasant, more healthful, more saving to the heart.[49]

IV. ABSOLUTION: FREEING THE HEART

The penitentials do not give us much information about the actual moment of reconciliation or absolution. For this reason, there is some debate amongst scholars as to whether Celtic penance did have any recognised ritual or formula of absolution at all. Certainly, no such formula is offered in the penitentials or related material.

The lack of a definitive formula, however, should not be allowed to cast doubt upon the fact that penitents were in fact absolved under the Celtic system. We may, judging by the texts frequent allusions to this matter, assume that there was some rudimentary rite of reconciliation with absolution and that this took place after the penitent had completed his penance.

In a series of canons Columbanus uses the following formulae to describe this part of the penitential process:

(a) '. . . after making satisfaction let him (the penitent) be restored to the altar after the judgement of the priest.'

(b) '. . . let him do penance . . . and let his guilt be wiped off by the priest.'

(c) '. . . let him do penance . . . , let his guilt be remitted to him and let the priest pray for him and so let him be restored to the altar.'[50]

We can see, therefore, that the completion of penance, signals the moment in which the penitent may return to his confessor for absolution. Moreover, the penitentialist identifies three elements which are a part of the confessor's action. These are: a juridical decision, a wiping away or remission and prayer.

An Act of Judgement

The first of these, namely the juridical decision, is often referred to throughout the penitential literature. The phrase *iudicio sacerdotis* appears at least ten times in the early texts alone. This tells us several things. Firstly, the agent of absolution and reconciliation was usually the confessor, that is, a priest and not the bishop. Secondly, absolution was granted after the assigned act or acts of penance had been completed. Thirdly, this moment of reconciliation was as private as was the initial confession of sin. Fourthly and finally, the penitentialists were clear about the juridical character of the confessor's office.

Thus, the term 'according to the judgement of the priest' indicates an implicit awareness of the use and effect of the 'power of keys' which proclaims the pardoning of the sinner. This binding and loosing could be seen on the one hand as an expression of totality, suggesting total power to forgive sins; or as temporarily barring or 'excommunicating' in order to bring about a subsequent profound conversion. In this way, the sinner would be made to experience his alienation from the Christian community so that he might be the better disposed to return. There was here, in other words, a recognition of the juridical power entrusted to the minister of the Church and exercised in the name of God.

The new *Ordo*, in turn, informs us: 'Through the sign of absolution God grants pardon to the sinner who in sacramental confession manifests his change of heart to the Church's minister and thus the sacrament of penance is completed.'[51] The penitentialists, it would seem, are in broad agreement with this definition except for the fact that they required the 'change of heart' to be manifested not alone in 'confession' but also in the completion of the assigned acts of penance. Hence Finnian's stipulation that 'One must not go to the altar until one's penance has been completed,'[52] and his further requirement that even those who are nearing death (*in ultimo spiritu*) are to be granted absolution and communion only on the condition that they first make a vow that they will finish the prescribed penance in the event of recovery (Vi.34).

Therefore, the notion of an act of 'granting pardon' seems to have been accepted by all the penitentials. The Second Synod of St Patrick advises great caution and prudence to those who have been assigned the power of loosing and binding (*potestas alligandi et solvendi*: Pa.II,2). This said, however, one must look long and hard to find further concrete references. The penitentials, it would seem, took for granted the reader's awareness of the importance and nature of absolution.

Thus, where the notion of judgement does appear it more usually refers to the role of the confessor in establishing the nature and severity of the penitent's faults and of the allotment of acts of penance in proportion to the nature of his sin and of his personal status. Further, this is, as we have already noted, often tempered by the imagery of medicine, cure and healing.

The penitential texts, therefore, as a rule, do not emphasize the notion of judgement since penance for them was seen less in terms of a juridical process for getting rid of sin than as a form of personal correction and conversion to the Gospel message.[53]

An Act of Purification and Liberation

The second aspect of the moment of absolution which we have noted in Columbanus is the notion of 'wiping away' sins. The term adopted by the penitentialist here (*abstergere*), that is, to wipe off or cleanse away, is again used by him when he describes the correct disposition for participation at the Eucharist. He explains that the good Christian must first be cleansed from his interior vices. There is the notion here of a final purifying or cleansing of the person after the rigours of penance in order to face once more the task of the Christian life. Again, the cleansing here is seen in terms of a preparation for a fuller participation in the Christian community and way of life. The focus, then, remains forward-looking and future-oriented.

The fact too that Columbanus attributes the activity of 'wiping away' and 'remitting' to the confessor is also significant. It indicates that the priest's words are not merely words about reconciliation and forgiveness but are instead words which actually reconcile and forgive as they are spoken. The priest's words are, therefore, to be seen as an effective manifestation of God's mercy and they are pronounced by the confessor who acts with power and authority in his name.

This notion is, in turn, shared by Finnian who informs us: '. . . we say sins can be absolved in secret. . .' (Vi.10) and by a directive of the aforementioned Second Synod of St Patrick which rules that 'we ought to believe that those who have lapsed from the faith are not to be absolved unless they are first received with imposition of hands by a Bishop.'[54]

Interestingly, these are the only instances where the term *absoluere* is used in this sense. The term is more usually employed by Columbanus in the context of the setting free of slaves where he prescribes the freeing of servants from the 'yoke of bondage' (Co.B.20). The parallels between the absolution of the slave liberated from the yoke of bondage and the penitent who is freed from the yoke of sin clearly suggest another rich dimension to the Celtic understanding of forgiveness and reconciliation.

The Bigotian text represents a further development in this matter. It describes the necessary prerequisites for communion thus:

> . . . everyone after confessing his faults and destroying them and after the grace of God has come and the heavenly father and the Church are present with him shall then . . . receive the sacrifice.[55]

The order is clear. First comes the confession of sin, second the destruction of sin through acts of penance, and third the coming of God's grace which renders present the Father and the Church. It is this final moment which is enacted in the absolution. There is an awareness here that the pardoning of the sinner comes from the Father and that the sinner is united, or rather, re-united with the whole Church to which he is restored in a living communion by the moment of absolution.

An Act of Prayer

This brings us to the third aspect of absolution noted by Columbanus, namely, prayer. As we have already pointed out, we do not have any idea of the formula which was used by the confessor at this juncture nor indeed whether any such formula existed at all. What is clear, however, is that the priest did pray at this stage. This, in itself, underlines the fact that the entire penitential exercise took place within an atmosphere of worship. Finnian begins his penitential by invoking the Holy Trinity and here too the end of the penitential process becomes a prayer. Thus, prayer initiates and completes the penitential exercises and disposes the penitent to re-insert himself into the living communion of the Church.

This restoration, as we have noted, usually took the form of removal of the bans of excommunication. The term *iungatur altario* signified such a removal and in real terms it seems to have meant rejoining the congregation as an equal member rather than necessarily or specifically suggesting a re-admission to sacramental communion.[56]

The link with sacramental communion is, on the other hand, explicitly alluded to in some texts. For instance, Gildas indicates that the repentant deacon or presbyter who has fulfilled the requisite penance 'may receive the eucharist and come for the kiss of peace and sing the psalms with the brethren lest his soul perish utterly from lacking for so long a time the celestial medicine'.[57] And the Bigotian text in turn explains that '. . . there are three ways in which the just are separated from the unjust, by the mass, the table and the kiss of peace.'[58]

For all intents and purposes, the reconciliation of the penitent would have first been publicly recognised when he approached the altar for communion. Moreover, this was no mere coincidence. The penitentialists, and Celtic theology in general, asserted a strong link between penance and Eucharist. The Eucharist was recognised as the place where the individual could enter into communion with Christ and thus be transformed by way of this communion. This on-going, saving and reconciling activity of Christ in the Eucharist is underlined by its description as 'the celestial medicine'.

Thus, the sinner who had repented and had already received the healing power of penance would, after his conversion, continue to be sustained by the 'celestial medicine' of the Eucharist. Of course, those who had not yet confessed their sin and converted to the virtuous life could not participate, since sin, which was a sign of division, discord and selfish satisfaction could never be in harmony with that event which commemorated and proposed a style of communion, brotherhood and self-giving in Christ.

Nonetheless, even those who did participate were aware that they were but repentant sinners or, as the later Columbanus might say, *pilgrims* on the road to sanctity. Therefore, they too would find sustenance in the Eucharist which would help them to reinforce and strengthen their personal conversion which was initially begun in the confession of their sins. If the penitentials did, as we have argued throughout, propose penance as an attitude of life, then the Eucharist was very much a part of this attitude since, in itself, it was a sign which showed the need for continuous and progressive conversion.

Absolution and the Conversion Process

We may say, therefore, that despite the lack of evidence for a formula of absolution in Celtic penance, in essence absolution and reconciliation of the penitent did take place. Furthermore, once the sinner had been thus reconciled, the whole incident was considered closed and the individual by virtue of his practice of the 'contrary virtue' would have been strengthened and sharpened for the daily battle against sin and for the call to conversion which was a central aspect of the Christian vocation.

In a sense, then, where the new *Ordo* states that the return of the absolved sinner is 'finally expressed in a renewed and more fervent sharing at the Lord's table', we can see that this is a point of continuity with the Celtic model of penance.[59]

V. THE ROLE OF THE COMMUNITY IN THE CELEBRATION OF PENANCE

We have said, in the previous section, that when the penitent had completed his penance 'the heavenly Father and the Church' were said to be 'present with him'. This, therefore, gives rise to the query as to what exactly was the role of the Church as Christian community in the process of penance under the Celtic system. Much has been made of the fact that the Celtic model tended to place emphasis on the individual and particular needs of each penitent. One might validly ask, therefore, whether the broader Christian community had any real input into the penitential process.

Solidarity in Prayer

In fact, there would seem to have been a twofold input by the Church: the Christian community cooperated in the conversion of the sinner by its prayer and support and by its example.

The first aspect, namely that of prayer, is referred to at several junctures in the penitential literature. Cummean lists the prayerful intercession of Christians as one of the ways in which sins may be remitted (Cu.pr.9). He cites from the celebrated passage in the Letter of St James which runs:

> Is any among you sick? Let him call for the elders of the Church and let them pray over him anointing him with oil in the name of the Lord . . . and if he has committed sins he will be forgiven. (Therefore confess your sins to one another and pray for one another that you may be healed).

Evidently, the penitentialist sees a role here for the whole Christian community beyond the official ministry of her priests. All are entitled, and indeed expected, to pray for each other in order that together they might obtain both the conversion of the sinner and divine grace for his forgiveness and reconciliation. Further, each member of the community is to be so closely bound to his brothers in Christ that he experiences regret for their sins also. The Bigotian text explains that genuine sorrow is that sadness which we feel 'when we are sorry for our sins and for the sins of others' and that we 'should sigh for our sins and for our neighbour's ignorance'.[60]

This sorrow, then, should be the basis for an apostolic attitude of prayer, that is to say, prayer which not merely focusses upon our own needs but which also includes the needs of others. Prayer, like all other works of love and mercy, should take into consideration one's needy neighbour. And the repentant sinner who is undertaking a path of penance is undoubtedly in need of such spiritual sustenance and support. Moreover, prayer in community will of its very nature include prayer for sinner's and even one's enemies since in this way the whole community will be united in one common action of imitating Christ and rendering honour to the Father. Columbanus in his *Rule* recommends that his followers should pray:

> . . . first for our own sins, then for all Christian people, then for priests . . . for those who do alms, next for the concord of kings, lastly for our enemies, that God reckon it not to them for sin that they persecute and slander us, since 'they know not what they do'.[61]

This prayer is itself expressive of a broader desire for reconciliation between all men and women, a desire to overcome divisions and enmity. Further, it is with good reason that Columbanus echoes the forgiving words of Christ on the cross toward his persecutors, 'Father, forgive them for they know not what they do', because Christ himself overcame sin by death. The sacrifice of Christ who consented to being crucified for our sake saved us from the condemnation due to our sins. Therefore, not alone is Christ the model for Christians but by entering into his death and resurrection Christians are redeemed and reconciled into the holy people of God. This holy people or Church, moreover, while never condoning sin, does not consider itself a community of the perfect: 'Whilst we are placed there in the flesh, we cannot be to perfection, unless the eighth day come; that is unless the time of the future world arrive.'[62]

And so the battle against sin must be fought daily. In this struggle the whole person, and indeed the whole Church, is involved. Therefore, it will be a characteristic of Christians that they intercede for sinners. Their prayer will be at once an act of solidarity for their brethren in need and also an act of faith in the mercy and reconciling love of God. It enters into the activity of Christ and gives expression to the Christian ideal of mutual forgiveness. For this reason, the Old Irish text states that penitents are entitled to and indeed required to seek the prayers of others by way of spiritual support:

> There is required of them (penitents) also remorse and lamentation for their sins, and that they should desire their brethren to pray God for them that their sins may be forgiven through penance and penitence.[63]

Solidarity in Acceptance and Example

Another way in which the community 'participated' in some sense in the conversion of the sinner was by welcoming the penitent back into its communion of love. Finnian prescribes that the sinner who has been sent out into exile is to be 'received into his own country' (Vi.23) upon completion of the assigned penance. Similarly, all sinners having repented and carried out the requisite penance are to be 'received into communion' (Vi.34–35).

We should note here too that the onus is being placed squarely upon the community which is to welcome back the sinner. The penitentialist is placing the emphasis here upon hospitality. This quality, which was one of the hallmarks of Celtic monasticism, must, according to Finnian, find a particular expression in that moment wherein the repentant sinner returns to communion with other Christians. In this way, it is hoped, he will experience something of the heavenly joy and welcome which accompanies his conversion and home-coming.

We have said that the other aspect of the Christian community's role in penance is example. The community centred upon the monastery aimed at becoming a forgiving, reconciling and ever-penitential centre of Christian life. The penitential literature makes no secret of the fact that it is seeking to win souls for Christ. Finnian reminds his followers:

> We are not to cease to snatch the prey from the mouth of the lion or the dragon, that is the devil, who ceases not to snatch at the prey of our souls, even though we may have to follow up and strive (for his soul) at the very end of a man's life.[64]

Despite the melodramatic nature of the imagery here, the underlying message is quite clear. All are to see it as part of their Christian duty to win and win *back* sinners to the Gospel message. The Bigotian text reminds us: 'Remember how great a merit it is to you to convert a sinner from the error of his way.'[65] This echoes the words of St James, who affirms that the Christian who seeks to reconcile and save others, by this very activity, also furthers his own salvation.

Hence, in a real sense the founding fathers of Irish monasticism had a vision of the monastery and surrounding Christian community as being a place of *being* as well as of *doing*. The monastic Church could not content itself with being a mere dispensary of penance and of absolution to individuals. Instead, it had to be, as a community, committed to the idea of conversion. All were called to do penance and to convert others daily. This is reflected also in those penances (which we have already catalogued) where the penitent was required to convert other sinners. Every Christian was to be concerned for his brothers' and sisters' salvation as well as for his own. A Christian was entitled, also, to point out to his neighbour the latter's sin and to exhort him to do penance provided his correction was done for 'the sake of blaming the evil and confirming the good'.[66]

Solidarity in Shared Pilgrim Status

This, in turn, reinforced the notion that all were pilgrims on the road to salvation. Everyone had to "live as though he died daily".[67] And the example *par excellence* of this way of life was provided by the Irish monks themselves, who unlike their desert forefathers did not completely abandon the world but merely remained a little apart from it, that they might provide a witness of ascetic life valid for all. In this type of Christian community, even the differences and divisions of ecclesiastical rank were muted. In the Irish Church, even the bishop was, in a sense, merely one of the monks, consecrated for the sacramental moments which required episcopal office but in other matters remaining firmly under the jurisdiction of the abbot.

This close association of the Celtic monks with the society to which they gave spiritual counsel and guidance was a hallmark of their pastoral approach: 'By the very fact of their existence in the midst of such a people, still more or less pagan, they set up the permanent vision and challenge of a Christianity seriously lived out and preached through personal example.'[68]

Further, in this ascetic and intensely spiritual context ecclesiastical rank and clerical status came very much in second place to the individual's personal faith response to the Gospel and to the call to conversion. Throughout the penitential literature we have abundant evidence of an identification of priest and people, cleric and lay, single and spoused, all united in the doing of penance. There is a realisation that all are pilgrims striving after a better moral life. It is not as though one is the 'possessor' of spiritual power and the other is being asked somehow to 'measure up'; instead, both are pilgrims who must help each other along the penitential road.

The principal divisions of the penitential literature are not those of status, rank, age or even sex; they are, rather, the divisions of the various kinds of vice and sin and the virtues with which they are to be combatted. The Irish monastery was the *locus*, then, for a remarkable union. A primitive people newly evangelised (previously given to superstition and pagan cult) were now joining in the activity of ascetic penance alongside monks of long standing Christian maturity.

Monks rubbed shoulders with the married, bishops with laymen, and saints with sinners. People repenting of distractions at prayer did penance beside those guilty of sexual indiscretions.

What was happening here was truly a symbol of reconciliation and unity. The monastery and *eo ipso* the Church was being opened up to the people. The Celtic Christian community was bridging the gap between the official Church and the masses in a way that even the old churches of Europe had been unable to do among 'civilized' people. Not only was penance being re-interpreted here but the inter-relation of monastery (Church) and society was being re-interpreted as well.

The essential traits of Celtic Christianity consisted in:

(a) a social initiative of the monks acting in the spirit of the prophets,
(b) a thorough ritualisation of the life of the people,
(c) the bringing to bear of the ascetic way of life upon the Christian community at large, in order to effect a 'moral shaping' of the lives of the faithful.[59]

Therefore, Irish monasticism was in close contact with the world and actively entered into it with ascetic and moral demands. By appealing to the traditional Celtic values of fasting and fighting spirit, and successfully welding these with a pilgrim spirituality and theology, it managed to win masses of people to the Christian message. People who had previously relied upon the druidic schools for instruction and inspiration now saw in the monastery a more worthy ideal. Perhaps then, the outstanding missionary successes of the Celtic monks is explained, at least in part, by the fact that the Celtic Church was already missionary at home.

What we are essentially saying is that in the Celtic Church unitive and reconciliatory activity was not simply confined to the activity of the anamchara or confessor but was in fact more typically representative of the whole ethos of Celtic spirituality and penitential theology.

VI. THE CONFESSOR

From what we have said so far, it is clear that the monastic practice of soul guidance had a substantial influence on the later development of private confession. Consequently, it is not surprising that the roles of confessor and penitent were in turn influenced by the preceding relationship between the anamchara and his consulter. Within this context, penance was viewed from the outset in terms of a medicinal measure, which was to promote healing and spiritual development.

The monastic confessor was not envisaged solely in terms of a judge who deliberated over the crime before deciding the sentence; rather his role was perceived to be threefold, that of physician, judge and fellow-sufferer. All three roles are clearly manifest in the penitential literature.

The Confessor as Physician

The penitential manuals are replete with the imagery of healing. Penance is a form of healing, and since the confessor is the minister of penance, then he is to be seen as a physician or healer. Columbanus traces the similarities between the work of physical and spiritual doctors. He reasons:

> For as doctors of the body compound their medicines in diverse kinds; thus they heal wounds in one manner, sicknesses in another, boils in another, eye diseases in another, fractures in another, burns in another. So also should spiritual doctors treat with diverse kinds of cures the wounds of souls, their sicknesses (offences), pains, ailments and infirmities.[70]

According to this doctrine, the confessor was to see himself in a healing role. Furthermore, he had to be a wise healer; one who was adept at individual diagnosis and accurate in his prescription of the medicinal remedy.

The penitent would go to the confessor as a patient would to the doctor, prepared to accept what treatment he prescribed even where such treatment entailed extremely harsh measures such as a period of quarantine where there was a risk of contagion to the Christian community. As spiritual doctor (*medicus animarum*), the confessor had to steer a course between, on the one hand, not unduly burdening the penitent and, on the other hand, prescribing an effective cure. By modern standards Celtic penitents would seem to have been very heavily burdened indeed. And yet the penitentialists remind us that the task of 'healing souls' also entails 'punishing sins', for these are, as it were, two sides of the same coin.

Further, this task will necessarily require great competence and experience on the part of the confessor since the problematic of ministering to penitents is clearly manifold (*multiplex est*) on account of 'both the diversity of sins and the difference in the virtues and qualities of sinners'.[71] The point here is, that as well as requiring great spiritual strength, the role of 'physician of souls' also demands a certain amount of skill and aptitude in the understanding of human nature. In other words, the confessor must have the ability to get to the heart of the matter and to discern the root of the penitent's sin.

We can see, then, a distinct parallel between the outlook of the Celtic penitentialists and that of the new *Ordo* which affirms: 'Discernment of spirits is a deep knowledge of God's action in the hearts of men; it is a gift of the Spirit as well as the fruit of charity.'[72] This is in perfect harmony with Columbanus' assertion that 'this gift belongs to a few, namely . . . to restore what is weak to a complete state of health'[73] and with his later insistence on the centrality of discernment/discretion in the leading of the good moral life.

Evidently, the confessor must dispose of finely honed powers of discernment in order that he might fully appreciate the penitent's spiritual situation and then gently educate his moral awareness so that he hears and responds to Christ's call to conversion, first in the inner depths of his heart and then in his external life. To put it another way, the confessor must be capable of discerning what it takes for the individual to resume his pilgrim path. It is in this context, that Cummean asserts that: 'warning, exhortation, teaching and instruction' are all a part of the confessor's role.

That is not to say, however, that the confessor is called upon to give subjective advice or merely personal opinion. Instead Finnian is anxious to point out that all 'remedies of penance' should have as their ultimate grounding 'the pronouncement of scripture' and the 'thought of learned men'. Similarly Columbanus explains that discretion or discernment means nothing other than 'weighing all actions in the scales of justice'.[74]

Like the doctor of the body, the *medicus animarum* disposes of a scientific basis for his healing activity. He does not dispense mere personal or subjective views, but brings his knowledge of the Scriptures and Tradition to bear upon his words. This done, confessor and penitent can then together make a realistic assessment of the roots of the latter's sin and identify new patterns of behaviour that will bring about changes which will truly heal.

The Confessor as Judge

Evidently, the confessor was expected to assess the extent of the sinner's guilt. This he was to do by seeking to build up a more complete picture of the circumstances surrounding the sin and the sinner's own background. The reasons for this investigation were not solely punitive; instead it was hoped that by having more information at his disposal, the confessor would be better able to make a sound judgement and to enjoin a suitable penance aimed at helping the penitent to overcome his particular areas of moral failing. Cummean outlines all the considerations which are to be taken into account, if the confessor is to be a good judge.

> This is to be carefully observed in all penance: the length of time anyone remains in his faults; what learning he has received; by what passion he is assailed; how great is his strength; with what intensity of weeping he is afflicted and with what oppression he has been driven to sin.[75]

It is obvious, then, that the confessor was expected to make a judgement concerning the penance which was to be undertaken and that this judgement could be more or less severe, involving, for example, in its harshest forms, the loss of ecclesiastical rank or even excommunication. Even in such instances penance was not so much perceived as divine punishment; rather, the penitent was himself perceived to be the author of his own misfortune and consequently the harsh penance served to underline the necessity of a powerful, personal effort to reverse the logic of sin.

Columbanus reminds his followers that it is a statement of terrible import which tells us that everyone shall at the end time be punished or rewarded 'according to his deeds'. For, asserts Columbanus, if our own deeds are to be the only criterion of our final judgement then they shall surely evince a severe punishment. Instead we must hope for the judgement of Christ for his judgement is always one of mercy: 'for who can be justified and not need the mercy of his Judge, when he dwells in the body of sin?'[76]

In other words, where the penitentials speak of judgement we would be mistaken to think in terms of a modern court-room scene. For, to speak of judgement is to proclaim the mercy of God in Christ. The judgement of Christ is, indeed, to be welcomed for his judgement is concerned above all with saving the sinner. God, affirms the Bigotian text, is the 'righteous judge' (Bi.26.pr). Divine justice instead of condemning the sinner actually renders him 'just' once more.

The confessor, then, as judge is more concerned with carefully proportioning the penitential remedy than with condemning. He is, by virtue of his being 'other', able to assess the problematic of the penitent's sin with a certain objectivity and then impose a sentence which will eventually rehabilitate the sinner. It is interesting to note, in this context, that the penitential texts when dealing with the punishing of sins use the term *animadversione*. And yet the same term is used in a different context and with a slightly different nuance where the texts seek to underline the necessity of the confessor to *observe* and *be aware* of the various qualities and failings of the penitent.

Thus, over and above his role as *medicus animarum* or soul-doctor, the confessor also had to be an *animadversor*. Moreover, as *animadversor* he was not simply exercising a punitive role but was rather drawing upon his ability to observe objectively the penitent's situation and accordingly to prescribe a remedial course of action. The roles of anamchara and *animadversor* were not therefore mutually exclusive but on the contrary complementary. The confessor was called upon to be a friend to the penitent, not a false friend who said only what the penitent wanted to hear, but rather a friend who, because of his 'otherness' had the perspicacity to discern the roots of his sin and the courage to set him upon the road to recovery even where that road was long and arduous.

Clearly then, although judgement is a recurring image throughout the penitential texts, it does not have quite the same negative connotation as in a modern court of civil justice. Nonetheless, it probably did, in practice, prove to be the Achilles' heel of the Celtic penitential system. Once the penitential texts were taken out of their original theological and spiritual context of healing and cure, it was then but a small step toward seeing these manuals as mere lists of punishment and measures of expiation. In this way, the notions of inner conversion, turning back to God, and transforming the external dimensions of life (which were so dear to the hearts of Columbanus and his brethren) became overshadowed and often forgotten.

A further contribution to this deterioration of the penitential ideal may be seen in the physical shifting of the Celtic penitential system from their original geographical and social context in Ireland and Britain to mainland Europe. For instance, in Celtic society the judge or brehon was an 'arbitrator, umpire, and expounder of the law rather than a judge in the modern acceptation'.[77] A brehon's pronouncement was rather more a declaration of law and justice as applied to the facts before him than a sentence in the strict sense of the word. It is easy to see, then, how the Celtic model of law and justice would have favoured an understanding of the judge as one who clarifies and speaks authoritatively, and how this was, in turn, considerably different from our modern emphasis where the judge is he or she who must pronounce sentence.

Therefore, both the roles of physician and judge envisaged close collaboration between priest and penitent in preparing the penitential pilgrimage back to the virtuous, moral life.

The Confessor as Fellow-Sufferer

The Celtic understanding of the confessor as fellow-sufferer has its origins in the spiritual tradition surrounding the anamchara. Although the term 'fellow-sufferer' does not appear in the penitential literature, much evidence of what the term denotes is to be found there. For instance, Cummean reminds his confessors that 'sorrowful lamentation', on their part, must be one of the principle motives for correcting sinners; otherwise they will forfeit the title 'physicians of souls' and become mere 'detractors' instead (Cu.VIII;16).

Similarly, the author of the later *Penitential of Theodore* (q.v.) warns against a proud or intransigent attitude on the part of the confessor and reminds him instead that he too is a sinner: 'If any presbyter denies penance to the dying, he is answerable for their souls since the Lord saith. On whatever day the sinner is converted, he shall live and not die.'[78]

Perhaps though, the clearest statement of the confessor as fellow-sufferer is to be found in a monastic rule written by Carthage (d. 639). He counsels the confessor to take his role very seriously and to himself enter into the sinner's fight against his sin: 'If any of you be anybody's soul-friend, do not sell his soul. Let them confess to you candidly and devoutly . . . Pay for them the price of fasting and praying. If you do not you will pay for your own sins . . .'[79]

The Bigotian author, in turn, echoes this sentiment affirming in words taken from Leviticus: 'The priest who offers this and brings about reconciliation, it shall be for his own sin.'[80] There is, then, on the one hand an unmistakable recognition that the priest or confessor is but himself a sinner in need of repentance and, on the other hand, a call to a fraternal solidarity between minister and penitent. Hence, the Celtic practice never loses sight of the truly sacramental nature of penance.

The penitential texts are geared toward rendering the confessor a better instrument in God's hand, a true steward and channel of God's mercy and a genuine anamchara or soul-friend to the penitent. For, whilst it is clear that the role of confessor is not coterminous with the earlier role of anamchara, nevertheless, it is equally clear that the confessor was expected to take upon himself the humility, wisdom, and holiness which were fundamental to the practice of *anamchairdeas* (soul-friendship). This, in turn, served to highlight the personal dimension and in particular the fact that the penitent encountered the merciful Christ through the mediation of the priest.

The confessor had to receive the penitent with that generous hospitality which was typical of Celtic monasticism and to listen to him as a friend, that is to say, paying attention with the heart in a spirit of receptivity. There is even evidence in some penitential texts that at times the confessor would offer the penitent a meal and vice versa. Having created a propitious climate for effective dialogue to take place, the penitent would then confess his sins. At this juncture the priest would then have to call upon his powers of discretion and judgement in order to prescribe a suitable cure.

There was, therefore, within the ministry of confessing a creative tension between, on the one hand, what we have called the roles of *medicus animarum* (doctor) and *animadversor* (judge) and, on the other hand, that of *anamchara* (fellow-sufferer, friend). The good confessor had to cultivate and master all three aspects in order to minister effectively. Therefore, Columbanus in his *Rule* criticises those who admonish their brethren too severely: 'Let him who corrects ungently be taken note of until he asks pardon from the brother who has been reproved, with thirty strokes also or fifteen psalms.'[81]

Correction and guidance had always to be of a truly fraternal nature. And whereas the new *Ordo* places emphasis on the paternal function of the confessor, the Celtic texts tend to opt more for a fraternal aspect. The confessor had to be in solidarity with the sinner, striving to overcome sin himself. There is good reason to believe that like the desert fathers before them, Celtic confessors even went to the point of joining in fasts and in prayers for their penitents. And whilst this does not receive explicit treatment in the Celtic literature, later penitentials do recommend this form of solidarity and supportive activity lest confessors themselves should fall into that category of sinner '. . . who place insupportable burdens on men's shoulders and fail to move a finger to lift them'.[82]

Confessors in the Celtic system, then, were to be always conscious of their own sinfulness and unworthiness. They were, in effect, what we might nowadays call 'wounded healers'. Wounded themselves by sin, the Irish monks fought nevertheless heroically to overcome their moral failings, so that they might become martyrs in the Celtic sense —living witnesses to other Christians who sought to live a virtuous life. Moreover, because of their humility, self-effacement and wisdom, they were chosen as confessors so that, despite their weakness, they could be effective ministers of God's forgiving and healing grace. The following lines taken from Columbanus' *Rule* are typical of the ideal of humility and self-abnegation to which all Celtic monks aspired: 'These are the words of the sons of God, (let) nothing be in rivalry, as the apostle says, nor in vainglory, but in lowliness of spirit each reckoning the other better than himself.'[83]

VII. THE PENITENT

Since the penitentials were designed to be handbooks for the confessor, it is perhaps not surprising that the penitent is never directly addressed there. It is clear from the texts, however, that penitents could be either monk cleric or lay and they often make provision for this distinction. Later material refers to married men accepting counsel from a monk adviser, as well as undertaking to practise a certain amount of asceticism in their lives.[84]

The Penitent: Representative of All Social Strata

Penances for monks tend to differ considerably from those for laity. Columbanus, for instance, divided his penitential into two sections: the first for monks, the second for clerics and laity. Finnian, on the other hand, intended his penitential manual to be used only in connection with clerics and laity. The absence of any provision for monks in this document, is very telling and suggests that the document was aimed at non-monk penitents. Cummean's manual and the penitential in old Irish treat clerics according to their ecclesiastical rank and the laity according to their class and social status.[85]

Thus, by the time of writing the penitential documents, the laity were already availing themselves of penance. Clearly, the pre-existing form of monastic confession and direction played a key role in the evolution of this penitential discipline. Further, the Irish had also at their disposal the anamchara tradition. Laity, and especially decision makers, were already accustomed to consulting their counsellors for advice on important matters.

In addition, there was the Celtic predilection for asceticism and fasting as a means to overcome sin. The scene was truly set, then, for a shift in the parameters of penitential discipline and doctrine. The Irish monks found themselves equipped with various elements of theological and traditional learning and confronted with a newly evangelised people who were hungry for the curative power of penance. The following are the 'tools' which they had at their disposal:

(a) The pre-existing monastic practice of *manifestatio conscientiae*, which had both a devotional and corrective purpose.
(b) The Celtic concept of anamchara or soul-friend with its traditional emphasis on counselling and guidance and its availability to all people whether monk, cleric or lay.
(c) The shared monastic and Celtic traditions of ascetic activity out of which the Irish Church developed its unique understanding of the theology of martyrdom, as a means of striving toward the perfect moral life.

Given the coexistence of these factors, it is, I believe, easier to understand why the role of the penitent was now broadened to embrace all manner of people who professed to follow Christ. As one historian has observed:

> Even though the monks recognised the difference between their own forms of discipline and those which could be reasonably be expected of lay people, the task of establishing Church law outside the monastery cannot have been an easy one. We might (therefore) expect the monks to have tried to ease the process by making the most of similarities between their disciplinary traditions and those native customs which seemed analogous to them.[86]

The monks, then, seem to have exploited to the full the obvious links between the roles of confessor and soul-friend. It appears, in fact, that they succeeded in welding together various elements from different traditions, both spiritual and secular. In so doing, they produced an understanding of penance which was truly unique and broadened the notion of penitent to include all Christians who sought divine forgiveness.

The Penitent: Representative of the Church

This fact, in itself, served to strengthen the fraternal bond between confessor and penitent. Both were fellow sufferers, both were involved in the same sinfulness and the same struggle, and the priest ministered to the sinner out of his own simplicity and poverty. Thus, while it is true that the priest as confessor represented in a particular way the Church and the Christian community insofar as he ministered to the sinner, discerned his weakness, prescribed a cure and eventually welcomed back into communion with other Christians, yet, in a real sense, the penitent was also representative of the Christian community, which always recognised its need for renewal, reform and purification.

The penitent was a sign of man's conversion to God; in and through his penance, he did in a particular way what the whole monastic Church sought to do in a more global fashion. The penitent's confession, prayer and penance were a microcosm of that *sacrificium laudis* which the monastic Church sought to live out on a daily basis. In a very immediate way, the penitent became one who bore living witness to the ideal of conversion and he did this within a monastic context where all sought to make this ideal an attitude of life. The penitent's confession and repentance were themselves a sign of the Celtic Church's very *raison d'être*.

In the moment of confession, the penitent confronted himself with another person and, through that other person with, 'the pronouncement of Scripture and . . . the opinion of very learned men' (Vi.ps.). He was confronted, moreover, with the call to conversion, the call to be a disciple, a pilgrim or as Columbanus would have it 'a living image of God'. In doing this, he was confronting himself ultimately with the call to holiness to which the whole Church aspired:

> True love is not in word only but in deed and in truth. Therefore let us restore to our God, our Father, his own image, since He is holy, according to the saying be ye Holy since I am holy.[87]

As a result of this personal encounter or confrontation, the penitent was enabled to see precisely where he was and precisely where he had still to go. In essence, it entailed a candid admission of his sinfulness and moral weakness and fragmentation of his spiritual life. And yet this very admission of weakness was, itself, a very real step forward.

In his confession of sin and his acceptance of the remedial penitential measure, the sinner echoed the example of Christ, who accepted his cross, and in so doing he knew that he would eventually also share in the resurrection of Christ who had conquered sin. Columbanus reminds his followers of the insertion of all Christians into the saving death of Christ: 'See and understand how difficult it is for this age to be conquered, since a saint is freed from it not otherwise than by the death of Christ.'[88]

In this sense, then, the penitent in the Celtic system typified the whole Christian community which, as a pilgrim people, had to accept hardship and battle against sin and weakness, in order to one day rise with Christ.

CHAPTER FIVE

THE PENITENTIALS AND THE SACRAMENT OF PENANCE TODAY

I. SYMBOL AS CHALLENGE

Having posed the question as to which elements of Celtic penance may 'dialogue' with contemporary thought, we can almost immediately eliminate some areas from our enquiry. For instance, the calculation of precise numbers of days, weeks and years of penance will not offer much fresh inspiration to the modern theologian, neither will the excessive rigorism of the early Celts find a receptive audience today. One area, however, which does prove very enriching and beneficial to contemporary theology is the level of symbol.[1]

As I see it, it is precisely symbol which provides the hermeneutical key enabling us to understand the richness of the ancient Celtic texts and, at the same time, to apply the fruits of our work to the theology and practice of penance today. In this chapter, then, we shall take the words of Ricoeur as starting point, namely that: 'the preferred language of fault appears to be indirect and based on imagery'. Thus a consideration of symbol allows us at once to respect the original thrust of the penitential texts whilst at the same time discovering within them a meaning and significance for contemporary mankind.

Symbol and the Penitentials

The Celtic penitential literature, as we have already seen, essentially presents us with three paradigms or models for understanding sin and conversion:[2]

(1) The first symbol is that of disease and wholeness where sin is understood as illness, penance as curative and the confessor as healer or physician of souls.

(2) The second is that of judgement and justice where sin is considered as offence, penance as reparation and the confessor as merciful judge or *animadversor*.

(3) The third is the image of life-pilgrimage and suffering. Here sin is seen as a wandering from the right path, penance thus becomes re-orientation and the confessor is portrayed as a fellow-traveller, fellow-sufferer or *anamchara*.

This chapter will discuss the merits and weaknesses of each of these models and show how they serve to summarize and encapsulate the value of the penitential texts.

Together with modern theologians, Celtic scribes would be at pains to point out that no one model or metaphor should achieve dominance over the rest. On the contrary, the texts themselves bear witness to the integration of all three models and many secondary or peripheral models.

Symbol as a Vehicle for Theology

At once the strength and the peculiarity of these models is that none has the definitive key to the understanding of sin and conversion. Instead, each symbol dialogues, modifies, or, as Ricoeur puts it, struggles with the others. And, out of the dynamics of this struggle emerges a 'spontaneous hermeneutics' which affords us a clearer understanding of the problematic of sin and repentance.[3]

Furthermore, to speak at all of models or symbols is already to distance ourselves in some sense from the penitential texts. In this final chapter we are purposely withdrawing from the Celtic world and returning to present-day preoccupations, so it behoves us to focus on those elements of Celtic penitential theology which might prove fruitful for the contemporary theologian and pastor. In so doing, we shall seek to respect the original 'enigma' of the symbols whilst at the same time indicating ways and means by which these same symbols might shed light on the experience of contemporary man and woman.[4]

Symbol as Method: the Strengths

The great strength of this methodology is that it affords us the means of going beyond the limitations of our own particular outlook and entering into fruitful conversation with another age which had a radically different outlook. A further advantage still is that dialogue need not stop at present-day experience, but may also point toward possible future developments in theology and praxis. In other words, the symbol has, at once, an explanatory and an exploratory function. It sheds light on and synthesizes biblical and historical data and may be applied to whatever our experience tells us of the Christian way of life. And, because of its underlying continuity and consistency, the symbol or model can foment new future-oriented theological insights. The hermeneutical enterprise eventually gives way to a heuristic one in that the good symbol endures and can dialogue or converse with people of all eras.

In short, the symbol or model is never fully fathomable; it is not a perfectly transparent sign but is instead opaque. Enigmatic symbols therefore, by their nature, will ever yield fresh insights to fresh enquiries. Or, better still, as Ricoeur succinctly expresses it: 'symbols give rise to thought'.[5]

Inevitably, other students of the subject will draw conclusions different from mine. I shall be content to have introduced the reader, whether pastor, penitent or theologian, to the essential core of Celtic penitential theology, enabling him to set up his own dialogue between this rich, historical tradition and his own personal, practical or pedagogical experience of sin and penance. Only in this way, can we seriously hope that the insights and riches of this critical moment in the history of penance might reach a wider audience and thus be re-discovered and re-deployed at the service of all Christians who seek to respond to Christ's call to conversion.

Symbol as Method: the Weaknesses

The main weaknesses of this approach lie in the fact that we can be tempted to lay too much store by any one model or paradigm. Our acceptance of one paradigm should entail an openness to others, otherwise we are merely indulging in idolatry.[6] No single paradigm is, in itself, capable of resolving all theological and pastoral difficulties. Each model of penance and conversion has its own inadequacies. The Celtic penitentialists were themselves aware of this (though they obviously did not share our thematic approach) and, for this very reason, three models co-exist side by side together with several secondary models as well. Each of the Celtic models, as we shall see, gels in some sense with the others.

A further weakness resides in the fact that the modern reader approaches texts with the notion that models or paradigms are detailed and well-worked out systematic explanations of theological problems. This is not at all true of the Celtic texts. Given the nature of the penitentials, the reader must first carefully sift through the mosaic of canons, exhortations and aphorisms, as we have attempted to do, and from this select the predominant strands of imagery and ideas which sew this patchwork of legal, moral and spiritual maxims into a coherent whole.

Neither must we claim here that the models set out here are unique to Celtic penitential literature. Rather, as we have already seen, Celtic Christians gleaned what wisdom they could from those patristic sources available to them.[7] What is clear, however, is that each of the models presented here was significantly moulded and modified by Celtic monasticism and put to work at the service of penitential theology at what proved to be a critical historical juncture for this discipline.

Other Levels of Challenge

Finally, the reader might well be forgiven for asking whether there are not more practical conclusions to be drawn from our study of the penitentials than those to be found at the level of symbol. Our response to this query is twofold. Firstly, the symbol, while operating primarily at the level of imagery, once accepted by the individual leads to very practical conclusions indeed. Secondly, we shall make provision at the end of this chapter for consideration of the more global or wide-ranging observations which might be drawn from our study and which may prove fruitful for the sacrament of penance today.

In the presentation of the three 'Celtic' models referred to, we shall limit ourselves to indicating briefly where these models are to be found (we have already devoted adequate space to textual exegesis in the preceding chapters and, besides, our principal aim here is to focus on the common ground between these Celtic models and contemporary doctrine on sin and penance).[8]

II. THE JURIDICAL MODEL

The juridical model, as we have already noted, is widespread throughout the penitential literature. Because, this model is intrinsically tied to the notion of divine justice and not mere human justice, the portrayal of Christ as just but merciful judge is uppermost.

Strengths of the Juridical Model

This model of penance has several strengths; firstly, it emphasizes the vertical dimension of penance and demonstrates how this must always take precedence over the horizontal aspect: it reminds us that in confessing his sins to the minister of the Church the penitent dialogues with Christ and on him 'takes place the judgement which on the cross was passed on the sins of the world'.[9] It shows that no penitential or ascetic activity is intelligible, much less efficacious, if it does not spring from God's helping and healing grace. Transgressions against God and his Church can, then, only be truly remedied by a definitive and authentic word of forgiveness in the name of Jesus Christ and on his authority.

This model also links the power of authoritative forgiveness with those to whom the Church, and ultimately Christ, has entrusted this ministry. Confession of sins is, therefore, fundamentally and primarily concerned with the remission of these sins; hence the emphasis is laid on the gratuitous and supernatural nature of this remission: each time the penitent confesses his sin, he acknowledges the fact that only in this way can he ultimately discover the merciful and forgiving God.

Moreover, this model also highlights the immediate aspect of the conversion process; namely, that God's forgiving grace comes to the penitent via the decision of the minister of the Christian community. That is to say, there is an effective juridical 'verdict' on behalf of the Church through her ordained representative. This, in turn, underlines the seriousness of the role of the minister; he must be capable of being an *animadversor*, one who can discern, listen and respond objectively to the penitent's confession.[10] Not just 'any' impartial listener, he makes an authoritative, corrective and discerning intervention into the life of the penitent in order to distinguish good from evil and place them in context. In this context, it is again interesting to re-call Columbanus' insistence on the need to cultivate the skill of discernment.[11]

The penitent, for his part, must make sufficient admission of his situation of sin and accept responsibility for it. Confession of sins is, thus, precisely an acceptance of one's personal responsibility as a Christian. When paragoned with the contemporary situation, this approach has the great merit of steering clear of a temptation toward generalisation and excessive emphasis of collective guilt. It seeks not to conceal guilt under various euphemistic disguises but rather to confess it, to atone for it and to desist from it. It affords the penitent the possibility for radical reformation and re-orientation of his moral life.

Further, it underlines the conviction that behavioural limits are good and wholesome and that human activity flourishes within certain bounds. In other words, true freedom is seen to be, as Columbanus would have it, at the ideal 'mean-point' between restriction and licence.[12] The Christian does not then seek to break out of these limits but, on the contrary, hopes and prays that God will transform him within these bounds. Ultimately, in this model of penance, God's spirit is imaged as an ordering of human chaos, the in-breaking of divine justice to our world, overcoming sin and death and thus enabling our ultimate return to wholeness.

Weaknesses of the Juridical Model

The main problem with allowing this model to stand on its own is that in its emphasis of the vertical and immediate aspects of penance, it is all too easy for the horizontal and continuous aspects to be neglected: conversion needs to be an on-going process, springing from the moment of confession and becoming, eventually, an attitude of life.

A misrepresentation of the juridical model tends to transpose civil juridical procedures to the sacramental event. Inordinate emphasis is laid, therefore, on the turning away from the old man (Adam) and insufficient emphasis is placed on the need to turn toward the new man (Christ).[13] This misrepresentation obscures the fact that the Christians, like the ancient Celts of old, must work upon the *metanoia* event throughout their lives.

Instead, too much is made of the moment of absolution, with the ensuing danger of reductionism. In such a scenario, confession becomes an objectively mechanical process. The minister's function is too easily reduced to that of examining magistrate, characterised by his acts of accusation rather than by his act of mercy. Celtic asceticism and penitential praxis, for all its severity, was not, I believe, guilty of this form of reductionism.

In Celtic penance absolution came about only after the penitent had made a serious effort to radically transform his lifestyle. The *reatus poenae* (burden of punishment) was, by means of the 'principle of contraries', transferred into the domain of the penitent's moral behaviour. Instead of undertaking merely token penance, the penitent was charged (at least in theory) with the task of personal corrective behaviour which was, in effect, a form of on-going conversion and re-orientation. By the time the Celtic penitent reached the moment of absolution he had demonstrated to the Christian community, and to himself, a degree of self-discipline and self-mastery which suggested that he would be not so susceptible to this form of temptation in the future.[14]

The Celtic monks and penitentialists (who abhorred the sorcery of the druids) were intent on demonstrating that true conversion was not a magical event. To be sure, God's forgiving grace was gratuitous, and could not be earned, but the efficacy of the penitent's conversion was nonetheless measured and limited by his own internal dispositions.

Nevertheless, the weakness remained, at least in germ, in this model of penance. This meant that when the Celtic penitential practice was later transposed into other societies, which enjoyed different and more sophisticated civil legal systems from that of Celtic society, the way lay open for the advent of an unhealthy legalism and the language of sin and penance became lost in a commercial logic of offences and penalties. This was later given a forceful expression within Celtic society in the practice of commutations, which marked a serious deterioration of the original ideal.[15]

The Juridical Model and Contemporary Doctrine

Even a cursory reading of conciliar and post-conciliar documents will demonstrate that the juridical imagery has certainly not been abandoned today. What has happened, however, is that this symbol is now being complemented, and completed, by other symbols. Nonetheless, private confession remains the place where Christians 'obtain pardon from God's mercy for the offence committed against him' (LG11).

Emphasis is laid too on the necessity for all Christians to recognise their capacity for sin. Before one can become detached from one's sins, one has to acknowledge and recognise them for what they are: 'for it is not possible to deal with sins in abstract terms' (RP13). Thus, the minister of penance has the responsibility of bringing the penitent to knowledge of himself.[16] In doing this, he makes present 'the judge of the living and the dead, who judges according to the truth and not according to appearances'. In this new found self-awareness, the penitent will see more clearly the areas in which he or she transgresses God's law.

This consideration of sin, from the point of view of the punishment it merits, is, therefore, a valid (though by no means the only) way of discovering more about sin. It is a perspective, moreover, which has strong theological and biblical roots (RP17).[17] Essentially, what is important is that the notions of wilful wrong-doing, disobedience or rejection of the sovereignty of God should not be lost; since these concepts ultimately help us to understand what sin is all about.

Contemporary, Church teaching, therefore, wants to promote a 'healthy sense of sin' (RP19) so that Christians will always remain sufficiently honest with themselves, admitting their offences, and sufficiently courageous to seek forgiveness and pardon through the minister in the sacred tribunal of penance. Emphasis is placed, however, on the fact that one may only speak of 'tribunal' here in an analogous fashion. For, the sinner confesses his sin within 'a tribunal of mercy rather than of strict and rigorous justice' (RP31). Further, when one considers how this tribunal functions one discovers 'over and above the character of judgement a healing of a medicinal character'.[18]

Thus, the link is established between the imagery of judgement and that of healing. The corrective and curative aspects of penance are not mutually exclusive; they are intrinsically linked. The requirements of the spiritual judge and spiritual physician are similar in that both need a knowledge of the sinner's heart to be able to judge and to absolve, to cure and to heal. Let us postpone, however, further consideration of the healing imagery until our next section, where we shall deal with it in some detail.

The Juridical Model: Conclusion

So, the juridical model of penance fulfils an important and irreplaceable role in the theology of the sacrament of penance. In the language of the Celtic texts, there is still need today for the *animadversor*—one who stands over against the penitent and, because of his 'otherness' and his capacity for discernment, can help him toward self-discovery and self-knowledge; one who is not afraid to recognise that evil does sometimes find a place in the human heart, thus turning the self into a kind of God and giving rise to pride, avarice, lust and aggression, which are the effects of serving this false God;[19] one who enables the individual to 'name' his sin, in the conviction that, already in the naming process, the penitent rediscovers and re-affirms his personal responsibility and thereby takes the first step toward excising his sin and amending his life.

According to this perspective, then, law remains an essential element in Christian morality but, equally, over-emphasis on the law is decidedly unhealthy. Legalism is, by definition, idolatry and *eo ipso* sinful. The minister of penance has no place for merely vindictive punishment, but seeks, instead, to impart God's mercy and enable the penitent to take corrective action, to turn again toward his fellow man and woman and ultimately to turn back to Christ.

III. THE MODEL OF DISEASE AND HEALING

The imagery of disease and healing is, as we have often pointed out, by far the most predominant imagery in the penitentials.[20]

Strengths of the Healing Model

The primary strength of this symbol is that it at once complements and counterbalances the sister metaphor of judgement and mercy.

Whereas, the latter places the emphasis on the corrective nature of penance, the former tends to stress the curative dimension.

Our textual analysis has shown that the penitent himself was understood to exercise an important role in 'curing' his moral life and that in so doing he had to take corrective measures. Thus, there is no absolute division between cure and correction. What this model of penance does, is place the corrective aspect of penitential activity within a more global, all-embracing notion of cure or care.[21] In this way the imagery revives the notion of penance as process, and serves to integrate the ideas of healing, caring, curing and suffering.

This model serves to bridge the gap between the other two models of penance. For it retains the essence of the juridical model by describing the moment of confession as a healing encounter with the risen Christ, while also underlining the need for the penitent to continue to cultivate a morally healthy lifestyle, as he makes his life pilgrimage towards spiritual wholeness. The healing model of penance has rich, biblical and patristic roots; the Gospels are replete with stories which present Jesus as healer. The very etymology of the title 'saviour' itself connotes healing.[22] Evidently then, in this paradigm the minister is seen to be an instrument of Christ's healing power. Whereas the juridical model defines his role in terms of *animadversio*, this perspective emphasizes the gift of *animacuratio*. To discover a penitential cure, the physician of souls must be able to make some form of diagnosis; he must pinpoint those areas of the penitent's moral behaviour which need to be examined and healed so as to bring about a true conversion.

So, as we have seen throughout our textual exegesis, this model has the merit combining the horizontal and vertical dimensions of penance. The penitent here becomes actively involved in his own conversion; he is called upon to make profound adjustments to his outlook and lifestyle to return to spiritual health. Yet he cannot accomplish this task alone but instead must follow the prescription of the 'physician of souls' who shares in the healing power of the divine Physician.

Moreover, the minister here does not merely propose ideals to be aspired to but rather concrete steps to be taken to heart by the penitent. This finds its most pithy and powerful expression in the so-called 'principle of contraries'.[23] Thus, between them, confessor and penitent undertake a reconstruction of the latter's moral life.

Despite the preponderance of austere practices, which the modern reader might find hard to stomach, these penitentialists do demonstrate a sympathetic knowledge of human nature as well as a 'desire to deliver men and women from the mental obsessions and social maladjustment caused by their misdeeds.'[24] This desire was in turn supported by a scientific approach (however rudimentary), in which the spiritual doctor had first of all to know (*cognoscere*) the various illnesses, then treat them (*curare*) and finally, restore (*revocare*) the sinner to a state of complete, mental health.[25]

Again, it is not difficult to see how this approach dovetails with Columbanus' notion of discretion. The cure of souls was a gift, by no means possessed by all, through which the spiritual doctor, by exercising his discretion, was able to apply the 'principle of contraries' to individual cases. There is a timeless quality about this procedure which, however much obscured by jargon or theological refinements over the centuries, still remains at the heart of the sacrament of penance today.[26]

A further positive aspect of this model is the attention it gives to the roots of sin, to the tension between sin and grace and to the re-shaping of one's life according to deep motivations. There is an attempt, even in the penitentials, to come to terms with a profounder type of conversion or *metanoia*. The octade of sins, borrowed from Cassian, formed the backbone of the Celtic categories of sin. As such, they also provide a useful corrective to the notion of sin as merely infraction or infringement of law.

By contrast to the later listing of the Ten Commandments, as a model for the examination of conscience, the capital sins were viewed not so much as deeds to be admitted but as tendencies of the heart which were to be found behind one's actions. In this light, we can best understand Columbanus' exhortation that 'just as we must beware of mortal and fleshly sins . . . so also must we refrain and cleanse ourselves from interior vices and the sicknesses of the ailing soul' (Co.B.30). The sinner was, above all, to become aware of these tendencies, confess his sins before God and ultimately seek to convert the underlying tendencies into behaviour which was morally acceptable and spiritually advantageous.

In the penitentials, this effort to get at the root of conduct and misconduct seems to have been at least as important as the precise enumeration of misdeeds and sinful actions. Thus, the curative philosophy seems to hold that the basic human instincts and drives, which in particular instances may lead to sins of pride, gluttony, lust and so forth, may equally, with the aid of the medicine of penance be re-directed to enhance the spiritual life of the penitent rather than hinder it.

This approach by extension implies that there are sins of moral failure, of not doing enough, of not caring enough, of not serving enough, of not loving enough. The penitent orients his life toward the virtuous dispositions but, insofar as he fails to realise these, he is constantly reminded of his woundedness and sinfulness.

A final advantage of this paradigm is what the modern commentator might call its 'holistic' dimension. There appears to be a shared conviction among the penitentialists that, just as one's sinful choices are reflected at several levels of being; physical, mental, emotional and spiritual; so too must all of these levels be involved in the curative, penitential process. The result is that the repentant sinner becomes aware that true conversion will make very real demands upon him; it is never simply an intellectual or theoretical concept.

Weaknesses of the Healing Model

As with the juridical model, the medicinal model of penance also has its share of disadvantages, especially that misinterpretation which would portray sin as having no reference to one's own active freedom. The result would be to somehow attempt to shift responsibility for one's misdeeds to a 'dark, impersonal, anonymous fate or to an Ego, from which one cannot escape'.[27] The penitentials, in harmony with patristic and biblical precedents, use healing imagery to describe the way out of the morass of sin. Nowhere is there an attempt to negate individual responsibility: they put forward the view that the sinner must hold himself responsible for his misdemeanours.

Thus, whether one is a priest or a layman, powerful or lowly, male or female, all must first acknowledge that they have sinned of their own volition before they can have recourse to the salutary medicine of penance. Sin then, whilst it is understood as wounding the sinner, may not be seen as a vague, amorphous evil for which no one is responsible, no one guilty and about which no moral questions may be asked.[28]

Instead, the penitentials are vehemently opposed to the concealment of sin under various euphemistic disguises, so much so that the language is at times of a candour and degree of explicitness which the modern reader finds shocking. The penitentialists' motive, however, is not principally to shock but to bring home to the penitent the need to recognise and acknowledge his sin, to realise that he is his brother's keeper. For, it is only at that moment when he begins to accept responsibility for his guilt and his sinfulness that the possibility of radical reformation of his moral life opens up before him.

Hence, despite the apparent severity of this position it is, nevertheless, a hope-filled one for it enables the penitent to transcend his self-centredness and to own his guilt. No matter how serious the sin, the knowledge that one has 'done' it itself implies the reassuring hope that one can 'undo' it. The person remains a responsible subject who can take positive steps as well as negative ones and who, therefore, is not the helpless prey of an all-embracing and crippling evil.[29]

A further possible weakness of the healing model is that of casuistry. Indeed, the penitentials themselves, are quite definitely a form of casuistry. Unfortunately, for the modern commentator, it is quite difficult to consider this term without thinking immediately of its many negative connotations. Considered objectively, however, it is not difficult to see the reasoning behind the casuist approach. The physician of souls, like the physician of the body, needs to be able to bridge the gap 'between theory and practice, between abstract reflection and the concrete life-situation'.[30]

Further, he needs to be able to pass on, in some methodical fashion, his findings, in order that future generations may learn from his attempts at interpreting and applying ethical principles and norms to concrete situations. In this regard, the sacrament of penance becomes the locus *par excellence* of casuistry for the pastor. Various putative scenarios are outlined in the penitential texts and these serve as models or as an information resource for the confessor. The need for such an aid was reinforced in eras and situations, such as that of Celtic society, where confessors themselves did not always enjoy a satisfactory degree of instruction. The penitentials, then, had the merit of enabling the minister to concretise moral teaching, apply it to the case of a particular individual, and even instruct and help to form the conscience of that individual where this was necessary.

Inevitably, the difficulty here, though, was one of reductionism. Given that each individual sinner was precisely that, namely an individual, then no two situations no matter how similar, are identical. Casuistry, thus, runs the risk of stereotyping and mechanising the moment of confession. Instead of becoming an aid and guide, casuistry can deteriorate into legalism and minimalism.[31] It is not our intention to argue here that this did not happen in Celtic penance. It is, however, clear to the reader of the penitentials that this was certainly not their author's intention.

Columbanus insists that he knows only 'in part' and that his penitential is but an aid to others (Co.B.pr.). Finnian likewise insists upon the 'poverty of his talent' and looks forward to future up-dating and up-grading of his findings by 'diligent searchers' (Vi.ps.) Both Cummean and the Bigotian author add the important rider that in all penance the following factors are to be considered: 'the length of time anyone remains in his faults; what learning he has received; by what passion he is assailed; how great is his strength; with what intensity of weeping he is afflicted and with what oppression he has been driven to sin' (Cu.ps.1. and Bi.pr.2). There is here, then, at the very least, a sincere attempt on the part of the penitentialists, to highlight the danger of a blind application of their prescriptions.

The penitentialists themselves are acutely aware of the limitations of their manuals. Let us however put ourselves in the shoes of the founding fathers of the Celtic Church if we may. Having advocated the parallels between doctors of the soul and doctors of the body, they needed some way of ensuring that spiritual physicians adhered to ethical principles and norms which were based upon scripture and tradition. The *libri poenitentiales* fulfilled this need, albeit in a rudimentary fashion. The penitentials were aware of the risks of legalism and mechanism incumbent upon their work; but it was a risk they were prepared to take, for, as they saw it, the alternative was chaos.[32]

The Healing Model and Contemporary Doctrine

As well as being the predominant imagery of the penitential texts the model of healing has also enjoyed a resurgence in recent Church documents. The language of disease and wholeness has become an increasingly significant image in the twentieth century. The Church is understood to be 'wounded' by the sins of Christians (LG11). Moreover, man in his inmost self is also wounded by original sin (RP2). The truly Christian approach resides not merely in gazing upon this woundedness but in 'mending divisions, healing the wounds and re-establishing at all levels a sincere reconciliation (RP3). We are told, however, that all attempts at reconciliation are, ultimately, to be measured in terms of their efficacy and completeness by the 'extent that they reach—in order to heal it—that original wound which is the root of all other wounds: namely sin' (RP3).

The wound of sin, moreover, is essentially caused by an act of disobedience, and it has a twofold expression—within the penitent himself, and in his relationship with his neighbour (RP15). To heal this woundedness, the Christian has the privilege of recourse to the sacrament of penance where the minister acts *in persona Christi.* And the Christ made present here is 'the physician who heals and comforts' (RP29).[33]

Indeed, Church doctrine is at pains to point out that the juridical model of penance must always be tempered by the healing one. Attention is drawn to the frequency with which Christ himself is presented as healer in the Gospels, as well as to patristic predilection for this metaphor.[34] And this, in turn, leads to the conclusion that the priest in his role of healer 'must aquaint himself with the condition of the sick person in order to treat and heal him'.[35]

The Healing Model: Conclusion

We may, then, conclude our survey of the model of healing by saying that it is now enjoying a renewed interest. Its importance, as a sister image which dialogues and tempers the juridical model, is now being officially stressed. The priest's role, moreover, as *medicus animarum* is recognised as distinct from that of *animadversor* and therefore requiring diverse talents. Further, there is a very real sense in which we can say the 'cure of souls' is not simply a metaphor, but that Christians truly are made whole and rendered more spiritually healthy, when they courageously face up to their own responsibility for the wounds of sin and evil, and have recourse to the salutary medicine of penance.[36]

IV. THE PILGRIMAGE MODEL

The third and final model of Celtic penance is not so immediately apparent in the texts as the other models; yet it is perhaps the one that model which is the most quintessentially Celtic.

The Pilgrimage Model: Secondary Themes

Part of the difficulty in perceiving it is that it comprises a number of secondary metaphors which, when taken in isolation, prove difficult to interpret but, once placed in harmonious relationship with other imagery, form a mosaic in which all of life is seen as a form of pilgrimage. It is precisely along this life path that each Christian must make his pilgrim's progress. In this regard, the imagery of pilgrimage in Columbanus' *Instructiones* is of great value as an aid to interpreting the penitential texts.

We may take as our starting point the words of the apostle that we are but 'strangers and exiles on the earth . . . seeking a homeland' (Heb 11:13–14).[37] Throughout our earthly pilgrimage we need to bear witness to this fact and continue to strive toward the heavenly city.

This is recognized by both the Scriptures and the penitentials as no easy task, for the Christian life cannot exist apart from trial and suffering. Recognising that every Christian must, in some sense, experience a 'wandering in the desert' before attaining 'the promised land', it becomes apparent that he must be equipped mentally and spiritually to survive this desert ordeal. He must, in the words of Columbanus, 'refrain and cleanse (himself) from interior vices and the sicknesses of the ailing soul before the covenant of true peace and the bond of eternal salvation' (Co.B.30).[38]

The penitentials are really the handbooks of the desert experience. In this model, the minister is viewed above all as the fellow-traveller, fellow-pilgrim, fellow-sufferer, or, to use the Celtic term, *anamchara* (soul-friend). The emphasis in this model is predominantly one of solidarity. Both minister and penitent are, ultimately, pilgrims on the same pilgrim path. The important thing is to persevere, to remain steadfast, to stand ready and even to do battle with the forces of evil. Thus, a secondary image becomes that of battle. The Celtic values of heroism and valour are put to work in the struggle against sin and vice.[39]

But man is also morally weak, fragile, incomplete. He needs support and sustenance. Hence, the role of *anamchara* who receives the weary pilgrim with hospitality and restores him. Here, the emphasis is placed, not so much on the saving judgement or salutary medicine but on the fraternal witness and compassion of the *anamchara*. Again, the notion of Celtic or green martyrdom is uppermost here; one must bear *living* witness to the Gospel. And the trait *par excellence* of this testimony is spiritual humility, *paupertas* (Patrick), or *humilitas* (Columbanus).

Thus, the fortitude of the confessor, and therefore of the Christian, is born not out of his own strength but out of a keen awareness of his own weakness, which is, itself, a living confession of our need to participate in the saving power of Christ, who is ultimately *the* Way of all Christians.

Strengths of the Pilgrimage Model

The advantages of this model are several.[40] Firstly, the horizontal or continuous dimension of penance is fully explored. Emphasis is placed on the fact that penance is tied, ultimately, not to abstract principle but to real human beings in history. Confession of sins, in turn, tends to be seen as a means not an end. In confessing his sin, the sinner acknowledges his distance from God, and God bridges this distance with his mercy. But in the immediate moment of saving sacramental encounter, the penitent becomes strengthened, so that he is able to strive after the good moral life with renewed purpose and vigour.

In this way, this model of penance situates the confession of sin within the basic human yearning for life, love and freedom; so, conversion cannot be a merely momentary experience but, instead, must be a more dynamic one which reaches out into a life-long project of struggle to overcome hatred, pride, selfishness, lust and so forth. In a very real way, conversion is understood as a change of heart which re-fashions the whole of existence and by means of which Christ becomes the compass point by which one steers.[41] The centre of gravity of the penitent's life can no longer be self-centredness but, rather, the practice of those virtues which in themselves encompass the truly Christian life.

In the Celtic tradition, this re-shaping of life was given expression above all in the ascetic life. Christians practised discipline in order to become better disciples. The ascetic life was understood to be the struggle against all interior evil and the suppression of the more dangerous natural urges in order that the spiritual person might develop more fully. There is, then, the quest here for that creative harmony between the different forces in man. And it will, no doubt, have occurred to the reader, that the ideal mean-point sought after by Columbanus was not all that different from that *mesotes*, which the ancient Greeks understood to be the very essence of virtue.

Yet, as we have seen in the previous chapter, for the Celtic Christian, ascetic activity had also to be a taking up of the Cross of Christ. The Christian who undertook ascetic activity could not justify this apart from the saving death of Christ. Instead, he tried to live as though he 'died daily' to demonstrate his awareness of the transitory nature of things.[42] Through personal sacrifice each individual Christian in his or her own way said 'yes' to the Cross in their own lives and, in so doing, strove to imitate more perfectly the Saviour.

A further advantage of this penitential model is its depiction of the minister. In this model, he fulfils a markedly prophetic role. The *anamchara* is above all a companion, a brother in Christ, helping and counselling, consoling and admonishing, bearing with the penitent and bearing witness to Christ in an existential exposition of the Gospel message.[43] There is a strong sense of solidarity in the understanding of *diakonia* or ministry here. For the priest, too, remains a pilgrim. He is *in via*, on the road. He too is in a state of becoming and in search of perfection. Like the penitent, the priest journeys from the sinful *a quo* toward the future glorious *ad quem*. For the priest, as much as for the penitent, the words of the first apostle ring true, namely that 'testing and suffering remain the crucible of faith' (1 Pet 1:7).

More so than with the ministries of *animadversio* and *animacuratio*; *anamchairdeas* lays emphasis on life-witness. The priest's own attitude and his readiness for his own conversion become crucial here. On the other hand, in the moment of confession the minister, by virtue of his acting *in persona Christi*, makes present to the penitent the fact that God himself has become incarnate, so as to join us on our earthly pilgrimage. This model has the merit of fixing our attention on the fact that God became man for our sake; that Christ too experienced temptation and suffering, and that, for this reason, he has real *compassion* and *sympathy* for those who are tempted, where these words are understood according to their true significance, namely to share the same *pathos*, the same emotion, and ultimately to suffer with the other.[44]

The Church, in turn, is imaged here (like the Celtic monastic Church of old) as a Church of sinners, but a Church nevertheless, which is also holy, for it is the privileged community wherein Christians encounter the saving grace of Christ. In this model, the Church bears guilt with the sinner, suffers by it and helps to atone for it, and, in her prayer, seeks after those sinners who are still indifferent to the call to repentance. The Church is the 'Church of poverty, humility, temptation, suffering and persecution following in this way her crucified Lord'. In this suffering of fault in Christ crucified, there is, in some sense, a manifestation of the cross of Christ in the world and a sharing of its burden.[45]

What becomes essential here is perseverance; hence the ancient Celtic emphasis on the secondary ikons of soldier and martyr as incarnations of the heroic will to persevere. This, in turn, highlights another merit of this model of penance, namely that the minister is not portrayed in terms of superiority. To be sure, the *anamchara* is, in some sense, a master; but the term is only applicable insofar as he is a master of his own discipline, one who perseveres, he is not master of the penitent but, instead, with him must strive to discern the will of the divine Master.

Unlike *animacuratio*, which places the emphasis on skill, and *animadversio*, which accentuates the need for wisdom, *anamchairdeas* by contrast, stresses above all the the importance of a resolute will.[46] The minister, or *anamchara,* must himself be one who comes through the fire of real suffering and self-sacrifice whilst, at the same time, growing ever more open to the saving and forgiving grace of Christ, and one who always reserves, in his heart, a sincere hospitality for the stranger, the fellow-pilgrim, the fellow-sufferer.

Weaknesses of the Pilgrimage Model

As with the previous two models of penance, this one has drawbacks. The first of these resides in the practice of asceticism, which is easily open to misinterpretation, the danger being that asceticism would come to be understood as an end in itself, rather than as a means to conversion. The ensuing problem is that God is 'bracketed out' and the role of divine grace is disregarded. For, 'it is perfectly possible to justify moral asceticism in the eyes of the world and independently of Christian belief.'[47] By this stage, of course, we are hard on the heels of Pelagius and earned forgiveness is just around the corner.

In fact, it is true that several commentators have not spared the Celtic penitentialists this criticism.[48] Nonetheless, I tend to side with the majority view on this point which holds that in the first place Irish penitential theology was not sufficiently well developed to be concerned with a sophisticated soteriology, and, in particular, with the relationship between saving grace and human free will which so taxed the minds of Pelagius and Augustine. Celtic penance was, quite simply, more concerned with praxis than with doctrine. Secondly, it is evident from the penitentials themselves that moral perfection was not the Celtic ideal in quite the same way as it might have been for the early monks on the desert fringes of Hellenic Christianity.

The Irish monks lived at the centre of Irish society and, as such, had no illusions about ever escaping completely from sin and temptation. Each of the penitentialists, in turn, despite his mastery of the ascetic way of life, is keenly conscious of his imperfection. Columbanus, Gall, and Columba, the great holy men of Celtic tradition, are frequently irascible, stubborn and even violent men and in this regard they behave no better than the holy men of the Old Testament.[49]

This, however, does suggest a second potential disadvantage, namely that there could somehow be a two-tiered approach to the Christian life and to salvation. One has, at times, the distinct impression, on reading the early Celtic penitential and spiritual literature, that Irish churchmen saw themselves as something of 'an elite sub-group of a Christian community that reached beyond the bounds of any single, physical settlement'.[50]

Again, whilst, on the face of it, this is clearly a flawed approach, it is somewhat doubtful as to whether it is wholly true of the Irish situation. It is true that Finnian, Columbanus, Cummean and their monks did see themselves as being called to a more rigorous and demanding lifestyle than laymen and clerics, but this calling was precisely so in order that they might become green martyrs—or living witnesses. Their vocation was not to abandon society, but to remain within it challenging and edifying it in the process. Thus, there was established a mutual dependence, the laity provided vocations, economic support and in some sense the very raison d'être of the monastery; in return, the monastery and its monks provided inspiration as well as a place of spiritual encounter and healing counsel. In the Ireland of the penitentials the monastic community and the larger Christian community became so interwoven that it was virtually impossible to think of one without the other.

Another potential flaw of this model, to which we must give some attention, concerns the role of the minister. For, the question arises as to how exactly the minister is to interpret practically his call to be a fellow-sufferer. While this unquestionably represents the more humane dimension of Celtic penance, it is not without its difficulties. Historically, one of these difficulties was the question of commutations through which a substantial reduction of a prescribed penance could be obtained by the penitent's having recourse to his soul friend who, in turn, accepted some of the penitential burden.[51] The merits of this practice are obvious in terms of a compassionate pastoral approach intended to off-set the severity of some of the penitential canons. Nonetheless, history has also shown the inherent weaknesses in such a policy since it quite easily fell foul of commercialism and abuse.

There is no reason, however, why a modern theology and praxis of penance, which sets much less store on the severity of penances, should not retain the symbol of fellow-sufferer and pilgrim, while, at the same time, jettisoning the practice of commutations, which no longer squares adequately with our understanding of sin and its remission.

Excursus: The Pilgrimage Model and Fundamental Option

A final question, to which we must give some consideration, here before setting the model of pilgrimage aside concerns how precisely the sinner was understood to sin. More particularly, in a model which emphasizes the continuous rather than the immediate aspect of personal, moral behaviour, we may ask ourselves whether or not there is something here akin to what the modern scholar might call a theology of the fundamental option.[52] At one level, our immediate answer must be no, since in Celtic penance there is no clear explanation of how divine grace, personal freedom and personal choices interact in the way, for example, that modern theology has sought to tackle this problem. At another level, however, we can piece together various strands of imagery and view the moral choices and responses which the Celtic Christian had to make according to the understanding of vocation in these texts.

Again, it is Columbanus' pilgrim imagery which evokes the question most forcefully. In his eighth sermon he affirms: 'Let this principle abide with us, that on the road we so live as travellers, as pilgrims, as guests of the world, entangled by no lusts, longing with no earthly desires, but let us fill our minds with heavenly and spiritual impressions.'[53] Thus, the Christian life is considered to be an onward progression toward eventual glorification. But a subsequent sermon combines this with another strand of imagery: 'Let us not be the painters of another's image . . . For righteousness and unrighteousness . . . are opposed to one another. Then lest perhaps we should import into ourselves despotic images let Christ paint his image in us.'[54]

The secondary strand of imagery here is emphasizing the overall, negative effect of sin upon the Christian's moral personality rather than simply highlighting individual sinful acts. Each Christian is, therefore, called to be a 'painter of God's image' but, at the same time, runs the risk of painting the despot's image. There is, then, a struggle within the individual between the forces of good and evil. And to the extent that there exists this 'despotic' force, sin is not simply a question of categorial acts. Instead, the subject must continually struggle against the more pervasive sinful foe: 'For this is a time of war; for no one should expect rest in warfare . . .'[55] Thus, we can see that as in Augustine's *Confessions*, so too in Columbanus' *Instructiones*, acts are placed in the setting of the person's ineradicable desire for the good, which is at root the thirst for God.

At best, I think we can say that Columbanus is striving to emphasise the personal component in sinful activity. In common with Paul (Rom 7:3–25) the sinful condition of humanity is the backdrop of his thought. The sinful acts of man are, in some sense, the expression of a force that is hostile to God and his message. Thus, the basic sin is estrangement from God. Through baptism, however, Christ's victory over sin is renewed in every Christian. Thus, Christ alone can save man from the tyranny and slavery of sin, but it is up to each individual to make a choice for a life of holiness. After the style of Pascal, Columbanus presents the human enigma thus: 'Your life is a net for you, you are ensnared willing or unwilling, in yourself you have the matter of entanglement, in yourself you do not have the means of release' (Co.Inst.III).[56]

The Christian, however, freed from the slavery of sin, can co-operate with divine grace, and make a basic decision for the holy life in order to 'restore the image of God' at the end of his life. But this life-long project must be realised in and through concrete words, deeds and thoughts: 'For the love of God is the restoration of his image. But he loves God who observes his commands . . . And true love is not in word only but in deed and in truth' (Co.Inst.XI).[57]

We may say, then, that in Celtic penance and, more particularly, in Columbanus, there is a more profound understanding of sin than simply sinful act. The texts do not contain the notion of the fundamental option, as such, in the complex and theologically sophisticated sense with which contemporary moralists understand the term. But the Christian is called, all the same, to a life of holiness and in this life he does battle with sin. At times, he may fall foul of the sinful despot and this will express itself in sinful actions, some of which are described as *peccatis capitalibus.*[58] It then behoves the sinner to have recourse to the medicine of penance so that the despot's image may be cast out and the image of Christ become uppermost again.

It is precisely at this juncture in Celtic penance that the three paradigms of judgement, medicine and pilgrimage do battle, as it were. Consequently, there is a tension, at this point, as to how precisely these paradigms interact. As a general rule, though, we can say that the so-called 'capital sins' tend to be considered as signs of a moral life which has already fallen into the slavery of the sinful despot.

On the other hand, lesser sins such as those of disobedience, despondency and anger are seen to be more at the level of sinful attitude than act. Hence, indefinite penances are prescribed depending on the duration of the sinful attitude and according to the maxim: 'as long a time as a person remains in sin so long is he to do penance' (Gi.14).[59] And this maxim is, I believe, the bridging element which allows the Celtic penitentialist to see categorial sins as signs or expressions of an underlying sinful attitude which must be opposed, in an on-going fashion, with virtuous exercise according to the principle of contraries. There is, at least, a rudimentary understanding here of both the metaphysical and historical (or chronological) dimensions of sin. Ultimately, the texts, however, go no further toward explaining the interaction of these two dimensions within the personal subject, than to allow the three penitential paradigms to exist side by side, in the hope that, in this way, they might wage a more effective battle against sin in both its particular and general expressions.

The Pilgrimage Model and Contemporary Doctrine

Having discussed at some length the merits and disadvantages of this model of penance, we must now consider how it might find an echo in more recent Church documents. Firstly, we can say that the basic anthropological categories of the Celtic 'pilgrim' model are in harmony with those of the Constitution on the Church in the Modern World (*Gaudium et Spes*). Section 13 of this document recognises that the 'whole life of men, both individual and social, shows itself to be a struggle, and a dramatic one, between good and evil between light and darkness' (GS13). And a later section (GS37), takes up again the imagery of the 'battle field', pointing out that Christian life is an onward progression, in which: 'all human activities . . . must be purified and perfected by the cross and resurrection of Christ.' And a later section still reminds us that the whole Church is engaged in an earthly pilgrimage (GS45).

Thus, the basic thrust of the two sets of imagery are broadly similar. Man's life is a pilgrimage in which he must do battle against sin and its signs. And the Church, in turn, has a historical character, wherein she is understood as the Church of 'poverty, humility, temptation, suffering and persecution following in the way of her crucified Lord'.[60]

The model of passage or pilgrimage does not find quite the same level of direct reference and treatment in the post-synodal exhortation *Reconciliatio et Paenitentia* as did the models of healing and merciful judgement. Nevertheless, there are some very striking parallels here, at the level of language and imagery, which suggest that the model of pilgrimage is not alone compatible with, but in fact contained within this document. For instance, the early pages are replete with references to the on-going dimension of penance. 'One's whole existence', we are told, must become penitential. There must be a 'continuous striving for what is better'. Moreover, penance cannot remain simply an intellectual idea, but must, instead, become enfleshed at the level of 'deeds and acts'. For this reason, asceticism is advocated, which is to be understood as the 'concrete daily effort' of the Christian to 'lose his or her own life for Christ'.[61]

A subsequent section invites us to consider the *mysterium crucis* as the 'loftiest drama where Christ suffers . . . the tragedy of the division of man from God' (RP7). And this, in turn, gives rise to a call for all Christians to be 'disciples of Christ' and to be anxious to give the 'proof of concrete living witness'. (RP9) Christians are, therefore, ambassadors for Christ (2 Cor 5:20) and *eo ipso* called to be ambassadors of reconciliation.

Section 12 of this document points out that all Christians are on 'pilgrimage through the world' and are called to 'get up again after every fall' (RP12). Pilgrimage, then, implies a sense of solidarity both in the negative sense, that each 'individual's sin in some way affects others', and in the positive sense, that 'every soul which rises above itself raises up the world' (RP16).[62] Chapter Two is equally striking in its resonance of the symbol of passage. It calls to mind the Pauline expression *mysterium pietatis* which, ultimately, it asserts, is 'the very mystery of Christ' (RP20). Moreover, the document affirms that *mysterium pietatis* is precisely a 'path' (RP22) which opens the Christian intellect to conversion, understood 'not as lofty abstractions but as concrete Christian values' (RP21).

The third part of the exhortation, which concerns more directly the pastoral ministry of penance and reconciliation, holds that the Christ who is made present to the penitent in the sacrament of penance, is the 'brother of man' and the 'shepherd intent on finding the lost sheep' (RP29).[63] This depiction of Christ as brother and Christ as leader, approximates, quite closely, to the Celtic notion of *anamchara* where Christ, of course, is seen as the *anamchara par excellence*. Further, the document asserts that this means, in turn, that the minister is called to be a fellow-traveller; he must 'first travel the path' in order to 'lead others along the path of Christian perfection.' (RP29) And, precisely in this role of fellow-traveller, the minister bears witness to the social nature of the sacrament and to the fact that 'the whole Church—militant, suffering and glorious in heaven-comes to the aid of the penitent' (RP31. iv).

Both priest and penitent, moreover, are called to be fellow-sufferers with Christ in that both are to make a 'serious effort to crucify the "old man" so that the "new" can be born by the power of Christ'. Ultimately, this exhortation argues that Christian penance can only be truly authentic if it 'takes as its model Christ, who though he was innocent chose the path of poverty, patience austerity and, one can say, the penitential life' (RP26).

At this point, we may say that, during the course of the last few pages, it has been our aim to demonstrate that this latter model, proposed by *Reconciliatio et Paenitentia*, and the Celtic model of pilgrimage and passage are, broadly speaking, one and the same thing.

The Pilgrimage Model: Conclusion

As we mentioned at the beginning of this section, the 'pilgrimage' model as presented in Celtic penitential literature is perhaps the most typically Celtic of all the models and consequently represents a significant component of the challenge which that literature holds for the sacrament of penance today. As a model of penance, it also emphasises the duty of every Christian, and in particular of the Christian minister, to help those who are in danger of despairing, to rediscover their own value, dignity and destiny. By extension it implies that it is also the Christian's task to overcome everything which threatens to diminish and obstruct our pilgrimage toward fulfilment in Christ.

Further, it underlines the fact that this task cannot be carried out without self-sacrifice and without a profound desire to place oneself at the service of others. There is a recognition that sacrifice, suffering and human failure are a part of Christian life, but also that sin does not have the last word. Suffering and voluntary sacrifice are a reminder of that inner suffering and pain of remorse and contrition. Yet, there is an awareness too that without suffering that 'growth which we call repentance would be impossible'.[64]

Austere penances and ascetic practices are, thus, an acknowledgement that all effort and pain can, ultimately, become a *way* in which we attempt to undo the evil we have done and repair the distortion and falsehood within ourselves. Moreover, the minister, and ultimately the Church, through their role as fellow-sufferer with the sinner, make visibly manifest a profound understanding of the human condition and thereby become a tangible sign of the forgiveness of God, which actively seeks out the sinner (Lk 15). In this way, too, repentance and forgiveness do not simply belong exclusively within the sacrament of penance but spill over also into the Christian's daily life.

In short, what we are saying here is that the Celtic image of pilgrimage affords a vision of the Christian life wherein the individual will inevitably encounter suffering and sin, but where he has also the means, through penance, to cleave to that graced process, whereby he is freed from the un-Christ-like elements 'which impede the growth of his humanity into the kingdom'.[65] Forgiveness of sin, thus understood, is not simply a cancellation of offence but a painting of the image of Christ within us, who 'is the goal of human history and of civilisation, the centre of mankind, the joy of all hearts and the fulfilment of all aspirations' (GS 45).

V. CONTEMPORARY PASTORAL CHALLENGES

Some General Anthropological Problems

Irish Christians today, and indeed Christians everywhere, have one important factor in common with the early Christians of newly-evangelised Celtic Ireland: they both are witnesses to a time of great change. In the aftermath of Marx, Freud and Nietzche man looks at himself differently, understands himself differently and, to some extent, interprets his faith differently. The crisis of the sacrament of penance today is symptomatic of the crisis in Christianity generally which, in turn, itself reflects a more all-pervasive crisis in the self-identity of Western man. For, despite his relentless search for freedom 'man remains alone, thrown back upon himself and his problems'.[66] In the secular arena, the futility and impotence of this freedom is evidenced at four levels.

Political At the level of the family the most basic political unit, our century has seen a shift away from the authoritarian, Victorian, *pater-familias* model of Western family toward the more democratic, modern concept of 'nuclear' family. A similar shift has occurred at the level of national government, away from absolute monarchy, toward the constitutional variety and ultimately toward democracy.[67]

Generally, in the Western world, the quest for freedom has moved from the national to the personal level. But the quest has not been an unqualified success. Whilst democracies have brought people a degree of freedom never experienced before, that same freedom did not yield the results which were expected. 'It has produced instead rebellion, violence and terrorism as well as universal permissiveness of every kind: free love, divorce, abortion, drugs, euthanasia, suicide.'[68]

Psychological Whilst Western man was busily pursuing his new-found political freedom, both personal and collective, two major movements in psychology were casting serious doubts on the validity of freedom itself as a meaningful term. Mankind began to discover the various conditioning factors which had been insidiously eroding his mental space. Hence, he gradually became more aware of his biological, hereditary, social, cultural, religious and psychological background.

The psychoanalytics and the behaviourists each, in turn, proffered explanations of the origin of guilt. At its worst, this was seen by one group (psychoanalytics) as removed from the realm of personal responsibility altogether. One did what one's desires drove one to do. 'Nobody was really responsible for sin; one might be responsible for a particular act, but one was not responsible for the fact that it was or seemed sinful.'[69]

The behaviourists, in turn, saw guilt as ultimately aroused by a process of conditioning. Certain themes of the mass-media and religious exhortation had conditioned us to condemn and think ill of ourselves, or so they believed. Again, at its worst, this painted a picture of man as a rather hapless, pathetic creature struggling to shed the psychological baggage of his oppressive past and to continue his quest for true freedom.

Philosophical The philosophical community also vigorously sought freedom from their religious and ethical shackles. In essence, this meant bad news for theists. Ours is the generation which inherited the indifferentism of the post-'God-is-dead' era. The God-elimination hypothesis set forth by Hegel, Feuerbach, Marx, Nietzche and others produced, in turn, scepticism, *ennui*, anthropocentrism and, ultimately, despair.

The philosophical discipline of ethics lived through an image-shattering, iconoclastic moment. In a world, where science became the reigning paradigm of knowledge the results in the pursuit of ethical systems were intuitionism, rationalism, logical positivism and ultimately emotivism, each of which were duly critiqued by rational argument and found wanting. Almost inevitably, then, nihilism and scepticism regarding inquiry into morality were the order of the day and ethics as a discipline slid into disarray.[70] Man's lonely isolation was complete.

Personal In a world, then where the individual was encouraged to sever his ties with his ethical, psychological and political patrimony there could really be only result: individualism. We live in an era where, at one level, the individual is king, independent and sovereign and where, at another level yet, he is a slave, unable to realize his freedom, seeking always after novel, materialist panaceas to assuage his metaphysical pain. Modern man is, therefore, a paradox. On the one hand, he jealously guards his independence, his privacy and his inner emotions, whereas, on the other hand, this privacy can lead to a lonely isolation which, in turn, translates itself into a deep need to confide in another person.

Modern psychoanalysis recognises this need and, indeed, posits it as a condition for a sane, balanced mind. And, whilst this need, itself, has always been a facet of human nature, it has, undoubtedly, attained a greater degree of acuity in the modern world. Evidence of this, is to be found in the proliferation of psychoanalysis in Western society and the proclivity of individuals to make anonymous, detailed and intimate confessions to radio chat shows and newspaper 'agony' columns.[71]

Modern man, therefore, at the very moment he experiences the intoxication of progress finds himself saddened and disquieted. He has not found the answers to the insatiable yearnings of the human heart; instead, he finds himself isolated, cut off, alone. In a very real sense, modern man has become the incarnation of the *incurvatio hominis*. He finds himself condemned to a certain conception of freedom which has estranged him. His freedom, thus, is useless to him, time also has lost its sense and man, consequently, is losing his taste for itself. In his solitude, he is at the mercy of his own 'egotistical, stifling concentration upon himself'.[72]

Some Specific Sacramental Problems

This profound questioning of the principles on which authority rests, did not, of course, leave the Church unscathed. We have already spoken of a 'crisis' in the sacrament of penance and in Christianity generally. The present reaction against rules of all kinds and the dramatic rejection of institutional authority has also found an echo among Christians. Many Christians felt bitter toward a certain expression of Christianity, closely connected with political models of power 'and ruling consciences by fear rather than love',[73] where the main emphasis was upon sins and punishments: a penal code rather than a way of life. In short, Christians too in Western society fell foul of the modern paradox.

At one level, they shook off the yoke and fear of their religious upbringing and began to live, instead, at the periphery of the institutional Church, isolating themselves somewhat from what it said and did. At another level, Christians still felt burdened, lost, abandoned, confused and alone. They too experienced the need to confide in another person who would listen, advise and ultimately heal them. At this juncture, one must inevitably pose the following question: given the existence of a Christian population which experienced the need to unburden itself, why was there not an increased recourse to the sacrament of penance, rather than the crisis which we can still clearly witness today?

One answer to this question is suggested by developing our foregoing discussion of the models of penance. We may say that part of the problem resides in the fact that the juridical model of penance was given too great an emphasis and, indeed, was often misconstrued. Many Christians did not feel inclined to avail of the sacrament of penance, for the sacrament itself, as they saw it, formed part of that authoritarian world which they had rejected. Thus, whilst society at the level of the family and government witnessed a shift in emphasis away from imperialist models of authority and toward democracy, the Church, by contrast, was slower to shed its symbols of power.

This situation was, of course, remedied by the Second Vatican Council which began to put forward as its principal paradigm of Church the 'people of God' model.[74] It too, as we have already seen, spoke of the Church as both holy and sinful, as needing repentance and reform (LG 8). There was, then, a major shift away from a hierarchical (imperialist) model and toward a democratic (solidarity) perspective. By this stage, however, the sacrament of penance was already in the throes of crisis and, in any case, the new thinking at the level of ecclesiology did not seem to be echoed by a corresponding re-think at the level of penitential theology.

What we are saying, then, in essence, is that the older model of penance, with its excessive emphasis on the juridical aspect, gave rise to some specific problems which, I believe, have not yet been fully resolved. Essentially, the main problem was one of reductionism in various guises.

Absolutionism At times, what should have been an important moment of healing encounter with Christ was marred by an excessive mechanism, automatism, and, what some commentators have called, the absolutionism mentality. In its worst expression, this resulted in penitents seeking merely to be absolved from sin rather than to undertake a profound personal programme of conversion.

Thus, that aspect of confession which makes it a nodal point, an encounter with Christ along our faith journey, was somehow neglected and reduced to an unhealthy juridicism; so that, the act of absolution occupied an exaggerated and disproportionate place in the sacramental process. The result was a tendency toward verbalism, where the penitent merely verbalised all areas of weakness, rather than concentrated instead on the true obstacles to his moral progress; and the confessor, in turn, almost invariably prescribed a verbal act of satisfaction.

And so, a kind of spiritual Cartesianism ensued where the penitential process became over-intellectualised in the worst sense of the word. Penitents no longer found the means within the sacrament of penance to rebuild their lives. They had no really significant part in the sacramental encounter and no collaboration in the reconstruction of their moral lives. They *received* absolution, rather than involved themselves more actively in their own conversion.

Legalism There was, also, the exaggerated preoccupation with the validity of the sacrament. This obviously led to a form of legalism. The emphasis on the integrity of the confession of sins, according to number and kind, was also indicative of a certain concept of justice and of authority not easily reconcilable with the biblical imagery of divine mercy.[75] Moral guidelines and prescriptions, which were meant to enable a free response to God, often came to be regarded by penitents as ends in themselves.

The reductionism here is evident; at its worst, legalism reduced God to law. The penitent too easily lost sight of the fact that it is values which are primary, not laws. This, in turn, gave rise to minimalism; where Christians believed they had not sinned so long as they had not infringed a law. 'With so much emphasis on identifiable and measurable sins less attention was paid to general sinfulness, either in the individual person, or in the community as a whole.'[76] And, in thus measuring one's goodness by the yardstick of law, it was relatively easy for the authoritarian person to suppose that he or she had already achieved the threshold of sanctity.

Paternalism A further form of reductionism was evidenced at the level of the minister's role. This, in its worst expressions, manifested itself in a form of clerical paternalism which neglected the fact that the penitent was a 'partner' in the sacramental event.[77] A penitent could here be left with the impression that the priest was a member of a ruling *élite*, entrusted with total power and authority. Moreover, a disproportionate emphasis upon the concept of the 'power of keys', portrayed the priest as being able to, at his own whim, 'supply or withhold the means of grace and thus to deny or confer what is needed for salvation—a truly terrifying power over the faithful'.[78]

In short, given that the minister of penance remained, predominantly, an authority figure in what was increasingly becoming an anti-authoritarian, social climate, it is not altogether surprising that the sacrament of penance should have entered the crisis in which it still finds itself.

Individualism A further expression of reductionism, at least until recent times, was a form of individualism. Whilst throughout the history of the sacrament there was a growing awareness of its personal character, this unfortunately had the effect of 'pushing the ecclesial dimension of the sacrament into the background of consciousness for a long time.'[79] Certainly, this imbalance has now been redressed, at least at the level of ecclesiology, by the Second Vatican Council; however, one suspects that this change has not as yet fully percolated through to penitential praxis and doctrine.

Infantilism One final problem which has left its mark on contemporary penitential praxis is what we may refer to as infantilism, denoting a certain lack of maturity and depth in the sacramental encounter. In the main, due to a deficient pedagogy, it meant that the penitent's confession of sins became fossilised, with little or no variation in the schema of sins from youth to adulthood and on into old age. Thus, there was no sense of a continuing faith journey in which the penitent was penetrating ever deeper into the mystery of his or her faith; neither was there sufficient attention to the occasional crises and 'trough experiences' which inevitably accompany a serious faith commitment.

3. *Some Pastoral Proposals from Celtic Penance*

It now behoves us to offer some pointers as to how the wisdom of the Celtic monks might be rehabilitated pastorally and placed at the disposition of the sacrament of penance today. What follows should not be taken as an exhaustive survey of the points of dialogue between Celtic and modern penance but as an indication of the areas which, I think, should be included in any serious evaluation of the subject.

Pedagogy Further to what we have already said, regarding the delay in the theological fruits of the Second Vatican Council's deliberations on penance filtering through to the pastoral level, it is clear that there is a need for a fuller pedagogy among both clergy and laity on the subject. One area which immediately suggests itself is preaching, for, in 'preaching, the word of reconciliation is proclaimed and God's forgiveness is offered. Preaching is an essential part of the cure of souls.'[80]

It is no accident that we have sought to interpret the penitentials in the light of the other Celtic spiritual and homiletical material. To divorce the sacrament of penance from the other corporate expressions of the Church's life, and from the proclamation of the Word of God, is to place it in a false context. Even the penitential literature, as we have seen, was at pains to include scriptural and patristic sanction for its pronouncements, despite its rudimentary knowledge of and limited access to these sources. Further, as we have noted, the penitentials linked penance to Eucharist (Co.B.30) and to Baptism (Cu.pr.2). And both Cummean and the Bigotian text went so far as to list up to eleven other ways in which reconciling and forgiving activity was expressed in the life of the Church (Cu.2.13; Bi.pr.30–32).

In this regard, we can also learn from the Celtic concept of 'green martyrdom'. Although the term today will, undoubtedly, be unfashionable its central idea remains sound theology, namely a life of witness to the value of conversion. Hence, the Christian life is understood as a continual conversion, a constant turning again and again to God as author and sustainer of all life. And, 'the goal of this conversion process is to experience afresh our graced nature and our relatedness to one another in Christ.'[81] The ideals of the ancient Celtic, living martyrs and those of modern-day penitential theology, are reducible to the same central idea: that 'the people of God become in this world a sign of conversion to God' (Ordo,4).

Education, of course, must involve not alone laity but also priests. One Celtic notion which can bear much fruit here is the Columban concept of *discretio* or discernment (Co.Reg.Mon.VIII). Columbanus saw this as the mediating virtue between extremes of licence and restriction. A good moral pedagogy will still favour a continuous growth of the individual's conscience, such that he or she is capable of moral discernment in the concrete situations of everyday life. More importantly, a true appreciation of the meaning of discernment should lead to wiser confessors.

Here, above all, there is room for a renewed application of the *healing* metaphor. The confessor needs to be capable of discerning the root cause of the penitent's sin and to bring to bear his religious and moral vision, together with his life experience and critical faculties, upon the particular problematic of each penitent; and to do so in a manner which invites an opening of the heart in trust, so that the sinful ailment might thus be healed.[82] This, in turn, will inevitably imply a focus on sinful attitudes rather than categorial sins or infringements alone. It is interesting to note that the penitentials are situated within a framework where eight vices and virtues form the moral backdrop, that is to say, not simply a series of laws or commandments such as the Decalogue. Thus, penitents were more readily enabled to focus upon new patterns of behaviour that would bring about the changes which truly heal.

The confessor, himself, in the Celtic tradition was also expected to be one who could open his heart to another. This, as we have seen, required a disposition characterised by *paupertas* or *humilitas* which, in turn, rendered him more receptive to the penitent. Also, the confessor in Celtic penance had, above all, to be a person of prayer if he were to have true discernment: 'Discernment is a gift. But, our tradition clearly affirms that a regular regimen of prayer is a common condition for opening oneself to this gift.'[83]

Ministry In addition to his spiritual disposition, it is evident that there is need for a shift in the confessor's understanding of his ministry in order that it may be harmonised with conciliar doctrine on ecclesiology. Essentially, he will have to to try and promote two quite different elements—human dialogue and worship. Above all, he will need to be a visible sign of kindness and love, and must, therefore, exhibit an attitude of welcome. His own ministry, moreover, should try to embrace all three roles which we have outlined from the Celtic tradition namely: *animadversor*, *medicus*, and *anamchara*. Hence, he must strive to find that delicate balance of receptivity, discernment and confrontation which is the synthesis of these three models.

Here too, the modern confessor can learn from the Celtic emphasis on hospitality, so that he expresses human care and welcome as an instrument of God's forgiving love whilst giving moral direction and sustenance to lead the penitent back from isolation to the full life of the Christian community.[84] The priest can, thus, encourage the penitent to consider Christ, his passion and his style of life, in order to assume this style and character of life as a *fellow-sufferer*. In the simplicity and poverty of his own role as *fellow-pilgrim*, the priest must minister out of his own weakness, for the example which Christ himself gave us is 'the power of God mediated in human weakness which has an appeal for conversion of hearts and lives, that the use of human power and status does not have'.[85] For all the people of God, priests and people, are, ultimately, co-penitents and members of the same pilgrim Church.

Penitential activity Clearly, modern-day penitents will not warm to the severity of the penitentialist's prescriptions. One aspect of Celtic penance, however, which I believe may still be used to great effect is the 'principle of contraries'. This is not to say that we must try to make the penance fit the sin in a rigid, legalistic way; rather, we need to recognise the truth that there is a relationship between them. Further, the argument has often been made that any genuine movement of the spirit in a being composite of spirit and matter, must, in order to be genuine, have a visible, external and material component. Therefore, the penitent's internal conversion and change of heart and rejection of self-gratification must issue in an external penance which itself counters the sinful expression.

In this way, a penitent's conversion is made manifest in activity which actually demonstrates his desire to change and his wish to regain the harmony disturbed by sin in the first place. Acts of penance, then, should express a 'healing remedy for the root cause of sin so as to restore the harmony disrupted by sin and also point the penitent in the direction a reconciled life ought to take'.[86] In this manner, penitential activity is not a mere appendage to the sacrament and everyday life and becomes a powerful sign of sincerity and conversion.[87]

We have also argued, throughout this study, for a rediscovery of the three traditional expressions of penance: prayer, fasting and almsgiving. The modern implementation of this procedure, however, must seek to preserve the inner coherence and dynamism of all three elements much more forcefully than did the penitentials. One of the great weaknesses of the penitentialists' approach was that, despite having the 'principle of contraries' at their disposal, they too easily allowed the resulting acts of penance to be reduced to lengthy fasts. Prayer, fasting and almsgiving are inter-related. The concern evoked by prayer, and fostered by self-denial, should bring the penitent to make a renewed effort to love God and to express this in his relations with others, and to share with them whatever their needs, be they spiritual, emotional or material.

This leads one to a better understanding of Christian life as pilgrimage, in which every Christian must renounce himself, take up his cross and participate in the sufferings of Christ. He can, therefore, no longer live for himself 'but for Him who lived for him and gave Himself for him. He will have to live for his brethren.'[88]

This approach, moreover, upholds the 'bodiliness' of the Christian life. Our faith is not a matter for souls, ideas or wills only; it is so central that it has to be reflected in the way we live out our lives.[89] Thus, faith cannot be construed as merely an intellectual assent but must instead become a living witness. Fasting, prayer and almsgiving are each essential aspects of this witness: 'they are crucial acts of witness in a culture which distrusts the past, exalts the present and regards the future as more of the present.'[90] In and through these practices, the Christian summons the future where there will be no more fasting, only the heavenly banquet toward which we strive in our earthly pilgrimage.[91]

Liturgical life One final area of the Celtic tradition from which we can learn is the integration of penance into the liturgical cycle of the year. We have already noted how the Celtic monks had three *quadragesimae* in the year, as well as two special days for fasting each week. In a certain sense, penitential activity was the norm, rather than the exception, for most of the liturgical year.

The contemporary Church, likewise, must, I believe, find concrete, tangible forms, times and ways of calling Christians regularly to conversion and reflection. There is a need also to re-discover and re-interpret the rich patrimony of places of pilgrimage and penance. This must be done in an intelligent fashion in order to accentuate the fact that the daily or weekly pilgrimage is but a microcosm of one's life pilgrimage. Hence, penance and conversion may be seen as not solely confined to the sacrament of penance, but, instead, part of a broader and richer realm.

There are privileged times in the liturgical year such as Advent and Lent which contain in themselves a specific call to conversion. There are also exceptional times such as traditional days of pilgrimage, retreat, or parish renewal. And finally, there are the great feasts such as Christmas, Easter and commemoration of local and national saints. A good pastoral policy will seek to integrate a penitential component into the liturgical celebration of all of these moments.[92]

Moreover, building upon the Celtic penitentialists' integration of the *pietatis obsequia* and vicarious *goire* (obligation of the sinner to compensate his victim) into their penitential theology, a contemporary ministry of healing or reconciliation should also be carried over into all areas of pastoral work: visitation, ministry to the sick, imprisoned, lonely, distressed bereaved as well as the struggle for a more Christian and just society.[93]

Further, each Christian, not only the minister, must see himself as called upon to exercise this reconciling office in all spheres of his daily life. The penitent who confesses his sin will, therefore, not be seen as oblivious to the social dimensions of penance but, on the contrary, as taking the first step toward a renewed discovery and implementation of the same.

Finally, it is important that at least some of these expressions of conversion should entail a communal celebration of the sacrament of penance, since this will serve to highlight the significance of the communion of Christians who, through self-denial and penance, prepare themselves to sustain the burdens of sin and the effort of conversion of all others. One might object that this has nothing to do with the Celtic tradition, but in fact what we are seeking to re-discover here is something which was already a solid feature of the Celtic monastery, namely a solidarity among those who did penance, wherein it becomes clear that the whole Church is a pilgrim community that constantly needs to be purified and drawn closer to God.

Some Final Observations

I believe, then, that it is only in adopting this form of liturgical and pastoral approach that the moment of sacramental confession can be rescued from isolation and obscurity. Only in this way will we begin to see it again as situated at the cross-roads between liturgy and life and at the nexus between the Christian's individual response to Christ and his commitment to society. Christians of today need to measure their examination of conscience and their confession against the realities of personal and social life, and the fruits of this examination must spill over into their faith journeys.

Thus, a renewal of the sacrament of penance must go hand in hand with a renewal of penance and conversion as life-attitudes. There is need, then, for a re-awakening of the spirit of imitation of Jesus as well as an attitude of faith, hope and love.[94] It is change at this level, I believe, which will have the most profound effect in the renewal of penance today. Certainly, as we have said, concrete steps may be taken *vis-à-vis* the implementation of new liturgical norms and recommendations as well as the creative use of the various rites of penance. In the final analysis, however, I think a more profound change of mentality is called for. The sacrament of penance must be rehabilitated within the Christian life project. 'It must remain the place of struggle, the place where good and evil forces fight within man, the place where God's clash with the forces of evil is fought out in terms of personal dis-cipleship.'[95]

Ultimately, what we are saying is that there is no reason why contemporary priests and penitents cannot adopt as models for the sacrament of penance today the paradigms of merciful judgement, healing and pilgrimage. Contemplation of these models indicates that the Christian life entails considerable striving after spiritual discipline, wholeness and compassion. These models provide orientation points for understanding the many dimensions of the Christian struggle. They also make it easier for twentieth-century pilgrims to see themselves as making the same journey as 'countless others in ages long past and cultures astonishingly diverse'.[96]

Christian conversion, assisted by the wisdom of the sage, the skill of the surgeon and the patient compassion of the soul-friend remains among the most profound endeavours which mankind can ever undertake.

CONCLUSION

At the beginning of the previous chapter, we set ourselves the task of outlining the challenges which our survey of the Celtic penitential literature held for the theological and pastoral understanding of the sacrament of penance today. This done, we shall not take up this theme afresh here but shall instead, content ourselves with a brief synthesis of our work and an indication of what remains to be done in this field. Thus, what follows is but a brief reflection on what this study has been about.

We have sought to place the penitentials in their true cultural and historical *Sitz im Leben*. We have delved into the predecessor pre-Christian culture and have noted the heroic virtues, the symbolism and the imagery which were a part of the Celtic patrimony. And we have taken from this patrimony some key concepts which, we believe, serve as an interpretative key to the proper understanding of this historical moment.

Instead of assessing the penitential texts according to modern categories of sin and repentance, we have first attempted to recreate the framework which the penitentialists themselves took for granted. This framework, in essence, was based on two notions each taken from John Cassian. The first was his version of the eight vices, the second his 'principle of contraries'. By combining these two concepts, we discovered a *modus operandi* for textual analysis of the penitentials. Thus, individual canons were placed within their true context wherein they sought to wean the sinner away from the attractions of vice and orient him toward a particular virtue. This too, allowed us to understand the symbolism of healing, pilgrimage and battle in a more intelligent fashion.

Our textual analysis complete, we were then able to provide some food for thought for the modern scholar or pastor. This we did in two ways: one direct, the other indirect. The direct method consisted in taking the constitutive elements of the sacrament of penance, as we know it today, and demonstrating how these could be enriched and enhanced by the Celtic tradition. The indirect method (Chapter 5) takes cognizance of the fact that the language of confession is that of symbol and poetry, in that it attempts to embrace our experience of the Christian faith.

Thus, when one speaks of one's idea of sin, one immediately suggests also certain presuppositions about one's idea of God, the Church, the

Christian life and other people. A study such as ours cannot explore all these considerations, but the language of symbol does offer us a means by which sin and repentance can be integrated more fully into the entire Christian project. The ancient Celts did not draw neat demarcation lines between morality, spirituality, liturgy and theology generally, and, for that reason, we too have sought to view penance from within a broader spiritual framework.

We mentioned, at the outset, that the sacrament of penance is currently in a state of crisis. The thrust of this study has been to bring the wisdom of one moment of the Church's tradition to bear upon the contemporary situation. We believe that the wisdom of the past must inform the present and also reach out into the future. In our study of Celtic penance, we have sought to point out that the structures of penance are secondary to the fundamental experiences of conversion and reconciliation.

One cannot, therefore, advocate a return to the norms of the fifth or sixth centuries, for our culture, our learning, our preoccupations and our problems are all different from those of the Celtic world. It is nonetheless clear, however, that the modern pastor and penitent can learn much from the symbolic forms of that era. Furthermore, a true, existential and internal awareness of sin requires symbolic language, and this language in its various expressions establishes in a living way the connection between faith and morality. Undue emphasis on the keeping of rules or following instructions on ethical behaviour needs to be counter-balanced by myths and symbols which can evoke a true sense of solidarity among all Christians. It is precisely this symbolic power which can speak beyond logic to the heart of the Christian.

The symbols of Celtic Christianity, whilst at times harsh and severe, had the merit of reminding each Christian that they had to make their own journey. Thus, life was focussed, life was purposed. In journeying toward Christ, Christians also journeyed deeper into themselves and began to forge their personal moral identity. They lived with the possibility of sin; but they also had a remedy for sin, and after each fall arose stronger and better equipped to forge a new moral life.

The Celtic Christian, moreover, started from a keen awareness of his capacity for sin. His humility was not some exaggerated form of self-abasement, but rather stemmed from a consciousness of what it means to be human, to be in need. For that reason, the Christian journey, and *ergo* the moral journey, was never something to be made alone, but something to be undertaken in the company of those who understood and appreciated the struggles of the human situation. Thus, the preoccupation was not about avoiding sin totally, but upon forging the new man out of the moral struggle.

The moral life, therefore, was a cumulative achievement built upon an ever greater knowledge of self and upon an awareness of the significance and the effects of all of one's attitudes and activities. There was a wholesomeness here, a sense that every moment and activity of life could be an opportunity for sin, but that it might equally be seized upon as an opportunity for moral growth and moral development. Celtic spirituality generally, therefore, was an antidote to the more legalistic prescriptions of the penitentials.

It has been the thrust of our study that the Christian of today must re-learn the language of morality and that we can be aided in this project by the Celtic penitential tradition. In a world where Christians have become discontent with vehicles of meaning which are outmoded or archaic, there is a need for new symbols or a renewed understanding of traditional symbols. We have spoken of the crisis of faith which has taken place, but that in itself should not discourage us. The Celtic Church too, lived through a phase of crisis and confusion but emerged to forge a fresh understanding of man's call to repentance.

A crisis, in other words, is fundamentally a time to make decisions. The reader might find it odd that a study which takes as its subject-matter the sacrament of penance should make more general recommendations regarding our understanding of morality; yet, if there is one overwhelming conclusion to be drawn from our study of Celtic penance, it is precisely that the moment of penance and conversion must flow into and shape our whole moral life.

A renewal of the sacrament of penance must, therefore, begin with a renewal of the categories by which we understand the conversion process today. Modern Christians will not be content with the notion of a Church which 'dispenses' forgiveness; instead, the Church herself will need to renew her efforts to live as a visible sign of reconciliation. The sacrament of penance, precisely because it is 'sacrament', is properly understood not as a cancelling of misdemeanours but as a nodal point along the faith journey of every Christian.

We hope that the primary contribution of our study will have been to demonstrate that the doctrine of Celtic penance, and the broader Celtic spiritual patrimony, have lasting and important insights to share with the modern scholar and pastor. We have sought to demonstrate that a critique which stops at the 'legal' prescriptions of the penitentials does not do full justice to the wealth of wisdom con-tained therein. Instead, we have sought to integrate these texts into their true cultural and spiritual hinterland.

Further, we have suggested that the misrepresentation of the *libri paenitentiales* is itself a parable which can shed light on the contemporary crisis in penance. For, just as the Celtic manuals must be returned to their authentic context to be correctly interpreted, so too, we believe, the sacrament of penance must be returned to a harmony with the cultural and spiritual categories of contemporary Christians. We have suggested some pastoral proposals which may aid this process, but, ultimately, we believe that the real change must occur at the level of mentality. In seeking to rehabilitate Celtic penance we have, at the same time, sought also to rehabilitate the modern expression of this sacrament within a more cohesive and holistic expression of personal faith.

In his summary of the written and oral interventions, at the 1983 Synod of Bishops on the subject of Reconciliation and Penance, Cardinal Martini called for more theological investigation of themes such as the nature and structure of penance and the measuring of sin. Six months later, the report of the International Theological Commission on the same subject emphasised the need for more reflection on the history of the sacrament of penance. This present study has been born out of a desire to respond, in some way, to that need; however, it is only a partial response, for its subject matter is restricted to a particular historical and cultural theme. The categories and symbols of Celtic penance are only one fragment of the history of this sacrament, but we believe it to be an important fragment and one which can continue to inspire and enrich the penitential doctrine of all eras.

Throughout this study we have touched upon some areas which would bear considerable further investigation by the serious scholar in this field. For example, we have noted a certain evolution in thought from the earliest Welsh and Irish Latin language texts to the later Irish Gaelic language texts. An interesting further development here would be a comparison and evaluation with the Anglo Saxon and Frankish texts.

Many secondary themes and symbols have been elicited in our study of the penitentials and of the broader range of Hiberno-Latin spiritual literature. These remain, for the most part, undiscovered by the modern student. Further, the vast range of prayers and liturgical texts from the Celtic tradition, as well as exhortations to soul-friends, have received only a cursory mention in this work since they fall outside the bounds of our study. Nonetheless, it is my view that a rich pastoral handbook could be compiled from these sources.

More recent studies of Celtic spirituality have become increasingly aware of the holistic view of Christianity and in particular of conversion which is presented there. Some theologians have attempted to set up a dialogue between these categories and those of modern thinkers such as Lonergan especially with regard to the inter-relation of religious, moral and intellectual conversion. Certainly, this area could profitably bear further investigation and analysis.

At the linguistic level, there is a pressing need for further study of the Irish penitential texts, to catch up with the work done on Frankish and continental texts. It is with great interest, however, that we read of the publication of a new translation of the Irish penitentials at the same time as we, too, go to print. Ultimately, it is only when new editions become available that we will be able to evaluate the full meaning of penitentials and penance in medieval life and literature.

Finally, just as we have sought to interpret the meaning conveyed by a particular historical moment in the history of penance through the medium of symbol; so, too, the doctrine and practice of today would undoubtedly benefit greatly were similar studies to be carried out upon the other critical historical junctures in the history of this sacrament.

Today's Christian cannot be expected to see the world from the perspective of the Celtic monk nor, indeed, from the perspective of other ages long gone. He or she can, however, learn from the various expressions and emphases which different eras have given to long-standing theological themes. The modern theologian must be like the 'good householder' who brings out of his treasury things which are old and things which are new (Mt 13:52). We are not proposing a facile re-affirmation of the theology of Celtic monasticism, but, rather, a sensitivity to the ideals and ideas of their era which might, ultimately, enable the modern Christian to answer the Master's perennial call to 'repent and believe in the Gospel'.

NOTES

CHAPTER 1

1 For example see the explanation of the evolution of penitential doctrine given in Ladislas Orsy, *The Evolving Church and the Sacrament of Penance* (Denville, N.J.: Dimension Books, 1978).

2 Cf. Michael Curran, 'Early Irish Monasticism,' in *Irish Spirituality* ed. Michael Maher (Dublin: Veritas Publications, 1981), 10.

3 For a detailed analysis of this era of Irish History see Kathleen Hughes, *The Church in Early Irish Society* (London: Methuen, 1966).

4 'During this time I gave presents to the kings, besides which I gave pay to their sons who escorted me . . . ' *The Confession of Patrick* trans. C.H.H. Wright Appendix A, in Noel Dermot O'Donoghue, *Aristocracy of Soul. Patrick of Ireland* (London: Darton, Longman and Todd, 1987), 115.

5 For example, Paragraph 4 of the Confession contains references to Matthew, Acts, Joel, Hosea and Roman. Cf. O'Donoghue, *Aristocracy* 102.

6 A very detailed account of this structure is to be found in F.J. Byrne, *Irish Kings and High Kings* (London: Batsford, 1973).

7 The two most important sources today for the study of old Irish law are the *Senchus Mór* and *The Book of Acaill.* Cf. 'Bretha Cróilge' ed. D.A. Binchy, *Ériu*, xii (1934): 1–7.

8 Ludwig Bieler, *The Irish Penitentials* with an appendix by D.A. Binchy, (Dublin: Dublin Institute of Advanced Studies, 1963), 229. cc. 3–4.

9 For example, see Pa.II:10 'Whoever falls with rank shall arise without rank. Content with the name (of cleric) alone, he shall lose his ministry, except when by his sinning he has not withdrawn from the sight of God.'

10 For instance, Vi.33 'We are also obliged to serve the churches of the saints and, within our means, have pity on all who are in need; pilgrims are to be received into our houses as the Lord has commanded.'

11 See here Columbanus' system of grading penance according to rank. 'However if anyone has committed fornication with women . . . , if he is a cleric, three years, if a monk or a deacon, five years, if a priest seven, if a bishop twelve years' (Co.B.4).

12 The fast of distraint is dealt with at length in P.W. Joyce, *A Social History of Ancient Ireland* vol. 1 (Dublin and Melbourne: Gill and Son, 1920), 204–7.

13 Cf. A. and M. Anderson, eds. and trans. *Adamnan's Life of St Columba*, London, 1961.

14 A good introduction to Druidism may be found in Louis Debarge, *Le Syncrétisme Religieux: Druidisme et Christianisme* M.S.R. 46 (mars 1989): 5–21.

15 Ibid., 11. 'Selon cette doctrine si l'homme echoue dans sons parcours vers la plénitude, il conserve la possibilité de recommencer sa vie, mais en se soumettant à

trois nécessités: celle de souffrir, celle de choisir, celle de se renouveler. Ainsi chacun pourrait librement se racheter et poursuivre son évolution. Rien ne serait jamais damné pour l'éternité.'

16 Joyce devotes a full chapter to the study of Celtic warfare in Joyce, *Social History*, 72–154.

17 The terms 'bard' and 'fili' were not, however, synonymous. For an explanation of the differences involved here, see Joyce, *Social History*, 448ff.

18 Cf. J.T. Mc Neill, *The Celtic Churches; A History A.D. 200–1200* (Chicago: University of Chicago Press, 1974), 73.

19 'Selon la loi du ternaire deux choses ne s'excluent pas, mais ne sont que les degrés extrémes d'une seule et même réalité dont l'équilibre a été rompu. Il importait de rechercher le point d'harmonie et d'éviter à tout prix les ruptures. Debarge, *Le Syncrétisme* 12.

20 Finnian sets down the principle and explains it in his penitential (Vi.29). The principle may have been first used by Cassian. In Coll. xix. 14–15 he explains that anger and dejection, as well as other sins must be cured by the opposing virtuous dispositions. The fact that the 'Principle of Contraries' does not feature in the earlier, Welsh material suggests that the concept passed from Cassian via the island of Lérins into the Irish Church.

21 Bieler, *Irish Penitentials* 46 commenting on the language of the penitentials he observes: 'Isolated medical metaphors occur in almost all the texts of the present collection.'

22 Cf. Joyce, *Social History*, 10.

23 Mc Neill, *Celtic Churches*, 115ff.

24 J.T. Mc Neill and Helena M. Gamer, *Medieval Handbooks of Penance: A Translation of the 'Libri Poenitentiales' and Selections from Related Documents* (New York: Columbia University Press, 1938), 25.

25 For an historical survey of this period see Mc Neill, *Celtic Churches*, 69ff.

26 Text and translation in Bieler, *Irish Penitentials*, 54–59.

27 Pa.I.30. 'Any bishop who goes from his own parish to another must not presume to ordain unless he has received permission from him who holds jurisdiction in the place; on the Lord's day he shall offer the holy sacrifice only if he is invited to do so, and he shall be content to comply in this matter.' For further analysis of this document see Patrick J. Corish, ed., *A History of Irish Catholicism* (Dublin: Gill and Son, 1967), vol.1, *Saint Patrick and the Coming of Christianity* by Ludwig Bieler, 86.

28 'To any high-souled youth of the early sixth century, the attractions of Clonard seems to have been irresistible. Disciples in vast numbers (three thousand became the acccepted figure) grouped themselves around Finnian's cell:' John Ryan, *Irish Monasticism. Origins and Early Development* (Dublin and Cork: Talbot Press, 1931), 117.

29 Cassian refers many times to the monk as a 'miles Christi' and to monasticism as a 'militia Christi'. Cf. Cassian, *Conlationes* ed. Petschenig *C.S.E.L.* xiv (1886): especially i,1; iv,12; xxiv,26; and xvi,1.

30 The *Old Irish Penitential*, for instance, records that the bishop reconsecrates clerics who have already done penance: '. . . on account of the fewness of

persons in orders. All these orders are reconsecrated after doing penance, with the same functions; and they go under the hand of a bishop.' cf. O.I.IP.I:10.

31 The texts are as follows Gi.24, Cu.1, Da.7, and Hi.IV.1–9.

32 Kathleen Hughes, *The Church*, 74.

33 For a good explanation of the differences between the Celtic monastic Church and the older Latin Church see Brendan Bradshaw, 'The Wild and Woolly West: Early Irish Christianity and Latin Orthodoxy', chap. in *The Churches, Ireland and the Irish* ed. J.A. Watt (London: Blackwells,1988), 1–2.

34 The definitive study of Irish monasticism is still undoubtedly Ryan's *Irish Monasticism* and we make extensive use of it in this section of our study.

35 Ibid., 272–5.

36 Ibid., 316.

37 Watkins gives a good description of the relationship between the Celtic monastery and its hinterland in O.D. Watkins, *A History of Penance, Being a Study of Authorities for the Whole Church from A.D. 450 and for the Western Church to A.D. 1215*. 2 vols. (London and New York: Longmans, Green and Co., 1920), 2nd. vol. 608. ff.

38 Jonas, *Vita Sancti Colombani* ed. B. Krusch, (Leipzig: Neueus-Studien zur Christlich-Mittelalterlichen Chronologie, 1880), 161.

39 'Si quis surrexerit ad scandalum et diposuit in corde suo proximum percutere aut occidere, si clericus fuerit dimedium annum peniteat . . . si quis autem laicus fuerit ebdomadam dierum peniteat; quia homo seculi huius est, culpa levior in hoc mondo et premium minus in futuro.'

40 The teaching on the Celtic understanding of the three forms of martyrdom may be found in the 'Old Irish Homily': Stokes and Strachan, *Thesaurus Paelaeohibernicus. A Collection of Old-Irish Glosses, Scholia, Prose and Verse*, 8 vols. (Cambridge: 1903), ii, 246–7.

41 Bieler, *Irish Penitentials*. Examples of this are the canons which prohibit magic-making in Vi.18–20, Co.B.6 and the copious instructions against 'keening' in Bi.IV.6:2–6.

42 'But we must know that neither this bliss of martyrdom nor any other benefit that follows can be perfectly fulfilled by any save him who has given particular attention to this . . . ' (Co.Reg.Mon.IX.) in G.S.M. Walker ed. and trans. *Sancti Colombani Opera* (Dublin: Dublin Institute of Advanced Studies, 1967).

43 These austere penances may be seen in the following canon from the *Old Irish Table of Commutations*: 'Commutation of a black fast (due) for grievous sin for one who cannot read: three hundred genuflections and three hundred properly administered blows with a scourge, at the end of each hundred a cross-vigil until the arms are weary': O.I.C.12.

44 Pádraig Ó Fiannachta, 'The Spirituality of the Céili Dé' in Maher, *Irish Spirituality*, 25.

45 '. . . coaptavit Vinniaus suis uisceralibus filiis dilectionis gratia vel religionis obtentu de scripturarum venis redundans, ut ab omnibus omnia deleantur hominibus facinora.'

46 Ryan, *Irish Monasticism*, 218.

47 See Cu. passim. in Bieler, *Irish Penitentials*, 109–135. We are referring in particular here to 'Cassian's' octade of vices since it was especially due to him that the Irish became familiar with this classification. In fact, they were originally devised by Evagrius Ponticus who identified them as: Gluttony, Lust, Covetousness, Sorrow, Anger, Spiritual Disgust, Vanity and Pride.

48 'Is colainn gan cheann duine gan anamchara' from Strachan, *Félire Oengusso Céili Dé. The Martyrology of Oengus the Culdee* (London: Henry Bradshaw Society, 1905).

49 Jean Leclerq, François Vandenbrouke and Louis Bouyer, *The Spirituality of the Middle Ages* (New York: Seabury,1988), 41.

50 'Laymen fancy that in order to get to heaven it is enough to give something to their soul-friends and that their soul-friends will thenceforth be at their command.' *Thesaurus Paelaeohibernicus* vii. 61.

51 G. Le Bras, 'Les Pénitentiels Irlandais' in *Le Miracle Irlandais* ed. Daniel-Rops (Tournai: Laffont), 188. 'Le système Irlandais de la pénitence privée a des répercussions bien au delà du domaine sacramentaire. Il accentue dans les rapports avec Dieu le sentiment d'un dialogue efficace'.

52 For a similar assessment of Celtic soul-friendship see R. Gula, *To Walk Together Again. The Sacrament of Reconciliation* (New York/Ramsey: Paulist Press, 1984), 208.

53 Plummer, *Vitae Sanctorum Hiberniae*; *Partim Haectenus Ineditae* (Oxon., 1910), xxx. 30.

54 *Ériu* II (1905): 64–65.

55 'Igitur inter parvum et nimium rationabilis est in medio mensura, revocans semper ab omni *utrimque* superfluo . . . Dum enim de utraque parte semper est continendum iuxta illud dictum "Continete vos a dextris et a sinistris".' And cf. Deut 5:32.

56 'Tanto maior potentia medici quanto magis creuit morbus egroti. Hinc procurantibus aliorum sanare vulnera solerter intuendum est cuius aetatis et sexus sit peccans, qua eruditione inbutus, qua fortitudine exstat, quali grauatione conpulsus est peccare, quali passione inpugnatur, quanto tempore in diliciis remansit, quali lacrimabilitate et labore affligitur et qualiter a mundialibus separatur.'

57 The contrast of cult between Irish and Latin spirituality is demonstrated in Bradshaw, *Wild and Woolly*, 15.

58 T.P. Oakley, 'Celtic Penance: Its Sources Affiliations and Influence' *I.E.R.* LII (1958): 584–85. We shall have cause to analyse the language of the penitentials at greater length, when evaluating their theological content in a later chapter.

59 Columbanus, writes: 'Idle then is a religion decorated with prostrations of the body, equally idle is the mere mortification of the flesh and the hollow devotion of the outward man unless it be accompanied by a fruitful moderation of the mind . . . ' Co.Inst.II.2.

60 Poschmann, *Penance and the Anointing of the Sick* (New York: Herder, 1964) 143.

61 '. . . let him wash away the guilt of his unsound communion, but if he did this in derision, that is after he was warned and forbidden by the priest not to . . .' Co.B.25.

62 Co.B.30. Columbanus exhorts regular confession saying, 'It is ordained that Confessions be made carefully, especially of mental disturbances, before going to mass, lest perhaps any should approach the altar unworthily.'

63 'It has been ordained . . . that we make confession before meat or before entering our beds or whenever it is opportune (of all failings, not only mortal ones, but also of minor omissions) since confession and penance free from death' (Co.Reg.Coen.I).

64 Orsy, *Evolving Church*, 36.

65 See Ryan, *Irish Monasticism*, especially 'Study in the Early Monasteries', 377–383.

66 See Columbanus' own justification for writing his penitential in Co.A.1. 'mensurae noscendae sunt paenitentiae, quarum sic ordo a sanctis traditur patribus ut iuxta magnitudinem culparum etiam longitudo statuatur paenitentiarum'.

67 The Bigotian text explains that it is precisely in examining the virtues and qualities of sinners that the work of the penitential physicians is best perceived: '. . . virtutum et qualitatum peccantium, sanctorum facta patrum ad Dominum revertentium a suis medentium peccatis, simul omisa verborum in brevi circuitione merito collegi vis . . .'. (Bi.pr.28).

68 The point is made in Quasten, Johannes, *Patrology* vol.III. The Golden age of Greek Patristic Literature (Westminister: Newman Press,1963) 171–2.

69 The historical arguments for this case are set down convincingly in Ryan, *Irish Monasticism*, 59–67.

70 O'Donoghue, *Aristocracy*, 105, para.16.

71 O'Donoghue, *Aristocracy*.

72 Ibid., 37.

73 Gerard Mitchell, 'The Origins of Irish Penance' I.T.Q. 22 (1955):8.

74 Gildas, *De Excidio Britanniae Epistolarum (vel praedicationum) Fragmenta* ed. Mommsen M.G.H. (Chron. Min. iii. 1894–8).

75 Gildas, *De Excidio*. 65.

76 Gildas, *De Excidio*. Fragment 3 260.

77 Columbanus, 'Epis. III ad Greg. Papam' M.G.H. 159.

78 The biography of David by Rhygyvarch (1057–99) is largely legendary. Useful biographical data on David may be found, however, in Nora K. Chadwick, 'Intellectual Life in West Wales in the Last Days of the Celtic Church,' chap. in *Studies in the Early British Church* (Cambridge: 1958), 121–82.

79 This view is advanced in Ryan, *Irish Monasticism*, 109.

80 Watkins, *A History*, 606.

81 J. Colgan, *Acta Sanctorum Hiberniae* (Louvain: 1645), 405.

82 Jonas, *Vita Sancti Colombani*. N.B. Texts and translations of all the other works may be found in Walker, *Sancti Colombani*.

83 'Vana est ergo nutibus colorata corporis religio, vana similiter corporalis sola afflictio . . .'

84 'Si enim modum abstinentia excesserit, vitium non virtus erit; virtus enim multa sustinet bona et continet.'

85 '. . . ita sine discretione viventibus excessus in promptu est, qui semper virtutibus in medio inter utramque nimietatem positis contrarius est.'

86 Columbanus also uses the term 'paupertas' in the course of his writings but here the term refers to Christian poverty in its stricter sense and not the broader patrician sense which embraces humility.

87 Text and translation: Bieler, *Irish Penitentials*.

88 Adamnán, *De Locis Sanctis* Text and translation ed. Denis Meehan (Dublin: Dublin Institute for Advanced Studies, 1958).

89 Text and translation: McNeill and Gamer, *Medieval Handbooks*.

90 F.W.H. Wasserschleben ed., *Die Bussordnungen der abendlandischen Kirche* (Halle:1951), reprint ed. (Graz:1958).

91 Wasserschleben, *Bussordnungen*.

92 Unfortunately it is hard to determine the exact dating of these texts. Given their authorship, however, we can conclude that they all date from the early sixth century.

93 These are, in fact, two different recensions of an original text which may date from anywhere between the years 550 and 650. Cf. Bieler, *The Irish Penitentials*, 7.

94 Auxilius and Isernius were bishops who came to Ireland in order to help Patrick with his programme of evangelisation.

95 James F. Kenney, *The Sources for the Early History of Ireland.* (New York: Columbia University Press, 1929), 241: 'It makes use of the Bible and perhaps of Cassian and some early Irish canons', and also Bieler, *Irish Penitentials*, 4: 'These "learned men" remain largely unknown except for some echoes of Cassian . . .'

96 Mitchell, 'St Columbanus on Penance' I.T.Q. 18 (1951) 43 'Its importance lies in the fact that it is not merely one of the chief sources of our information concerning the character of the penance administered by the Irish missionaries, but it was also the earliest penitential which we know to have been used on the Continent.'

97 The letters A and B refer to the monastic and non-monastic sections respectively which are believed, at one stage, to have become separated from each other. There is no longer much support for the view that there are in fact two distinct penitentials here. See Bieler, *Irish Penitentials*, 5.

98 Finbarr Clancy, 'The Irish Penitentials', *Milltown Studies* 21, Spring (1988) 95. Clancy points out here that the penitentials are all heavily influenced by the 'patristic triad' of apostasy, adultery and murder. Furthermore Cassian's 'octoade' especially as elaborated upon by Caesarius of Arles widened the focus to the eight capital sins.'

99 These affiliations will be examined more critically in the systematic assessment of the penitential material in the next chapter.

100 For a more complete discussion of these texts see Bieler, *Irish Penitentials*, 8–9.

101 However, if they were enacted on Adamnán's authority these canons could then reasonably be judged to belong to the late seventh century.

102 Ibid., 10. Bieler believes that this document pertains almost certainly to a seventh century synod and not to a fifth century one during the life or ministry of St Patrick.

103 Scholars have been unable to trace the authorship with any great accuracy here. The penitential appears to have come to the Continent from Ireland before being written down in its present form. Nevertheless, it is, for all intents and purposes, a Celtic document.

104 This is a penitential written in the old Irish language (i.e. sean Ghaeilge as opposed to modern nua Ghaeilge) and dating from the late eighth century.

CHAPTER 2

1 OIP.pr. Text and translation of this penitential are taken from the edition of E.J. Gwynn, *Ériu* VII (1914) 121–95. with occasional reference to the amended translation by D.A. Binchy in Bieler, *Irish Penitentials*, 258–76.

2 This was also the view of Evagrius and Cassian: 'Just as virtue forms a unity-Evagrius had compared it to the light of the sun streaming through different windows of a room — sins distinct in ascetical theory so hang together that a victory against one temptation however trivial will surely augment the power of the will to meet all temptations' O. Chadwick, *John Cassian: A Study in Primitive Monasticism* (Cambridge: University Press, 1950).

3 Cf. Cassian's *Conlationes* v.15,5.sqq. Note. The Bigotian credits Cassian with the division of vice into eight categories but bases its own treatment of same upon Theodore's Penitential.

4 Examples of the use of the variations in vocabulary are to be found as follows: 'Voracitas' Gi.7. Co.B.12. Bi.I:3,1. 'Manducare/ Bibere ad Vomitum' Co.B.22. 'Gula' Da.1. Co.B.24. Cu.I.tit. 'Gastrimargia' Bi.41.tit.

5 These scriptural quotations precede Cummean's analysis of this vice in Cu.I.1.

6 Bi.40.V. The thought however owes its origin also to Cassian. Cf. Cassian, *Conlationes* 16, 5ff.

7 'Qui autem superfluam ventris distentionem doloremque saturitatis sentit, .i. diem.' Cu.I.6.

8 Bieler lists the medical metaphors in Bieler, *Irish Penitentials*, 46–47; 'The second phenomenon is the frequent occurence of metaphors taken from medicine . . . Isolated medical metaphors occur in almost all the texts of the present collection.

9 See, for example, Gi.10; Da.4 and Bi.I.1.

10 Thus, for example, Da.2 chastises those who become drunk whereas the subsequent canon deals with penances for those responsible for another's drunkenness.

11 'Inebriati per ignorantiam, si per neglegentiam si per contemptum.' Da.2.

12 'Si quis laicus inebriaverit se . . . septimana in pane et aqua peniteat.' Co.B.22.

13 Note: this canon does contain an 'if' clause, however, (i.e. *si non satis penituerit*) which seems to suggest that the penance is only to be imposed where the sinner has not already done sufficient penance. Bieler suggests that this may be a corruption of the text and what is meant is that if the penitent apologises then he may no longer be considered a killer. On the other hand, it may be that the penitentialist is allowing for the fact that the sin may have already been confessed under another category such as hatred or anger and thus wishes to avoid penalising the penitent twice for the same sin.

14 'Si odii causa, ut homicida iudicetur.' Cu.I.3.

15 'Stupens elinguis caena privatur'. Gi.10.

16 The first two canons of the section dedicated to Gluttony correspond exactly with Te.I:1,1–5.

17 'Si quis episcopus aut aliquis ordinatus in consuetudine habuerit vitium ebrietatis aut destinat aut deponatur.' Bi.I:1.

18 'Qui accipit post cibum sacrificium,.vii. dies peniteat' Bi.I:3,1–4.

19 The text refers to '*immunditia animalium*' and the subject receives fairly widespread coverage in the penitentials. See for instance: Ad.8.ff. Bi.I:5,4. Bi.I:5,8.

20 For example see Gi.13 on the eating of carrion.

21 Ad.14. The Genesis teaching is also repeated in Lev 5:2. and Lev 17:10–14. See also Cummean's treatment of this subject in Cu.IX.16.

22 See Joyce, *A Social History*, vol II, 510.

23 Te.I.14,15. and see also P. Payer, *Sex and the Penitentials* (Toronto: University Press, 1984) 167 at footnote 76.

24 For more information on the 'bull feast' see Joyce, *A Social History*, vol.I, 236 and 245.

25 Bonosus was an heretical bishop of Naisus.

26 Cu.VIII.14–15. Note that Cummean sees verbosity as a sin of pride rather than of greed.

27 For instance: 'Qui causa invidiae detrachit vel libenter detrahentem audit . . .' Bi.VIII:2,2. We shall return to this matter in our analysis of 'Pride' in Chapter 3.

28 However, they are mentioned by the Bigotian author who in turn attributes them to Cassian.

29 That is by means of a *Questiuncula* or set of questions by which the confessor could decide the appropriate penance. See the oblique reference to same in Bi.I:1.

30 'Melius est enim expectare donec cor sanum fuerit' and again 'ita etiam ab interioribus vitiis et morbis languentis animae abstinendum est ac abstergendum'. But see also Co.B.pr. for the best statement of Columbanus' position in this regard.

31 'It e andso freptha in craóis .i. aine mesraigthe, congain cride, uaite séire, mence cestaigthe, frithaire, fled do bochtaib, didnad cech goirt . . .' OIP.I:1, c.

32 'It e immorro fodlai genethar ó ainmnit .i. fáilte spiraltaide, sochraide cuirp, glaine anmae, tó co toiscide cetfaide ecnai immed n-indtliuchta, saigid for runa Dé.' OIP.I:I,c.

33 See also Cummean on this 'prospective dimension' of penance: 'ab errore correxeris, a vitiis emendaveris et efficeris eum talem ut ei converso propitius fiat Deus . . .' Cu.ps.4.

34 Expiation of sin, eradication of vice and inculcation of virtues are ultimately connected in the penitential texts for example: Cu.pr.8. '. . . emendatio morum, hoc est abrenuntiatio uitiorum . . .'

35 See our discussion of this concept in Chapter One.

36 'Si quis in die Dominico per neglegentiam ieiunaverit ebdomadam totam debet ieiunare . . .' Bi.I:9,1.

37 In fact there is evidence that in the later expressions of Irish monasticism some over-zealous applicants to the monastery were actually turned away because they would not eat their allowance of food. See O'Dwyer, *Céili Dé: Spiritual Reform in Ireland 750–900*. A good description of the diet typical of an Irish Monastery may be found here also.

38 '. . . pane sine mensura et ferculo aliquatenus butero inpinguato die domnico, cæteris uero diebus paxmati panis mensura et misso parum inpinguato, horti holeribus, ouis paucis, Britannico formello utatur, himina Romana lactis pro fragilitate corporis istius eui, tenuclae uero uel battuti lactis sextario Romano sitis gratia et aquae talimpulo, si operarius est . . .' Gi.1.

39 Abstaining from wine and meat, Vi.3 and passim; from delicacies, Co.B.14. For further discussion of fasting and abstinence in Celtic monasticism see Gougaud, 'Le jeûne en Irlande' in *Dévotions et Pratiques Ascétiques au Moyen Age* (Paris, 1925) 143–54 and P. Grosjean, *Analecta Bollandiana* LXXVI (1958) 413–15.

40 '*Superpositio*' as a penance: see Gi.1 Gi.7 and Cu.II.2, whereas used metaphorically in Co.A.9.

41 For instance, Pa.I.29. The monastic days of fast have now given their names to three days of the week in modern Irish: Ceadaoin — the first fast (Wednesday); Aoine — the fast (Friday); Deardaoin — between the fasts (Thursday). See J. Ryan, *Ireland from the Earliest Times to A.D. 800* (Dublin: Browne and Nolan) 96.

42 Thus Finnian: '. . . peniteat cum pane et aqua per mensura in fletu et (lacrimis atque) orationibus die ac nocte et postulet de Domini misericordia si forte habeat remissionem peccatorum . . .' Vi.12.

43 Gougaud, *Les Chrétientés Celtiques* (Paris 1911). 'De telles privations pours des gens vivant dans les rudes climats du nord sont d'un héroisme qui stupefie.'

44 For example, Avaritia: Vi.27 Cu.III.3, whereas Filargia: Cu.III.tit.; Bi.III.tit.

45 'Air ise meccon aranfasat inna huli dubalcha istant.' OIP.III.1,b.

46 'nadchon tasici ass ani fochertar ind immata samlaid.' OIP.III.1,a.

47 '. . . ar is tene do loscuth is muir do badud is talam do slucud is leo du airchelath is best du biathad is claideb du fuidbiu du lemim is carcar du imchomet is slabrad do chuimriuch is cuithchi airricc archind bais coirp 7 anma.' OIP.III.1,a.

48 For instance, *furtum*: Co.B.7&19; Pa.I.15&32; Cu.III.1. whereas *rapacitas*: Bi.pr.2.tit. Whilst *furtum* is used most often to describe an actual theft, *rapacitas* tends to be employed where the proclivity or tendency toward theft is in question. Despite the predominance of canons regarding sexual misconduct in the penitentials, it is nonetheless clear that theft and murder are considered to be the greater crimes. For a similar view see Lisa Bitel, 'Sex, Sin and Celibacy in Early Medieval Ireland', *Proceedings of the Harvard Celtic Colloquium* viii (1987) 80.

49 He deems that such penitents are to do a full year's fasting on bread and water and salt and a further two years abstaining from meat and wine.

50 'Si autem non conversus fuerit, excommunicetur et anathema sit cum omnibus Christianis, exterminabitur de patria sua et virgis virgeatur usquequo convertatur si conpunctus fuerit.' Vi.31.

51 '. . . et sic in Pascha alterius anni communicet id est post duos annos, data tamen ante pauperibus de suo labore helemosina et sacerdoti paenitentiam iudicanti epula . . .' Co.B.19.

52 '. . . ut est aetas vel qualitas eruditionis.' Cu.III.2.

53 For example, Bi.III:1,3. 'Qualitas facientis iudicandum'.

54 '10. Isdem (puer parvulus) aliquid furti comedens .vii. diebus peniteat. 11. Si post vicesimum annum aliquid modicum furti huic accederit, .xx. diebus

peniteat. 12. Si vero in virili aetate aliquid simile accederit, .xl. diebus.' Cu.X.10–12.

55 '. . . quod enim Christus reprobat, ut quid miles Christi suscipiet? Ælimosinam namque praedonis invassi fletus extinguat.' Ad.15.

56 The more usual term here is 'Periuria' but 'Falsa testimonia' is also occasionally employed. Whereas the former normally describes perjury in the usual sense, the latter term tends also to embrace less serious instances of false accusation. Cf. Cu.III.8 and Cu.III.12. See also the next section of this chapter. And for further analysis of the subject see McNeill and Gamer, *Medieval Handbooks*, 38.

57 '. . . sed in presenti tempore caeleri medicina penitentiae prevenire oportet (de) perpetuas poenas in futuro . . .' Vi.22.

58 As we have seen in the first chapter the strata of Celtic society did also include a class of slaves. Nowhere in the penitentials is the practice of slavery expressly condemned, however the ruling that they should be set free as a form of penance seems to suggest that the penitentialists were at least coming to an awareness of the incongruity between slavery and the Christian message. There was an infrastructural problem here in that there were no prisons in Ireland and therefore reduction to a form of slavery was considered to be a reasonable form of punishment for criminals. See L. Ginnell, *The Brehon Laws* (Dublin 1917), esp. viii.

59 All these provisions may be found in Co.B.20 . . . This severe penance for laity is not however retained by Cummean: cf. Cu.III.8–11. Similarly Theodore replaces Columbanus' notion of 'acting out of fear' by a phrase which describes a situation of duress (*necessitate coactus*). This is deemed to be a mitigating factor and reduces the mandatory penance from eleven to three years.

60 'Qui in manu hominis periurat, apud Grecos nihil est; si vero in manu episcopi vel presbiteri vel diaconi seu in altari vel in cruce non consecrata, uno anno.' Bi.III:3,2–3.

61 'Falsa Testimonia' e.g. Co.A.8; Cu.III.12; Bi.III.4; whereas 'Mendacium' in Bi.III.5.tit. False testimony usually describes a situation where spurious accusations have been made whereas *mendacio* tends to apply to the whole range of sins against truth-telling. Worthy of note here also is the general distaste for all forms of dishonesty in the druidic predecessor culture. See L. Debarge, *Le Syncrétisme*, 11.

62 'Si quis falsum testimonium testificatus fuerit sciens, duobus annis paeniteat cum illius rei perditione vel redintegratione.' Co.A.8.

63 'Falsum testimonium dicens primo placeat proximo suo qualeque fratri inposuit tali iudicio damnetur iudice sacerdote.' Cu.III.12.

64 'Qui non implet quodlibet eorum pro quibus Dominus dicet: Venite benedicti patris mei, et reliqua, quanto tempore sic mansit tanto peniteat largusque vivat de cetero; sin autem, absidatur.'

65 The same penalty is also reserved for the cleric who fails to give his superfluous possessions to the poor.

66 'Clericus habens superflua donet ea pauperibus; sin autem, excommunicetur. Si vero post peniteat, tempore quo in contradictione fuit in penitentia semotus vivat' Bi.III:6,1–2. And it is interesting that the Irish monastic leaders were 'so

purified from all trait of avarice that none of them received lands and possessions for building monasteries unless they were compelled to do so by the temporal authorities'. See D. O'Laoghaire, 'Early Irish Spirituality', *Capuchin Annual* 36 (1969) 138.

67 The term employed here is 'usuram accipere' Da.13.

68 Cf. The prohibition on all israelites to accept interest from their brothers (Lev 25:36f; Deut 23:19) and likewise permission to lend to strangers (Deut 23:20).

69 'Usuram accipiens perdat ea quae accipit.' Da.13.

70 Co.B.pr.

71 See the following examples, Almsgiving: Cu.III.3.; Donation: Cu.III.4.; Chastisement, Confinement and Exile: Aq.3; Silence: Cu.III.17; Restitution: Vi.25; Liberation of slaves: Vi.22.

72 'Miser homo . . . ne fragili parcas vestimento, ne tibi tua praeferas. Plus te ames quam tua, plus animam quam res tuas . . . Quod enim tuum est, praeter animam? Noli ergo tuam perdere pro nihilo.' Co.Inst.III.

73 '. . . parvo extremae necessitatis censu in terris debent esse contenti, scientes lepram esse cupiditatem monachis imitatoribus filiorum prophetarum ac discipulo Christi proditionem atque perditionem apostolorum quoque dubiis sectatoribus mortem.' Co.Reg.Mon.IV.

74 See Finnian's exhortation to generosity in Vi.33.

75 The confessor's task is not only to eradicate sin but also to render the penitent open to the will of God after his repentance. cf. Cu.ps.4. and Bi.pr.34. '. . . et effeceris eum (peccatorem) talem ut ei converso propitius fiat Deus.'

76 Vi.32–33. And see also the *Old Irish Penitential* which rules: 'Christ says anyone who has much wealth or substance should distribute half of it to the poor.' OIP.III.5.

77 'Procuret economus de humanitate advenientibus adhibenda tam peregrinis quam reliquis fratribus, et omnes fratres parati sint ad ministrandum cum omni famulatu propter Deum.' Co.Reg.Coen.VIII.

78 'Mad intii adcobra rosá cléthe foirbthetad fodlai huli do bochtaib 7 adilcnechaib 7 tet i n-ailithri no bith innmnochta ind eclais oentath co te dochum nime.' OIP.III.6.

79 'Cleirech nó caillech bís ind eclais oentath lasambí ní for a leortu sechib ret taibreth di bochtaib . . .' OIP.III.10.

80 Cf. Ryan, *Irish Monasticism*, 244; 'All things considered there is reason to believe that about A.D. 600 many of the Irish monasteries were very poor and that none was really wealthy.

81 An English translation of this Rule may be found in De Bhaldraithe, Irish Monastic Rules (unpublished notes), School of Prayer (Dublin, 1986).

82 The term employed is *Ira*.

83 'Ira ferc ised ainm inna coicti dualchai marbus anmain duini amal tregtas foebar corp nduini is amlaid tregtas rind na ferca ind anmain co n-imolngai bás dosuidiu.'

84 'Offensus quis ab aliquo debet hoc indicare abati, non tamen accussantis sed medentis afectu, et abas decernat. Nam qui iram corde multo tempore retinet, in morte est.' Gi.17–18.

85 '. . . magna sunt peccata haec et capitalia et occidunt animam et demergunt eam in profundum inferni.' Vi.29.

86 'Dicit enim scriptura: Iracundia viri iustitiam Dei non operatur.' Vi.29.

87 'Homicida ille qui odit fratrem suum, quamdiu non repellit odium in pane et aqua sit et ei quem oderat caritate non ficta copuletur.' Cu.IV.4.

88 The terms used throughout the penitential texts are *homicidium* which we may take to mean unlawful killing in the usual sense and *parricidium* denoting the murder of a near relative. And indeed this is the gravest of all crimes to be found in the penitential literature.

89 See. Da.7. and Da.11. For the first category we are given no indication of the penance to be undertaken, but for the second the penitent must fast for three years.

90 The vicarious *goire* or obligation of the slayer to compensate his victim was also a provision of brehon law. See Bieler, *Irish Penitentials*, 243 at footnote 10. See the more detailed discussion of brehon law in Ginell, *Brehon Laws*, 109–116.

91 'Ecce ego vobis pro filio vestro; quęcumque dixeritis mihi faciam.' Vi.23.

92 'Si autem subito occiderit et non ex odio, et amici fuerunt ante . . .' Vi.24. The penance prescribed here by Finnian amounts to six year's exile three of which must be spent fasting and the other three abstaining from wine and meat.

93 '. . . per mensura in fletu et (lacrimis atque) orationibus die ac nocte et postulet de Domini misericordia si forte habeat remissionem peccatorum . . .' Vi 12.

94 Cf. Gen 4:14. 'Behold thou hast driven me this day away from the ground; and from thy face I shall be hidden; and I shall be a fugitive and a wanderer on the earth.'

95 This monetary compensation was twofold; The first part consisted of a mandatory wergild (eric) and the second a series of payments which were loosely based on the notion of an honour price which had to be paid to close relatives. See Thurneysen, *Irisches Recht*, 14.

96 'iuxta indulgentiam Novi Testamenti' Bi.IV:1,2. This is a repetition of Theodore's teaching on the subject; cf. Te.I:4,1–6.

97 This sin is referred to by the Bigotian author under the category 'De Occentibus Semet Ipsis' Bi.IV:1,4.cf. Te. II:10,1–3 Note this phrase as Callewaert points out demonstrates that in the penitential literature the division between abortive and contraceptive practices is very nebulous indeed. See further discussion in R.S. Callewaert, 'De Middleeuwse biechtboeken anticonceptionele praktijken' *Tijdschrift voor Theologie* 4(1964) 254–74. (trad. franc: 'Les Pénitentiels du Moyen Age et les pratiques anticonceptionelles': *La Vie Spirituelle Supplément* 74 (1965) 339–66) and J.T.Noonan, 'The Lessons of the Penitentials' *Contraception A History of its Treatment by the Catholic Theologians and Canonists* (Cambridge Mass.: Harvard Press, 1965) 152–70.

98 Thus 'Si homo vexatus a diabolo . . .' and on the other hand: 'Si autem pro disperatione vel pro timore aliquo vel pro causis ignotis.' and finally 'Qui voluntariae semet ipsum occiderit . . .'

99 Bi.IV:2,2–3. The phrase used is 'de perditio liquoris materiae filii.' Cf. also: Te.XIV,24–27; OIP.V.6; Hi.I.6. A fuller treatment of this subject by a

recognised scholar of the penitentials may be found in J.T. Noonan, 'An Almost Absolute Value in History', *The Morality of Abortion* (Cambridge, Mass.: Harvard Press, 1970), 1–59.

100 'Si mulier maleficio suo partum alicuius perdiderit . . .' Vi.20.

101 Cf. '2. Penitentia perditionis liquoris materiae infantis in utero mulieris .iii. anni in pane et aqua.' and '3. Penitentia perditionis carnis et animae in utero .xiii. peniteat in pane et aqua.'

102 But this is not true, however, of later penitential material; For example in the *Penitential Ascribed by Albers to Bede* we have the following canon: 'A mother who kills her child before the fortieth day shall do penance for one year. if it is after the child has become alive, as a murderess. But it makes a great difference whether a poor woman does it on account of the difficulty of supporting (the child) or a harlot for the sake of concealing her wickedness.' Be.II.11. The whole question is dealt with at length in the doctoral thesis of C.P. González, *Doctrina de S. Augustín sobre la malicia del aborto y su influencia en la disciplina penitencial de la Edad Media* (Salamanca 1959).

103 The subject is dealt with under the general title 'De Rixantibus' by the Bigotian author Bi.IV.3. See also Vi.5; Co.A.5&9; Cu.IV.9; Wa.A.8.

104 'Si autem clericus fuerit et percusserit fratrem suum aut proximum et sanguinem effuderit, unum est ut occiderit eum, sed non eadem penitentia . . .' Vi.8.

105 '. . . et orare se debet cum fletu et lacrimis ut misericordiam consequatur a Deo, quia dicit scriptura: Qui odit fratrem suum homicida est; quanto magis qui percutit.' Vi.8.

106 'Si autem laicus fuerit, .xl. dies peniteat et det aliquam pecuniam quem percutit, quantum arbitratus fuerit sacerdos aut iustus quisque.' Vi.9.

107 '. . . si autem non habet unde solvat, opera proximi sui primum agat quamdiu ille infirmus est medicumque quaerat et post sanitatem eius .xl. dies in pane et aqua peniteat.' Co.B.21.

108 'Si vero non habeat unde restituat haec, .i. annum peniteat.' Cu.IV.9–10.

109 Thus 'maldicere': Cu.IV.12; Bi.IV:5,1; Pa.II.4; 'acerviora verba proferre': Cu.IV.13; Bi.IV:5,2; 'Contristare fratrem': Cu.IV.1; Bi.IV.4.

110 'Qui mente tantum sentit commotionem, satis faciat ei qui illum commovit.' Cu.IV.15.

111 'Qui vero non vult confitere ei qui se commotavit, abscedatur pestifer ille a coetu sanctorum . . .' Cu.IV.16.

112 'De Clamore' cf. Bi.IV:pr.IV; Bi.IV.6.tit.; and Bi.IV:6,1.

113 On clan structure of early Ireland cf. chapter 1 in the section. 'Society in Ancient Ireland' and Joyce, *A Social History*, vol. 2, 3–19. But see also the superior view and critique of Joyce's position in E. MacNeill, *Celtic Ireland* (Dublin: Academy Press, 1921), esp. ch. 10, 'The Family Commune'.

114 'Ac homicida ille quod odit fratrum suum quamdiu non repellit odium in pane et aqua sit ei quem odierit caritate non ficta copuletur.'

115 Columbanus points out that no one ever criticises one whom he loves for 'criticism is the first-born of anger and thus the son of such a father ought justly to be exterminated.' and he reminds his followers that if as the apostle says one 'who does not love is in death' (1 Jn 3:14) then 'where shall he be

who criticises.' Co.Inst.XI. See A. de Vogüé, *Saint Colomban Règles et Pénitentiels Monastiques* (Bellefontaine: Vie Monastique, 1989): '. . . le plus grave est ce qui compromet la paix entre frères, ces disputes où l'on contredit l'autre et l'on soutient obstinément sa manière de voir.'

116 'Is sí dano sualaich roherbath du chathugud frisan dubalaich-si .i. cennsa co n-algini co neoch genithar úadi . . .' OIP.V:1,c.

117 'nihil amori Christi praeponere, iram non perficere, pacem falsam non dare . . . malum pro malo non redere . . . inimicos diligere.' Bi.pr.60–61 and see also Benedicti *Regula* 4.

118 '. . . pretiosa quaeque maiori cautela et diligentiori custodia indigent.'

119 'Ne forte itaque nobis tyrannicas introducamus imagines, Christus in nobis suam pingat imaginem, quippe dicendo: 'pacem meam do vobis, pacem meam relinquo vobis' Co.Inst.XI. and cf. Jn.14:27.

120 'Tristitae genera duo sunt: unum salutiferum, alterum mortiferum.' Bi.V:1,1.

121 'Salutiferum cum nos nostra peccata vel aliorum contristant et nobis lacrimarum habundantiam digna penitentia inducant.' Bi.V:1,2. For another account of health-giving remorse see Columbanus' sermon entitled *De Compunctione* in Walker, *Sancti Columbani*, 110–15.

122 'Mortiferum, cum orbitate amicorum aut demptione rerum corporalium aut dampno, si demptae sunt, contristamur.' Bi.V.1,3.

123 'Nech didu connach tibi diabul tria bron.' OIP.VI.2.

124 '. . . scilicet tristitia occidet vel consumit animam.' Vi.29.

125 'Et hoc vitium, ut quidam sapiens ait, emendatur sono psalmorum frequenter et praeceptis canonicis ex labiis iusti . . .' Bi.V:3,2.

126 See Joyce, *A Social History*, vol.II, 540.

127 Hence, Joyful Countenance and Glad Heart: Cu.VI.1; Bi.V:3,1. Fasting: Cu.VI.2; Bi.V:3,1. Temporary Exile: Cu.V.3; Bi.V:3,1. Fervent Prayer and Psalms: Bi.V:1,6; Bi.V:3,2.

128 See the Bigotian's starting premise 'Tristitiae genera duo sunt: unum salutiferum, alterum mortiferum.' The two forms of sadness are explained in the subsequent canons especially Bi.V:1,1 and Bi.V.3. For a discussion of the meaning of sadness in the OIP, see P. O'Dwyer, *Céili Dé*, 64–5.

129 '. . . ar antíi connessai a pectha fadesin 7 pectha a choibnesaim bid failid sidi la día for nim.' OIP.VI:1,b.

130 'Quae etiam disciplina disciplinarum est, quaeque aeterni temporis iucunditatem et aeterni gaudii amoenitatem praesenti merore comparat.' Co.Inst.IV.

CHAPTER 3

1 The preferred term is 'Fornicatione' see Cu.11 and Bi.11 but 'Luxuria' is also employed by the Bigotian text see Bi.pr.37. N.B. The serious student of this aspect of the penitentials will find in P. Payer, *Sex and the Penitentials*, the most comprehensive and detailed study yet undertaken on this subject.

2 'Nolite errare, quia neque fornicari neque idolis servientes neque adulteri neque masculorum concubitores neque fures neque avari neque ebriosi regnum Dei possidebunt.' Bi.pr.38.

3 'Luxuria tra hissed ainm inna dualcha tanaisi marbas anmain duini .i. arindí furumai sár for cach toil etir toil dé nad imradi ecna na crabad na suith inté bis fu cumachta 7 foa reir.'OIP.II:1.a.

4 'Praesbiter aut diaconus faciens fornicationem naturalem sive sodomitam praelato ante monachi voto .iii. peniteat.' Gi.1. Note the terms *fornicationem naturalem* and *sodomitam* are already recognised by the early Welsh author. And because of their juxtaposition here we take the term 'natural fornication' to indicate heterosexual intercourse whereas 'sodomy' clearly refers to the homosexual variety.

5 For example '. . . cum muliere disponsata Christo maritove sive . . . cum virgine vel vidua necdum disponsata.' Da.5.

6 The bride-price, called in Irish *tinol* or *tinscra*, in Welsh *agueddy* and in Latin *dos*, was a payment made by the bridegroom to the bride's parents. Cf. McNeil and Gamer, *Medieval Handbooks*, 37.

7 The sinner who fornicates with a consecrated virgin or married woman is to renounce the world for the remainder of his life, whereas if she is a virgin a year's penitential fasting plus the payment of the bride-price is the penance. See Da.5.

8 '. . . non minus peccatum eius est ut esset clericus ex iuventute sua et ita est cum puella aliena peccasset.' Vi.27.

9 '. . . et non intret amplius fornicari cum extranea femina quamdiu fuerit in hoc corpore.' Vi.36.

10 '. . . sed expectabit eum innupta patientia et castitate, si forte det Deus penitentiam in corde viri eius . . .' Vi.45. In terms of severity we may say that, as a general rule, where one party to a non-marital sexual relationship was married the penance was significantly greater than for 'simple fornication'.

11 'Aliter quidam aiunt intollerabilius: paenitentia concoitus mulieris alicuius mariti vivi .vii. annis cum pane et aqua.' Bi.II:5,2.

12 And the term 'unnatural fornication' is itself employed in the penitential literature see Bi.II:2 tit. 'De Fornicatione non Naturali'.

13 The term used here is 'Facere scelus virile ut Sodomite'. Literally: to do the male or sodomite crime. Lu.8.

14 Finnian prefers the term 'in terga vero fornicantes'. Literally: to fornicate in the rear. Vi.pr.2. Finnian, in common with all the Irish penitentialists is clearly referring to *male* homosexual acts. For the first mention of lesbian activity and the corresponding censures see Theodore: Te.I.2:12–13.

15 Columbanus describes the sin thus: 'Si . . . fornicaverit sicut sodomitae fecerunt.' Literally if he fornicated as the sodomites did. Co.B.3.

16 Columbanus explains: 'Si quis vero laicus fornicaverit sodomitico ritu, id est cum masculo coitu faemineo peccaverit . . .' Co.B.15. Columbanus also describes the details of the penances more fully than the other texts.

17 Note: the term *in terga* also refers to homosexual anal intercourse. Cf. note 14 supra. However, for the best discussion of the various nuances of language used by the penitentialists to describe sexual sin and in particular homosexual sin, see Payer, *Sex and the Penitentials*, 40–4.

18 The most popular choice of term here is '*Quoqinare* se' (coinquinare) e.g. Aq.2. And see subsequent footnotes for other linguistic variations.

19 'Qui voluntate obsceno liquore maculatus fuerit dormiendo . . .' Literally whoever was stained willingly by the indecent fluid while asleep. Gi.22 Given the leniency of the penance, though, it seems that ritual defilement rather than sin is the underlying issue.

20 Cf. 'Qui concupiscit mente tantum fornicari sed non potuit' Cu.II.11 and 'Si autem inpugnatione cogitationis violenter coinquinatus est.' Cu.II.13.

21 A distinction is made here between 'osculum simpliciter', 'osculum inlecebrosum' and 'osculum cum coinquinamento sive amplexo.' Cu.X.2. Literally: simple kissing; licentious kissing, and kissing with pollution or embrace. As with homosexual sin, so too, it is taken for granted here that the sin is between males.

22 Note the variation of terminology here: 'vero fornicationem imitantes et inritantes se invicem' Literally: imitating fornication and stimulating each other mutually and later 'se invicem manibus coinquinantes' Literally: mutually and manually polluting each other. Cu.X.4&7.

23 'Peccans cum pecode anno' Literally: He who sins with a beast. Gi.11.

24 However, this case is not simply one of bestiality but rather one of a boy having communicated after committing bestiality. Finnian includes no penance for the sin itself. Vi.pr.1.

25 Columbanus describes the sin as 'fornicare cum iumento' Literally: to sin with a beast of burden. Co.B.17.

26 Cf. Cu.II.6 and Bi.II:2,1. Thus we may agree with Brundage who asserts that the penitentials 'treated bestiality as a rather minor offence and frequently linked it with masturbation'. This, in turn, is probably a reflection on the rural character of Celtic medieval society where sexual opportunities with animals were more readily available than those with humans. J.A. Brundage, *Law, Sex and Christian Society in Medieval Europe* (Chicago: University Press, 1987), 168.

27 'Fornicantes labiis, quod dictum scelus . . .' Bi.II:2,4. And indeed there is much agreement among the texts that this is the worst of all sexual crimes: cf. Te.I.2:15; Vi.3; Cu.II.8; Cu.X.16.

28 'Qui mechator matris est .iii. annis cum peregrinatione perenni' Lu.6. The emphasis of the Celtic texts suggests that incest was understood only as sexual activity between close blood relations: mother, father, brother and sister. See also Cu.II.7 and Bi.II3:1–2. Only the later Theodore extends the range of prohibitions: Te.II.12:24–28.

29 'Si quis laicus infantem suum oppraesserit' Co.B.18 and Cu.X.9. where Cummean employs the same term in a slightly different context 'Puer parvulus oppressus a maiore annum'.

30 'De meretrice coiuge sic idem interpraetatus est, quod meretrix erit decusso proprii mariti iugo et secundi mariti iuncta vel tertii.' Ad.16.

31 There is some discussion, however, as to whether this text softens Vinnian's prohibition on divorce, perhaps allowing a spouse to divorce his adulterous wife. There are, however, textual difficulties. Cf. Bieler's discussion of same: Bieler, *Irish Penitentials*, 255 at footnote 15.

32 '. . . ut dicat, se servavit a ruina, dimedium annum peniteat cum pane et aqua.' Vi.14–15.

33 Cf. note 21 supra.

34 '. . . petat a Deo adiutorium per orationem et ieiunium diebus ac noctibus donec evanescat maligna cogitatio et sanus sit.' Vi.2.

35 'si fornicationem voluit . . ., quia effectus non expleuit voluntate iam peccavit in corde suo . . .' Vi.3.

36 'Qui diu inluditur fornicari a cogitatione tepidius ei repugnans . . .' Cu.II.14.

37 Note the difference between Cu.II.20 'Diligens mente tantum', literally: to love in mind only, and Cu.II.21 'Si autem dixit sed non est susceptus ab ea', literally: to have spoken but not to have been received by her.

38 '. . . si non necessitate luti largius abstergendi.' Co.B.27.

39 '. . . seniori vero etiam publice, sed altero pedes suos lavante, licet stando lavari.' Co.B.28.

40 For instance: Sexual abstinence Vi.37. Corporal punishment Co.B.27. Loss of rank Aq.1. Exile Cu.II.17. Chanting of Psalms Gi.22. Payment of compensation Da.6. Lying upon stone Da.11. Almsgiving Vi.36. Separation from spouse Vi.40. Prayers Vi.12.

41 '. . . vel XXX psalmos flectando genua unius cuiusque in fine cantat.' Bi.II:1,7.

42 '. . . et ita primum altario sacerdotis iudicio iungantur et suum torum tunc licito maritus ille cognoscat.' Co.B.18.

43 See the exception to this though in Da.5. where the penitents are enjoined to live 'dead to the world' for the rest of their lives. Given, however, that the penitents here are monks, this penance is not as severe as it appears at first sight.

44 'Qui diu inluditur fornicari a cogitatione tepidius ei repugnans . . . quantum exierit diuturnitas cogitationis, peniteat.' Cu.II.14.

45 Cf. Vi.37–39. and Cu.II.22–23. Finnian prefers the term 'non intret ad uxorem suam', whilst Cummean employs the more terse formula 'sine uxore propria peniteat.'

46 'semper ex intimo corde defleat culpam suam oboedientiamque prae omnibus libentissime excipiat' Cu.II.2.

47 'Post annum autem et dimidium eucharistiam sumat et ad pacem veniat et psalmos cum fratribus canat, ne penitus anima tanto tempore caelestis medicinae ieiuna interiat.' Cu.II.2.

48 '. . . id est congbaidet hi genas con-neuch genedir uad .i. forus comairle comlabrai cobsaid fosta fri anfontai tairngire fir fir do chomalath himradu dé feli aicnith nertath irsi miscais in chenntuir serc ind altair.' OIP.II:1,d.

49 'Contentiam esse in matrimonio precipimus et exortamur quia matrimonium sine continentia non ligitimum sed peccatum est' and '. . . id est in unitate carnis per generationem filiorum et non libidine concupiscentie carnalis.' Vi.46. And there is much evidence to suggest that continence is understood in very rigorous terms here. Sexual abstinence, for instance, was dictated by Lent, Advent, Pentecost, Easter, feast days, fast days, Sundays, hours of daylight and the menstrual cycle. For more information on the penitentials' understanding of the sexual life of the married see: J.L. Flandrin, *Un temps pour embrasser* (Paris, Editions du Seuil, 1983), passim. and Pierre J. Payer, 'Early Medieval Regulations Concerning Sexual Relations' *Journal of Medieval History* (180) 353–76.

50 '. . . et in futuro cum Christo regnabunt cum sanctum Abraham et Issac et Iacob, Iob, Noe omnibus sanctis . . .' Vi.46.

51 The reference here is to the Parable of the Sower which compares the human response to the Good News with the fruitfulness of seed which is sown in different soils. Hence married people who lead the devout Christian life are the seed which reproduce thirtyfold, whereas the sixtyfold are clergy and widows and the hundredfold, in turn, are the bishops, teachers and monks. Cf. Pa.II.18.

52 'Uxorem a viro non discedere dicimus sed si discesserit manere innuptam aut viro reconciliari secundum apostolum' Vi.42. Thus, divorce is disapproved of despite any number of unhappy situations. Marriage was always permanent in clerical eyes. And note also that the ruling may also have served as a denunciation of polygamy. See Lisa Bitel, *Sex, Sin and Celibacy*, 78.

53 '. . . sed expectabit eum innupta in omni patientia et castitate si forte det Deus penitentiam in corde viri eius.' Vi.45. The position of the Celtic Church is therefore at odds here with that of the patristic Church or at least with the interpretation of it proferred in G. Cereti, *Divorzio, Nuove Nozze e Penitenza nella Chiesa Primitiva* (Bologna: Dehoniane,1977) but see also the discussion in R. Laurentin, *Bilan du Concile. Histoire, Textes, Commentaires avec une chronique de la quatrième session* (Paris: 1966), esp. 81–90 and 395–7.

54 See Finnian's frequent use of the phrase 'quamdiu fuerit in corpore' (2 Pet 1:13) which prohibits further unions while one partner is still alive.

55 'Item: Non licet viro dimittere uxorem suam nisi ob quam causam fornicationis . . .' Pa II.26. and cf. Mt 19:3.

56 '. . . ne forte iuxta sancti sententiam Petri habeant oculos luxuriae plenos atque adulterii.' Co.Reg.Mon.VI.

57 Ibid. 'Deus enim spiritus in spiritu habitat ac mente, quem immaculatum viderit, in quo nulla sit adultera cogitatio nulla spiritus coinquinati macula, nulla peccati labes sit.'

58 The term preferred by the penitentialists here is 'Accidia'; see Bi.pr.45.

59 The term used for the idler is 'otiosus'; see Cu.VII.1, and for Gildas' discussion of motivation see Gi.15.

60 Work thus makes it possible at once to exercise charity and to serve the needy. 'Laborat manibus suis, ut habeat unde communicet indigentibus'. Bi.VI:1,1. and cf. Eph 4:28. For an illuminating discussion of what kind of work may have been entailed here see Ryan, *Irish Monasticism*, 360–83.

61 'Quia sicut fumo expelluntur apes, ut tollatur dulcitudo earum operis, ita et corporalis quies timorem Domini expellit ab anima et auferet ab ea omne opus bonum.' Bi.Vi:1,2. and cf. *Vitae Patrum* V. 10, 71 (Syncletica).

62 'Si mortem odis, cur somnum dilegis? Nam somnus assiduus emitatio mortis.' Bi.VI:2,1.

63 Ibid. 'In omni tempore glorificatur Deus'.

64 Note the term used by Cummean and the Bigotian author '*vagus instabilisque*' and see Cu.VI.2 and Bi.VI:3,1.

65 For example, Co.A.2–3. passim.

66 'Vagus instabilisque quis sanetur unius loci mansione operisque sedulitate.' Cu.VI.2.

67 'Accedia per stabilitatem corporis et cordis et cogitationis adiuuare potest.' Bi.VI:3,2–3. and cf. *Vitae Patrum*, V;2,9.

68 Bi.VI:3,4 and cf. *Vitae Patrum* V.2,1.

69 See *Vitae Patrum* V;7,15.

70 Bi.VI:3,6 and cf. *Vitae Patrum* V.7,30.

71 See Cu.IX.9 and Cu.IX.29.

72 For example: Work:Gi.16, Cu.IX.5; Vigils: Cu.VI.1, Bi.VI:2,2; Prayer: Cu.VI.1, Bi.VI:2,2; Earlier rising:Bi.VI:2,3 and Permanent Residence: Bi.VI:3,1.

73 See for instance Bi.VI:2,2. 'Sumnolentus cum vigiliis et orationibus sanetur.' and also Bi.VI:3,1. As well as the psalms the Celtic Church disposed of a magnificent body of 'new material' including hymns, antiphons and litanies. For further information on Celtic prayer see D. O'Laoghaire, 'The Celtic Monk at Prayer' *Monastic Studies* 14 123–43. and O'Laoghaire, 'Daily Intimacy with God an ever new aspect of Celtic Worship' *Studia Liturgica* 13(1979) 46–56.

74 'Numquid solo sermone quis suam domum a quolibet squalore mundabit aut sola loquela pulverulentos aggeres immundi ruderis submovebit? . . . Patientia ergo et diligentia et labor ac studium infatigabile.' Co.Inst.II.

75 The Bigotian author suggests 'Perseverentia, Studium Mentis, Patientia' and 'Studium scientiae legis Dei' as the virtues which are to be sought after. See Bi.pr.49.

76 'Accedia per stabilitatem corporis et cordis et cogitationis adiuuare potest.' Bi.VI:3,2.

77 Columbanus devotes a whole sermon to the notion of training (Co.Inst.IV), the thrust of which suggests that no goal in life is a worthy one unless it involves a lengthy period of training.

78 'Non quaeramus in via quod in patria futurum est; labor enim et fatigatio in itinere versatur, in patria requies et securitas paratur.' Co.Inst.V.

79 '. . . currat animus profectibus sicut vita cursibus, et ita animi augeatur maturitas, ut aetatis plenitudo; et sicut vitae circuli minuuntur, sic vitiorum numerus decrescat . . .' Co.Inst.VI.

80 Bi.pr.46. 'De Cenodoctia (nascuntur) contentiones, heresses, iactantia (et) presumptio novitatum.' whereas Bi.pr.47: 'De Superbia (nascuntur) contemptus, invidia, inobedientia, murmuratio (et) detractio.' N.B. Cummean prefers the term *iactantia* whereas the Bigotian author frequently interchanges between *cenodoctia* and *vana gloria* to describe the vice and makes *iactantia* a sub-section of this.

81 'De Contentione' cf. Cu.VII.1. and Bi.VII:1.

82 'Contentiosus etiam alterius sententiae subdat se, sin autem, anathemazatur ut regno Dei est alienorum.' Cu.VII.1.

83 'Qui aliam doctrinam extra scripturas vel heressim praesummit, alienatur ab ecclesia.' Bi.VII.2.

84 See footnote 80 supra and Bi.pr.46.

85 '". . . Air ciped dognem ar thucait cumtaich n" molta ho duinib is indocbail huaebrech n-anmnigter ar fochraic de namma ar molad o duinib amail asbeir Crist fadesin . . .' OIP.VII:1,a. And see the discussion of the OIP remedies in P.O'Dwyer, *Céili Dé*, 65.

86 Note also that Jesus' description of the just fast is closely allied to that of the prophet Isaiah (Is 5:4–5). 'Fasting like yours this day will not make your voice to be heard on high. Is such the fast that I choose a day for a man to humble himself.'

87 For example: fasting, silence and corporal punishment: Co.A.9; exclusion from the Christian community: Co.B.25; subjection to another: Cu.VII.1; acts of humility: Cu.VII.2; condemnation of heresy and conversion of others: Bi.VII:2; restraint in talk and food: Bi.VII:4.

88 'Contentiosus etiam alterius sententiae subdat se.' Cu.VII.I.

89 And see the same prescription echoed by the Bigotian text Bi.VII:1.

90 Such healing activity cannot be carried out (according to Columbanus) by someone using only his own efforts; instead it properly belongs to the scrutiny of others: 'quam nullus sibi ipsi per se potest tradere quia proprie aliorum est examinis.' (Co.Reg.Mon.IX).

91 '. . . et quos decipit ad fidem convertat.' Bi.VII:2.

92 '. . . et de modico verborum et ciborum et de nuditate saeculi et humilitate salvatur hoc vitium cenodoxiae.' Bi.VII:4. Cf. the later *Rule of Ailbhe* which advises 'their father is noble god, their mother is holy Church let it not be mouth-humility, let each have compassion on his brother' in E. De Bhaldraithe, *Monastic Rules.*

93 'His et illo farisei famosissimo se iustificantis exemplo colligitur quod interemtrix sit omnium bonorum vanitas et gloriatio elata, dum bona vane laudata farisei perierunt, et peccata publicani accusata evanuerunt. Non exeat igitur verbum grande de ore monachi, ne suus grandis pereat labor.' Co.Reg.Mon.V.

94 'Sine consilio nihil facias' Co.Reg.Mon.IX. and this in turn is taken from Sir 32:19–24.

95 'Duret igitur apud nos ista definitio, ut sic vivamus in via ut viatores, ut peregrini, ut hospites mundi, nullis haerentes cupiditatibus . . . sed caelestibus et spiritalibus formis animos nostros repleamus . . .' Co.Inst.VIII.

96 '. . . mansuetudo et dilectio Dei et proximorum pro invidia.' Vi.29.

97 'Samlitir dano a aicneth ind formait consindiri fri aicneth teneth ar is besad in tineth is cuma loisces a mbis issa 7 huassa 7 inna erchomair immatha samlaith a format is cummae frisoirc dundí bes isliu 7 bes huaisliu 7 bas cutruma combí náma da cach duiniu etir maith 7 saich etir cían ucus ocus.' OIP.IV:1,a. And note that the OIP. sees *Invidia* as one of the major vices, thus it takes the place of superbia in this version of the octoade of vices.

98 Ibid. 1,b. '. . . inna hiniri ní bi atreb do día inna cridiu nícon bía dano atreb dosum la día for nim.'

99 Cf. *Vitae Patrum* V.40,50–2. (Hyperichius).

100 'Susurrans serpens ad Euam de paradisso eam eiecit; huic ergo similis qui proximo suo obloquitur quando et audientis se animam perdit et suam non saluat. Bi.VIII:3.

101 'Ata dano cetharda arnid cüir taithbec ind uilc bís isin duiniu nád eroim a ícc tria guidi accus algini rodbu ar nach comet nach ali dÛ isin ulc sein rodbu ar chairiguth ind uilc fadesin rodbu ar demniguth in maith rodbu ar airchisecht indí dogní a n-olc.' OIP.IV.5

102 ''His aire is beithi menmae frisin fodor immun tuarai uare issed chetarráli diabul for adam 7 eva hi tosuch dommuin conid disuidiu dufuetar an obul dichmair conid ari rogabad al-lam a pardus dochum gortae, 7 bochtae 7 ítath 7 bais 7 hifirn asa cind.' OIP.IV.8.

103 'Qui superbos ceteros qualibet dispectione arguit, primo satis faciat eis, deinde ieiunet iudicio sacerdotis.' Cf. Cu.VIII.3 and Bi.VIII:1.

104 'Inoboediens maneat extra concilium sine cibo et pulset humiliter donec recipiatur.' Cf. Cu.VIII.4. and Bi.VIII:4; Note for further examples of sins of contempt see sections on Gluttony where priests are censured if they get drunk 'out of contempt' for their superiors, e.g.; Da.1–2. The Celtic understanding of obedience and disobedience and how this differed from other historical interpretations is set forth comprehensively in E. De Bhaldraithe, 'Obedience: The Doctrine of the Irish Monastic Rules' *Monastic Studies* 1, 63–84.

105 'Reticens peccatum fratris quod est ad mortem arguat eum cum fiducia et quanto tempore reticuit tanto in pane et aqua vivat.' Cu.VIII.19.

106 Textual references as follows: the reformed heretic: Cu.VIII.2; the proud censurer: Cu.VIII.3; the envious: Cu.VIII.7; the rebuker: Cu.VIII.21.

107 ". . . Deg teist di cách. Miscais ecnaich Innarbae fodoirt. Morath cach maith Tansem cach uile briathar algen menma aircisechtach di cach duine acht ní bas dír pecath.' OIP.IV:1,d.

108 '. . . quia si talis non fuerit oboedientia, non erit acceptabilis domino qui ait: 'Et qui non accipit crucem suam et sequitur me non est me dignus.' Co.Reg.Mon.I. For more on obedience see note 104 above.

109 'Quod autem declinat a bonitate condita et integritate hoc primum malum est, quod est superbia malitiae primae; cui contraria est piae bonitatis humilis existimatio suum creatorem agnoscentis et glorificantis, quod est rationabilis creaturae primum bonum.' Co.Reg.Mon.VIII.

110 'Humilitatis enim cordis requies animae est vitiis ac laboribus fatigatae ac unicum illius de tot malis refrigerium . . .' Co.Reg.Mon.IX. This Celtic mixture of humility and compassion is, I believe, one of the key symbols of the penitentials and points to a humanity and sensitivity in those texts which has been often overlooked. For a similar view see P. Payer, 'The Humanism of the Penitentials and the Continuity of the Penitential Tradition' *Medieval Studies* 46 (1984) 340–54.

CHAPTER 4

1 Text and translation of this document are taken from the *Rite of Penance (Approved for use in the dioceses of Ireland)* (Dublin: Veritas Publications, 1976).

2 See Luigi Della Torre, *Conversione e Riconciliazione* (Roma: Edizioni Paolini, 1983), 77 where there is some discussion of the document.

3 The penitentials in fact prefer the term 'compunction' for example: (Vi.17; Bi.pr.69) to that of 'contrition' as well as other terms which denote a sorrowful disposition. Whereas the etymological origins of the term contrition has the force of 'crushing' the hardened heart, compunction by contrast puts the emphasis more upon 'lancing' or 'piercing' the inflamed heart.

4 'In nomine Dei Patris et Filii et Spiritus Sancti. Si quis in corde suo per cogitationem peccaverit et confestim penituerit, percutiat pectus suum et petat a Deo veniam et satis faciat et sanus sit.' Vi.1.

5 See our discussion of this in chapter two under the heading of Dejection.

6 'Salutiferum cum nos nostra peccata vel aliorum contristant et nobis lacrimarum habundantiam digna penitentia inducant.' Bi.V:1,2.

7 'Tristitia vero utilis est, ut pro peccatis gemescamus et pro ignorantia proximorum et ut non cadamus a proposito et ut perfectionem bonitatis adtingamus.' Bi.V:1,5. And cf. Vitae Patrum V:10,71.

8 See Cu.pr.2–13; and the 'remissions' are again set forth in the Bigotian text at Bi.pr.30–31 but in a much abbreviated form.

9 See Cu.pr.5.

10 The argument here is taken from Gregory the Great, M. Moralia, xxiii.

11 'Tristes simus usque ad mortem cum Christo, ut tristitia nostra in gaudium convertatur.' Co.Inst.IV and cf. Jn 16:20.

12 '. . . tristes pro peccatis nostris, laeti propter spem vitae aeternae, tristes propter Christi absentiam, exsultantes similiter, quia legimus 'Videbimus eum sicuti est'. Licet enim praesentium frequentia tristificemur, victoria tamen utrorumque liberalis laetitia et nobile gaudium est.' Co.Inst.IV.

13 'Moriamur ergo, moriamur pro vita, quia Vita moritur pro mortuis, ut cum Paulo dicere possimus, "Vivo ego, iam non ego, vivit vero in me Christus."' Co.Inst.X.

14 See Ordo Intro. II:6,a. The Ordo is in effect describing here what is entailed by the term metanoia. Although this term never appears in the penitential literature, the essence or significance of the concept is certainly grasped by the penitentialists.

15 The painting metaphor is worked out by Columbanus in Co.Inst.XI; however, its origin is in the writings of Athanasius.

16 'De eo quod non vindicat Deus neque homines debent vindicari et in his qui cito convertunt de culpa ad penitentiam in Exodo legitur quod adoratione vituli . . .' Hi.III.8.

17 'Confessiones autem dari diligentius praecipitur maxime de commotionibus animi antequam ad missam eatur, ne forte quis accedat indignus ad altare, id est, si cor mundum non habuerit.' Co.B.30.

18 '. . . melius est enim expectare donec cor sanum fuerit . . . quam accedere audacter ad iudicium tribunalis.' Co.B.30.

19 '. . . ita etiam ab interioribus vitiis et morbis languentis animae abstinendum . . .' Co.B.30.

20 And indeed this criticism is voiced in Richard M.Gula, *To Walk Together Again*, 92.

21 Bieler, *Irish Penitentials*, 256 at footnote 12.

22 'Quinta criminum confessio psalmista testante 'confitebor adversum me iniustitiam meam Domino' et tu remiscisti impietatem peccati mei.' Cu.pr.6.

23 '. . . et Dei pii et boni ineffabilem misericordiam de profundo cordis nostri per Iesum Christum Filium suum infatigabiliter deprecemur . . .' Co.Inst.XII.

24 'Novate vobis novalia, et nolite seminare super spinas; quanto magis nos oportet agrum cordis nostri noxiis vitiorum passionibus emundare.' Columbanus is indebted to John Cassian for this metaphor from whose writings it immediately derives and indirectly to Jer 4:3 which is its scriptural source. See Walker, *Sancti Opera*, 69 at footnote 1.

25 '. . . et non sufficere credamus nobis terram corporis nostri ieiuniorum et vigilarum labore conficere, nisi in primis studeamus vitia corrigere moresque componere qui spem fructuum non terrae credimus sed caelo repositam.' Co.Inst.II.

26 'Quid ergo prodest exterioris hominis religio, nisi interioris quoque non adhibeatur emendatio?' Co.Inst. II.

27 'Quapropter nihil nobis utilius sciamus, quam ut omnibus diebus vitae nostrae vitam ancipitem retractantes . . . et verborum cogitatuumque nostrorum rationem agentes . . .' Co.Inst.IX.

28 'Se unusquisque consideret, ne liber et vivus in loco servi et crucifixi inveniatur et 'Unusquisque in quo vocatus est in eo permaneat apud Deum.' Co.Inst.X.' Cf. 1 Cor 7:20.

29 'Ispira corda nostra, rogo, Iesu noster, illa tui Spiritus aura, et vulnera nostras tua caritate animas, ut possit uniuscuiusque nostrum anima in veritate dicere, 'Indica mihi quem dilexit anima mea', quoniam vulnerata caritate ego sum.' Co.Inst.XIII. Cf. Song 1:6.

30 Confessio 3 and cf. Ps.107.

31 '. . . ut demus confessionem . . . quandocumque fuerit facile . . . quia confessio et paenitentia de morte liberant.' Co.Reg.Coen.1.

32 See Ordo Intro.II:6,b.

33 'Melius est enim expectare donec cor sanum fuerit et alienum a scandalo ac invidia fuerit . . .' Co.B.30.

34 Ordo Intro. II:6,c and cf. Paul VI Apostolic Constitution *Paenitemini*, 17 February 1966: AAS 58 (1966) 179.

35 'Qui verba acerviora protulerit in furore, non tamen iniuriosa, satis faciens fratri superponat.' Cu.IV.13.

36 'Nam et corporum medici diversis medicamenta generibus conponunt . . . Ita igitur etiam spiritales medici diversis curationum generibus animarum vulnera morbos (culpas) dolores, aegritudines infirmitates sanare debent.' Co.B.pr.

37 Cf. Ordo Intro.II:6,c. 'The kind and extent of the satisfaction should be suited to the personal condition of each penitent so that each one may restore the order which he disturbed and through the corresponding remedy be cured of the sickness from which he suffered.'

38 'De remediis vulnerum secundum priorum patrum diffinitiones dicturi sacri tibi eloqui mi fidelissime frater . . .' Cu.pr.1.

39 'Et hoc sapientibus in penitentia moderanda intuendum est, ne dignum scelus gladio ferula vindicent et dignum peccatum ferula gladio percutiant.' Bi.pr.3.

40 'De concordia virtutum quę genus humanum reparant ad regna caelorum apostolus.' Bi.pr.48.

41 'Qui vult animam suam salvam facere, perdet eam; nam qui perdiderit animam suam propter me, inveniet illam. Perdendum ergo est libenter quicquid diligimus praeter Christum pro Christo.' Co.Inst.X.

42 'Nullus autem potest sibimet mori, nisi Christus in illo vivat; si autem Christus in illo sit, sibimet vivere non potest. Vive in Christo ut Christus in te.' Co.Inst.X. Cf. Gal 2:20.

43 'Conaemdetar sruithe Erenn a riaglaib na screptrae pennatoir dilgind frepthae cech pecthae o bive commór.' OIP.pr.

44 See Ordo Intr.II.6,c. The text is in turn drawing here upon St Paul's exhortation to the Philippians where he explains the Christian orientation as 'forgetting what lies behind and straining forward to what lies ahead.' Phil 3:13.

45 'Sufficit autem pugnantibus adversarios vincere; si teipsum viceris, omnium victor es; si vero tui victor proprius es, tibi mortuus, Deo vivus comprobaris.' Co.Inst.X.

46 'Si enim vere Christi crucem assumpsisset, nihil ei horum licere animadverteret, quia et Christus in hoc exemplum dedit, ut nullus quod suum est quaerat, dicendo, Non sicut ego volo, sed sicut tu vis, et descendi non ut faciam voluntatem meam, sed voluntatem eius qui me misit.' Co.Inst.X. And cf. Jn.6:38.

47 '. . . labor enim et fatigatio in itinere versatur, in patria requies et securitas paratur.' Co.Inst.V.

48 '. . . unusqiusque sic vivere debet quasi cottidie moriatur.' Co.Inst.III.

49 '. . . Quid enim diligentius, quidve abundantius lex Dei mandavit quam dilectionem? . . . Quid dicemus pro excusatione? Numquid possumus dicere, laboriosum est, durum est? Non est labor dilectio; plus suave est, plus medicale est, plus salubre est cordi dilectio.' Co.Inst.XI.

50 '. . . et sic post satisfactionem iudicio sacerdotis iungatur altario' whereas (14) '. . . iii. annis paeniteat . . . et sic culpa illius per sacerdotem abstergatur.' and whereas (15) '. . . vii annis paeniteat . . . et ita dimittatur illa sua culpa et sacerdos oret pro illo, et sic iungatur altario.' Co.B.13–15.

51 See Ordo Intro.II:6,d.

52 'Non intrandum ad altare donec penitentia impleatur.' Vi.53.

53 See Gula, *To Walk*, 209. Gula shares this perspective.

54 'Non absolvendus autem lapsos a fide credamus nisi per inpositionem manus episcopi.' Pa.II,8.

55 '. . . id est unusquisque postquam confessus fuerit vitia et postquam ea subplantaverit et postquam gratia Dei venerit et pater celestis et aecclesia fuerint praesentes ei, tunc sanus in bono opere accipiat sacrificium.' Bi.IV:7.

56 See the basis for this position in Bieler, *Irish Penitentials*, 243 at footnote 6a.

57 '. . . eucharistiam summat, ad pacem veniat, psalmos cum fratribus canat, ne penitus anima tanto tempore caelestis medicinae (ieiuna) intereat.' Gi.1.

58 'Tribus modis separantur iusti ab iniustis: misa mensa pace . . .' Bi.pr.36.

59 See Ordo Intro.II,6. The Ordo in turn, links the image of renewing and sharing at the Lord's table with the parable of the Prodigal Son in Lk 15:11–32.

60 '. . . cum nos nostra peccata vel aliorum contristant.' Bi.V:1,1,2. and '. . . ut pro peccatis gemescamus et pro ignorantia proximorum.' Bi.V:1,5.

61 '. . . pro peccatis primum nostris, deinde pro omni populo christiano, deinde pro sacerdotibus . . . pro elemosinas facientibus, postea pro pace regnum, novissime pro inimicis, ne illis deus statuat in peccatum quod persecuntur et detrahunt nobis, quia 'nesciunt quid faciunt'.' Co.Reg.Mon.VII. and cf. Lk 23:34.

62 'In quo donec sumus in carne positi, ad liquidum puri esse non possumus, nisi octava venerit dies, id est, nisi futuri saeculi tempus advenerit . . .' Bi.pr.21.

63 'Dlegair doaib dano congain cridi 7 cói a pecad 7 tothlugud inna braithre in guidi dé léo conderaigter doib a pectai tria pennait 7 aithrigi.' OIP.ii.5.

64 'Non cessandum est eripere predam ex ore leonis vel draconis, id est de ore diabuli, qui predam nostre anime deripere non desinit, licet in extremo line vite hominis adfectandum (et) nitendum sit.' Vi.34.

65 Ceterum quanti memento meriti tibi est 'peccatorem ab errore convertere viae suae'. Bi.pr.29. and cf. Jas 5:20.

66 '. . . vel vituperatione mali bonique confirmandi obtentu . . .'. Cu.VIII, 16.

67 See note 48 supra.

68 See the excellent assessment of the primitive Irish Church by Albert Mirgeler, *Mutations of Western Christianity* (London: Burns and Oates, 1964), 68.

69 Here again I am indebted to Mirgeler for this perspective. See note 68 supra.

70 Co.B.pr. For Latin text see note 36 supra.

71 '. . . dum et tibi cura in peccata ulciscendi, hoc est medendi animas, sane multiplex est et in eo quod diversa sunt peccata et in discrepantia, ut dixi, virtutum et qualitatum peccantium . . .' Bi.pr.28.

72 See Ordo Intro.III;10,a. The Ordo draws this observation in part from St Paul's words in Philippians 1:9–10 where he prays 'that your love may abound more and more with knowledge and all discernment.'

73 'Sed quia haec paucorum sunt, . . . curare ad integrum salutis statum debilia revocare.' Co.B.pr.

74 'Et haec mensura verae discretionis omnes nostros pondere trutinans iusto actus . . .' Co.Reg.Mon.VIII. And note that for Columbanus 'discretion' and 'discernment' are quasi synonmous, he reasons thus: 'Discretio igitur discernendo nomen accepit eo quod ipsa in nobis discernit inter bona et mala . . .' Co.Reg.Mon.VIII.

75 'Sed hoc in omni paenitentia solerter intuendum est, quanto quis tempore in delictis remaneat, qua eruditione inbutus, qua inpugnatur passione, qualis existat fortitudine, qua videtur adfligi lacrimabilitate, quali compulsus est gravatione peccare.' Cu.ps.1.

76 'Quis enim potest per ignem iustificari et iudicis misericordia non egere, qui in 'corpore peccati' habitat?'Co.Inst.IX. And cf. Rom 6:6.

77 For the best and most reliable account of brehon law see Laurence Ginell, *The Brehon Laws* (Dublin, 1917) 52.

78 See McNeill and Gamer, *Medieval Handbooks*, 191–2, c.5.

79 E. de Bhaldraithe, 'Irish Monastic Rules' *Hallel* (1987): 47–92.

80 'Sacerdos qui offert illud et repropitiavit, erit pro delicto ipsius.' Bi.pr.32 and cf. Lev 19:22.

81 'Qui vero arguit non leniter, notetur donec petat veniam a fratra correpto et plagis XXX aut XV psalmos.' Co.Reg.Coen.XV.

82 See text in Watkins, *A History of Penance*, 598 and cf. Mt 23:4.

83 'Ecce verba filiorum dei, si 'nihil per contentionem', ut ait apostolus 'neque per inanem gloriam sed per humilitatem spiritus alter alterum existimans superiorem sibi.' Co.Reg.Coen.V. Cf. Phil 2:3.

84 For more information regarding the laity within the Irish monastery see Leclerq et al., *Spirituality*, 39–40.

85 See pp 30–36 which deal with the various penitential documents.

86 A.J. Frantzen, *The Literature of Penance in Anglosaxon England* (New Brunswick/ New Jersey: 1983), 32–3.

87 'Dilectio autem vera 'non verbo' est tantum 'sed opere et veritate'. Reddamus itaque Deo nostro, Patri nostro, suam imaginem inviolatam in sanctitate, quia ille sanctus est, iuxta illud, Sancti estote quia ego sanctus sum . . .' Co.Inst.XI. cf. 1 Jn 3:18.

88 'Vide et intellege quam difficile est vinci saeculum, dum non aliter, nisi Christi morte, sanctus de eo liberatur.' Co.Inst.IV.

CHAPTER 5

1 We are thinking in particular here of the sense in which Ricoeur use the term symbol i.e. a sign which entails a double intentionality, one literal and primary the other opaque and latent. See his explanation in Paul Ricoeur, *The Symbolism of Evil* (Boston: Beacon Press, 1969), 10–18 (orig. *La Symbolique du Mal*, Paris:1969).

2 These same paradigms have provided the framework for our discussion of the role of confessor in Ch.4; pp 153–160.

3 Ricoeur, *The Symbolism of Evil* Note: we interchange the terms 'model' and 'paradigm' in this chapter to denote the sub-group of imagery contained within each symbol. Our methodology here has been greatly aided by recourse to similar projects in other theological fields. Two of the most salient of these are: A. Dulles, *Models of the Church* (Dublin: G&M, 1976). and S. McFague, *Models of God* (London: SCM, 1987).

4 The term 'enigma' here is also Ricoeur's. See *Symbolism*, 16.

5 Ricoeur, *Symbolism*, 19.

6 See Dulles' excellent discussion of how best to approach the question of 'models' in theology in: Dulles, *Models of the Church* and in particular ch.1. 'The Use of Models in Ecclesiology', 13–30.

7 See Chapter 1 of this present work and in particular 1.1. 'The Historical Context of Celtic Penance' and 1.2. 'The Irish Monastery and Celtic Penance.'

8 Chapters Two and Three are in fact replete with all three strands of imagery. The very structure of these chapters is based upon the healing model whilst the language of 'merciful judgement' and 'compassion' also finds frequent expression there.

9 See Karl Rahner's illuminating discussion of both the strengths and dangers of the juridical view of penance in K. Rahner, 'Problems Concerning Confession' *Theological Investigations* III (London: DLT), 190–206.

10 But animadversor, of course, is to be understood here in the non-solely punitive sense which outlined already. See p. 157.

11 See Columbanus' thesis that true discernment consists in 'restraining . . . from all excess . . . and everywhere dividing justly between good and evil, whether both in eternal acts or between flesh and spirit in the inner life.' Co.Reg.Mon.VIII.

12 Cf. Co.Reg.Mon.VIII.

13 See the balanced critique of the juridical model of penance with some historical analysis in Dionisio Borobio, 'The Tridentine Model of Confession in its Historical Context' *Concilium* 190 (1987) 21–37.
14 See our discussion supra in 4.7. 'The Penitent'.
15 The best example of this may be found in D.A. Binchy, 'The Old-Irish Table of Commutations', *Ériu* XIX (1962) 47–72. The English translation of same is also contained in an appendix to Bieler, *Irish Penitentials*, 277–83.
16 RP. 29. See also Acts 10:42 and Jn 8:16 which are deemed to form the scriptural basis of this model.
17 Cf. Thomas Aquinas, *Summa Theologiae* I–II q. 72 a. 5. which is also cited in the document.
18 And note the Council of Trent always acknowledged the difference between the divine and human tribunals — through its use of the phrase 'ad instar actus iudicalis'. See RP at footnote 178 and the fuller discussion in Borobio, 'The Tridentine Model' 21–37.
19 A warning against a too-optimistic picture of man which does not take account of the 'dark side of our nature' is presented in Seán Fagan, *Has Sin Changed?* (Dublin: G&M, 1977) reprint 1988, 209–10.
20 See Bieler, *Irish Penitentials*, 46–47 which give some idea of the range and variation of which the medicinal metaphor is capable.
21 For further discussion of the medicinal metaphor and its application to penance see John T. McNeill, 'Medicine for Sin as Prescribed in the Penitentials' *Church History* I (1932) 14–26.
22 The point is well made by Gail Ramshaw-Schmidt who herself has some interesting comments to make about possible paradigms for penance see Ramshaw-Schmidt, 'Sin. One Image of Human Limitation' *Concilium* 190 (1987) 3–10.
23 See Vi.28; Cu.pr.15; Vi.ps. and Co.B.pr.
24 McNeill and Gamer, *Medieval Handbooks*, 46. McNeill, himself a compiler of the penitentials, is one of the first to detect a sympathetic, humanitarian emhasis in these texts. The position has subsequently been developed by Payer, Frantzen, Power and Billy among others.
25 As the reader will have already observed these three 'scientific principles' have, in essence, formed the framework of our textual analysis in Chapters 2 and 3.
26 See D. O'Laoghaire, 'Traditions of Spiritual Guidance: Soul Friendship' *The Way* 25 (1985) 157. The case for re-discovering and re-implementing the 'principle of contraries' is well argued here.
27 The dangers of this misrepresentation of sin and repentance from a theological perspective are catalogued and discussed in Rahner, 'Guilt and its Remission: The Borderland between Theology and Psychotherapy' *T.I.* II 135–74.
28 The dangers of such a concept of sin from a medical perspective are extensively discussed in Karl Menninger, *Whatever became of Sin?* (New York: Hawthorn, 1973), 187.
29 This inherent strength of the penitentials is set forth and discussed at some length in: David N. Power, 'The Sacramentalization of Penance' *Heythrop Journal* XVIII (1977) 10–12.

30 See K. Demmer, *Christi Vestigia Sequentes* (Roma: PUG, 1988), 220–23 which gives a good overview of the casuistry question — though not specifically of the Celtic penitential literature. And for the entire treatment of the casuist question I am indebted to the reflections of Demmer on this subject.

31 See Servais Pinckaers, *Les sources de la morale chrétienne* (Fribourg: Editions Universitaires, 1985), 280–1.

32 That is — not alone spiritual chaos but also social disorder. For one can hardly understand the penitential enterprise of Celtic Ireland without at least acknowledging the relation between the Church and public order in general. See Brundage, *Law, Sex and Christian Society*, 169.

33 RP 29 And see also Lk 5:31ff. which the document cites as the scriptural basis for this model.

34 In particular the document RP at 31:II refers to Lk 5:31f, Lk 9:2 and Is 53:4f. as biblical grounds as well as to Augustines *Sermons* especially 82 and 352 as patristic evidence.

35 Cf. RP 31:III and Co.B.pr. Note the message of these two texts is almost identical in the emphasis upon the confessor's need in his role as healer to know the condition of the penitent.

36 An increasing awareness is coming about in the medical world of the parallels between sin and disease; for an interesting exposition of the subject from the medical perspective see Selward Hiltner, 'Christian Understanding of Sin in the Light of Medicine and Psychiatry' *Medical Arts and Sciences* 35 (1966).

37 The best survey of the pilgrimage model and its scriptural roots, in my view, and one which has greatly helped to clarify my thoughts on this matter is that of C. Spicq. *Vida Cristiana y Peregrinación según el Nuevo Testamento* (Madrid: Autores Cristianos, 1977) orig. (*Vie Chrétienne et pérégrination selon le Nouveau Testament*, Paris: Ed. du Cerf, 1972).

38 '. . . ita etiam ab interioribus vitiis et morbis languentis animae abstinendum est ac abstergendum ante verae pacis coniunctionem et aeternae salutis conpaginem.'

39 See our discussion of these values in 1.3 supra.

40 An interesting assessment of the model may be found in Power, 'Confession as Ongoing Conversion' *Heythrop Journal* XVIII (1977) 180–90. Although we should note here that Power's understanding of 'passage' is slightly different to the one which I have presented here.

41 The image is 'coined' by Konrad Baumgartner in his article 'The Process of Conversion and its Ministries' *Concilium* 190 (1987) 41.

42 For a discussion of how asceticism may still be seen as a valid enterprise for contemporary Christians, as well as a survey of some historical expressions of same see K. Rahner, 'The Passion and Asceticism' (Thoughts on the theological basis of Christian asceticism) *T.I.* III 58–85.

43 See Haltigar's 'Instruction to Confessors': 'Nobody can help the man who has fallen beneath a burden, unless bowing down he gives them a hand; no doctor can heal wounds, if he is afraid of infection. Likewise, no priest or bishop can heal the wounds from which a sinner suffers, or take away the sin, if he does not suffer and pray and weep with him.' in C. Vogel, *Le Pécheur et la Pénitence au Moyen Age* (Paris: du Cerf, 1969), 51–2.

44 See Rahner's discussion of these concepts in Rahner, 'The Passion' 70–80.

45 This depiction of the whole Church as, in some sense, fellow-sufferer with Christ is set forth comprehensively in Rahner, 'The Sinful Church in the Decrees of Vatican II' *T.I.* VI. 281 ff.

46 See also here a similar enterprise and similar conclusions by Neville who outlines three ikons for philosophers in Robert C.Neville, *Soldier, Sage and Saint* (New York; Fordham Univ. Press, 1978).

47 See Rahner, 'The Passion' 63.

48 For instance: W Godel, 'Irisches Beten in frühen Mittelalter' *Zeitschrift für Katolische Theologie* 85(1963) 61–321 and 389–439.

49 On the question of Pelagius see Bradshaw, 'Wild and Woolly' 10. In fact, I believe, a fuller treatment of Celtic theology could argue cogently and convincingly for an account of nature, sin and redemption which would be quite orthodox. See a similar view in J. Mackey, *An Introduction to Celtic Christianity*, 17–19. And in the same work M. Forthomme Nicholson, 'Celtic Theology and Pelagius' 386–413.

50 See Bitel, 'Sex, Sin and Celibacy' 84–5. Bitel outlines and develops the approach which I have presented here.

51 One of the best examples of this practice may be seen in D. Binchy, 'The Old Irish Table'. See note 15 supra. And see also Hughes, *Sources*, 82–9.

52 For a comprehensive account of the expressions and emphases which this theorem has taken over the years see I. Fucek, *Il Peccato Oggi: Riflessione Teologico-Morale* (Roma: PUG, 1991), 174–89.

53 'Duret igitur apud nos ista definitio, ut sic vivamus in via ut viatores ut peregrini, ut hospites mundi, nullis haerentes cupiditatibus, nullis terrenis inhiantes desideriis, sed caelestibus et spiritalibus formis animos nostros repleamus.' Co.Inst.VIII.

54 'Ne simus alienae imaginis pictores . . . Pietas enim et impietas pax, et discordia, contraria sibi sunt. Ne forte itaque nobis tyrannicas introducamus imagines, Christus in nobis suam pingat imaginem.' Co.Inst.XI.

55 'Tempus enim hoc tempus belli est; ideo enim nemo putet securitatem in bello . . .' Co.Inst.X.

56 'Laqueus tibi tua vita, irretiris, velis nolis; in te habes quo compediris, in te non habes quo solveris.' Co.Inst.III.

57 'Dei enim dilectio imaginis eius renovatio. Deum autem diliget qui eius mandata custodit . . . Dilectio autem vera Non Verbo est tantum, sed opere et veritate.' Co.Inst.XI.

58 See Co.B.pr; Da.10; Vi.29; and Co.B.30.

59 'Sciendum est tamen quod quanto quis tempore moratur in peccatis tanto ei augenda penitentia est.'

60 Karl Rahner, 'The Sinful Church' *T.I.* VI 281. This article together with Rahner, 'The Pilgrim Church' *T.I.* VI provide a rich commentary on how a modern theology might understand both the shortcomings and the pilgrim character of the Church.

61 All these citations are taken from RP 4.

62 Cf. Elizabeth Lear, *Journal et pensées de chaque jour* (Paris:1918), 31. This source is indicated by the document.
63 The document cites the following scriptural basis for these understandings of the forgiving Christ: (a) Brother of man — Mt 12:49f; Mk 3:33f; Lk 8:20f; Rom 8:29. (b) The Good Shepherd — Mt 18:12f and Lk 15:4–6.
64 See Donal Murray, *Life and Sacrament: Reflections on the Catholic Vision*, (Delaware: Michael Glazier, 1983), 79.
65 Ibid. 52–3.
66 See René Latourelle, *Man and his Problems in the Light of Jesus Christ* (New York: Alba, 1982) (orig. *L'homme et ses problèmes dans la lumière du Christ*).
67 See a good analysis of this political shift later applied to the sacrament of penance in Gian Angelo Palo, 'Problematiche socio-culturale a riguardo del sacramento della Penitenza' in AA.VV., *La Crisi della Confessione* (Bologna: EDB, 1974).
68 Latourelle, *Man and his Problems*, 375.
69 See James P. Mackey, 'The Idea of Sin in the Modern World' in Denis O'Callaghan (ed.) *Sin and Repentance* (Dublin: Gill and Son, 1967), 66.
70 See Daniel Maguire, *The Moral Choice* (Minneapolis: Winston Press, 1979), esp. Chapters 1 and 2 for a good account of the demise of ethical systems. See also Macintyre, *After Virtue* for a similar critique from a different perspective.
71 For a good account of the modern 'paradox' see Adrien Nocent, *Le Sacrement de la Réconciliation dans l'Eglise de l'Occident* (Rome: S. Anselme, 1972), 5–7.
72 See the survey of the anthropological question in International Theological Commission Report 'Penance and Reconciliation' *Origins* 13 (1984) 31, 516.
73 Latourelle, *Man and his Problems*, 4.
74 See Avery Dulles, *Models of the Church*, 48f for a good discussion of this paradigm.
75 The point is well made in Palo, 'Problematiche' 28–30.
76 Sean Fagan, *Has Sin Changed?*, 64.
77 K Demmer, *Medicina Salutis: Appunti per la pastorale del Sacramento della riconciliazione* (Roma: P.U.G. 1987), 8–9.
78 Dulles, *Models of the Church*, 153.
79 I.T.C. *Penance and Reconciliation* 5.
80 See Leech, *Soul Friend*, 207.
81 Kevin Irwin 'The Good News of Repentance and Conversion' in Michael J. Henchal (ed.) *Repentance and Reconciliation in the Church* (Collegeville: Liturgical Press, 1987).
82 See Demmer *Interpretare e Agire: Fondamenti della Morale Cristiana* (Roma: Paoline, 1989) 228–229 (orig: *Deuten und handeln Grundlagen und Grundfragen der Fundamentalmoral*: Freiburg: Herder, 1985).
83 Gula, *To Walk*, 237.
84 For an excellent account of how the quality of 'hospitality' might be put to good use by the contemporary confessor see Gula, *To Walk*, 229–237.
85 Hellwig, *Sign*, 136.
86 Gula, *To Walk*, 244–245.
87 See Demmer, *Interpretare*, 229.

88 See Paul VI, *Poenitemini*, 1966, 180.

89 I believe it is precisely this 'bodily' component, for example, which is responsible for the popularity of pilgrimage to Lough Derg, Croagh Patrick and such like among young Irish people today.

90 Irwin 'The Good News' 42.

91 Cf. Rev 19:5–9.

92 See Marliangeas, *Réconciliation Aujourd'hui* 126 for further development of these pastoral and liturgical proposals.

93 See our discussion of these Celtic concepts in chapter II, in the section 'Anger: the symptoms'.

94 Cf. I.T.C. *Penance and Reconciliation*, 524.

95 Leech, *Soul Friend*, 209.

96 Kennedy, *A Sense*, 180.

BIBLIOGRAPHY

PRIMARY SOURCES

Anderson, A. and M. Anderson. eds. *Adamnan: Vita Sancti Colombae*, London, 1905.

Bieler, Ludwig. ed. *The Irish Penitentials*. Scriptores Latini Hiberniae, Dublin: Institute for Advanced Studies, 1963.

——, ed., 'The Old-Irish Table of Penitential Commutations' *Ériu* XIX (1962): 47–72.

——, ed., *The Works of St. Patrick and Hymn on St. Patrick by St. Secundinus*. Ancient Christian Writers, no.17. Westminster Md.: Newman Press, 1953.

Binchy, Daniel A., ed., 'Bretha Cróilge,' *Ériu*, XII (1934): 1–7.

de Bhaldraithe, E. ed. 'Irish Monastic Rules' *Hallel* (1987): 47–92.

de Vogüé, A., ed., *Jonas de Bobbio: Vie de Saint Colomban et de Ses Disciples*. Abbaye de Bellefontaine: Vie Monastique, 1988.

—— *Saint Colomban: Règles Et Pénitentiels Monastiques*. Abbaye de Bellefontaine: Vie Monastique, 1989.

Finsterwalder, P.W., ed., *Die Canones Theodori Cantuariensis und lhre Überlieferungsformen*. Weimar: 1929.

Gwynn, E.J., ed., 'An Irish Penitential' *Ériu* vii (1944): 121–95.

Haddan A.W., and W. Stubbs., eds., Councils and Ecclesiastical Documents Relating to Great Britain and Ireland. 3 vols in 4, Oxford: 1869–81.

Krusch, B., ed., *Jonas: Vita Sancti Colombani*. Leipzig: Neueus-Studien zur Christlich-Mittelalterlichen Chronologie, 1880.

Laporte, J., ed., *Le Pénitentiel de Saint Colomban. Introduction et Edition Critique*. Tournai: 1958.

Lawlor, H.J., ed., *The Manuscripts of the Vita S. Columbani*. (Trans. Roy) Dublin: Royal Irish Academy, xxxii, Sect.c. 1903.

Meehan, D., ed., *Adamnan: De Locis Sanctis*. Dublin: Dublin Institute for Advanced Studies, 1958.

Migne, ed., *Patrologie Cursus Completus; Series Latina*; 217 vols. including a large part of the poetic, epistolary, historical, philosophical and patristic Latin literature of the 1,000 years from Tertullian (d. 240) to Innocent III (d. 1216), Paris, 1844–55; with four vols. of Indices, 1862–4.

McNeill, J.T., and H.M. Gamer., eds., *Medieval Handbooks of Penance*. A translation of the principal libri poenitentiales and selections from related documents. Records of Civilization, Sources and Studies 29, New York: 1938.

Schmitz, H.J., ed., *Die Bussbücher und die Bussdisziplin der Kirche*. Mainz: 1883; repr. 1958.

—— *Die Bussbücher und das kanonische Bussverfahren*. Düsseldorf: 1898; repr. 1958.

Stokes, Whitley and Strachan, eds., *Thesaurus Paeleohibernicus: A Collection of Old-Irish Glosses, Scholia, Prose and Verse*. Cambridge: 1901–3.

Strachan, J., ed., *Félire Oengusso Céili Dé: The Martyrology of Oengus the Culdee*. London: Henry Bradshaw Society, 1905.

Vogel, C., ed., *Les 'Libri Paenitentiales'*. Turnhout: Typologie des sources du moyen âge occidental, 1978.

—— and Frantzen, A., eds., *Les 'Libri Paenitentiales' mise à jour*, Fesicule 27, Turnhout, 1985.

Walker, G., ed., *Sancti Colombani Opera*. Scriptores Latini Hiberniae 2, Dublin: Dublin Institute for Advanced Studies, 1967.

Wasserschleben, H., ed., *Die Bussordnungen der abendlandischen Kirche*. Halle, 1851.

Williams, Hugh, ed., *Gildae 'De excidio Brittaniae,' Fragmenta, 'Liber de Poenitentia,' accedit et 'Lorica Gildae'*. (Gildas, The Ruin of Britain, fragments from lost letters, the Penitential, together with the *Lorica of Gildas*.) 2 vols. Published for the Honourable Society of Cymmrodorion. London: Nutt, 1899–1901.

SECONDARY SOURCES

(A) Books

Adamson, I., *Bangor, Light of the World*. Belfast: Pretani Press, 1979.

Adnès, Pierre, *La Penitencia*. Madrid: La Editorial Católica, 1981.

Aridas, Chris, *Reconciliation: Celebrating God's Healing Forgiveness*. New York: Doubleday and Co., 1987.

Bellesheim, A., *Geschichte der katolische Kirche in Irland*, 3 vols. Mayence, 1883–91.

Best, Richard I., *Bibliography of Irish Philology and of Printed Irish Literature*. Dublin: National Library of Ireland, 1913.

Bieler, L., *Ireland, Harbinger of the Middle Ages*. London and New York: Oxford University Press, 1963.

Bischoff, B., *Mittelalterliche Studien 1*. Stuttgart, 1966.

Blanke, Fritz, *Columbanus und Gallus: Uhrgeschichte des Schweizerischen Christentums*. Zurich: Fretz and Wamuth, 1940.

Bourke, E., *Histoire de la Pénitence Sacrement*. Quebec, 1947.

Browe, P., *Beiträge zur Sexualethik des Mittelalters*. Breslau, 1932.

Brundage, James A., *Law Sex, and Christian Society in Medieval Europe*. Chicago: University of Chicago Press, 1987.

Bulloch, James, *The Life of the Celtic Church*. Edinburgh: St. Andrew Press, 1963.

Bullough, V. and J. Brundage, *Sexual Practices and the Medieval Church*. Buffalo, NY: Prometheus, 1982.

Byrne, F.J., *Irish Kings and High Kings*. London: Batsford, 1973.

Carmichael, A., *Carmina Gadelica*. 6 vols. Edinburgh, 1928.

Chadwick, N., The Age of the Saints in the Early Celtic Church. Oxford: University Press, 1961.

——, ed., *Studies in the Early British Church*. Cambridge: University Press, 1968.

——, ed., *Studies in Early British History*, Cambridge: University Press, 1954.

Chadwick, O. *John Cassian. A Study in Primitive Monasticism*. Cambridge: University Press, 1950.

Cereti, Giovanni, *Divorzio, Nuove Nozze e Penitenza nella Chiesa Primitiva*. Bologna: EDB, 1977.

Colgan, John, *Acta Sanctorum veteris et majoris Scotiae seu Hiberniae sanctorum insulae*. Lovanii, 1645.

——, 'De Monasteriis Hibernorum in exteras gentes' Fragment of Summary, ed. C. MacDonnell, *Proceedings Royal Irish Academy*, Vol. VI, 1853–57.

——, *Triadis Thaumaturgae seu divorum Patricii, Columbaae et Brigidae, Lovanii, 1647.*

Concannon, H., *The Life of St Columban, A Study Of Ancient Irish Monastic Life*. Dublin: 1915.

Corish, Patrick J., *A History of Irish Catholicism*. Vol.1, *St Patrick and the Coming of Christianity*, by Ludwig Bieler. Dublin: Gill and Son, 1967.

Daniel-Rops, *Le Miracle Irlandais*. Tournai: Laffont, 1958.

Delaney, Frank, *The Celts*. London: Grafton, 1986.

Delius, W., *Geschichte der irischen Kirche von ihren Anfangen bis zum 12 Jahrhundert*. Munich/Bale, 1974.

Della Torre, L., *Conversione e Riconciliazione nella Prassi della Chiesa*. Roma: Edizione Paoline, 1983.

Demmer, K., *Medicina Salutis. Appunti per la pastorale del Sacramento della riconciliazione*. Roma: Editrice P.U.G., 1987.

——, *Christi vestigia sequentes. Appunti di Teologia Morale Fundamentale*. Roma: P.U.G.,1988.

——, *Interpretare e agire. Fondamenti della morale cristiana*. Balsamo: Paoline, 1989. (orig. *Deuten und handeln. Grundlagen und Grundfragen der Fundamentalmoral*, 1985).

De Paor, Maire and Liam, *Early Christian Ireland*. London: Thames and Hudson, 1958.

Dillon, Myles and Nora Chadwick, *The Celtic Realms*. London: Weidenfeld and Nicholoson, 1967.

Dottin, G., *Les Littératures Celtiques*. Paris: Payot, 1924.

Duffy, J., *Patrick in His Own Words*. Dublin: Veritas, 1975.

Esposito, M., *Latin Learning in Medieval Ireland*. (trans. M. Lapidge; Collected Studies Series. Vol. 285), Aldershot: Variorum, 1988.

——, *Irish Books and learning in Medieval Europe*. (Ed.) M. Lapidge (Collected Studies Series. Vol. 1313), Aldershot: Variorum, 1990.

Fagan, Sean, *Has Sin Changed?. A Book On Forgiveness*. Dublin: Gill and Macmillan, 1977.

Favezza, Joseph A., *The Order of Penitents: Historical Roots and Pastoral Future*. Collegeville: The Liturgical Press, 1988.

Flandrin, J., *Les Amours Paysannes: Amour et Sexualité dans les Compagnes de L'Ancien France (XVI–XIXe Siècles)*. Paris: Gallimard/Juilliard, 1975.

——, *Le Sexe et L'Occident*. Paris: Editions du Seuil, 1981.

——, *Un Temps pour Embrasser: Aux Origines de la Morale Sexuelle Occidentale (VIe–XIe sicle)*. Paris: Editions du Seuil, 1981.

Flower, Robin, *The Irish Tradition*. Oxford: Clarendon Press, 1947.

Forshaw, H.P., *The Pastoral Ministry of the Priest-Confessor in the Early Middle Ages, 600–1100*. A study of the origin and development of the role of the priest-confessor in the administration of private ecclesiastical penance in the West. London: 1975.

Frantzen, A., *The Literature of Penance in Anglo-Saxon England*. New Brunswick: 1983.

Fucek, Ivan, *Il Peccato Oggi. Riflessione Teologico-Morale*. Roma: Editrice P.U.G., 1991.

Fuhrmann, Joseph P., *Irish Medieval Monasteries on the Continent*. Washington: Catholic University of America, 1927.

Geyer, Paul, *Adamnanus, Abt von Iona*. (Programm zu dem Jahresbericht des Gynasiums St-Anna in Augsburg), Augsburg, 1895.

González, C.P., *Doctrina de S. Augustín sobre la malicia del aborto y su influencia en la disciplina penitencial de la Edad Media*, Salamanca : 1959.

González Rivas, S., *La Penitencia en la Primitiva Iglesia Española*. Salamanca: Instituto San Raimundo de PeÒafort, 1949.

Gougaud, Louis, *Chrétientés Celtiques*. Paris: 1911.

—— *Gaelic Pioneers of Christianity. The Work and Influence of Irish Monks and Saints in Continental Europe (VI–XII. Cent.)*, Dublin: Gill and Son, 1923.

—— *Dévotions et Pratiques Ascétiques au Moyen Age*. Paris, 1925.

Gwynn, Aubrey and R.N. Hadcock *Medieval Religious Houses: Ireland*. with an appendix on early sites, London: Longmans, 1970; reprint Dublin: Irish Academic Press: 1988.

Gula, Richard M., *To Walk Together Again. The Sacrament of Reconciliation*. New York / Ramsey: Paulist Press, 1984.

Halligan, Nicholas, *Sacraments of Reconciliation: Vol. II Penance, Anointing of the Sick*. New York: Alba House,1973.

Hanson, R.P.C., *St. Patrick, His Origins and Career*. Oxford: Clarendon Press, 1968.

Häring, Bernard, *The Sacrament of Reconciliation*. Slough: Saint Paul Publications, 1980, reprint, 1987.

Healy, S., *Soundings in Irish Spirituality*. Dublin: Carmelite Centre of Spirituality, 1983.

Hellwig, Monika K., *Sign of Reconciliation and Conversion: The Sacrament of Penance for Our Times*. Delaware: Michael Glazier, 1982.

Henchal, Michael J., ed., *Repentance and Reconciliation in the Church*. Collegeville: The Liturgical Press, 1987.

Hughes, Kathleen, *Early Christian Ireland: Introduction to the Sources*. The Sources of History: Studies in the Use of Historical Evidence, London: Hodder and Stoughton, 1972.

——, *The Church in Early Irish Society*, London: Methuen, 1966.

——, and A. Hamlin., *Celtic Monasticism: The Modern Traveller to the Early Irish Church*. New York: Seabury, 1981.

Joyce, P.W., *A Social History of Ancient Ireland*. 2 vols. Dublin and Melbourne: Gill and Son, 1920.

Kelsey, Morton T., *Healing and Christianity in Ancient Thought and Modern Times*. New York: Harper and Row, 1973.

Kennedy, E., *A Sense of Life, A Sense of Sin*. New York: Image Books, 1976.

Kenney, James F., *The Sources for the Early History of Ireland. An Introduction and Guide*. Vol. One. Ecclesiastical, New York: Columbia University Press, 1929; reprint Dublin: Four Courts Press 1993.

Lapidge and Sharpe, *A Celtic-Latin Bibliography, A.D. 600*. Dublin, 1985.

Laurentin, R., *Bilan du Concile. Histoire, Textes, Commentaires avec une chronique de la quatrième session*. Paris: 1966.

Laux, J.J., *Der hl. Kolumban, sein Leben und seine Schriften*. Freiburg, 1919.

Leask, Harold L., *Irish Churches and Monastic Buildings*. Dundalk: Dundealgan Press, 1953, reprint, 1960.

Le Bras, G., *Institutions Ecclésiastiques de la Chrétienté Médiévale*. Paris: Bloud et Gay, 1959.

Leclerq, Vadenbrouke and Bouyer, *The Spirituality of the Middle Ages*. Series: A History of Christian Spirituality, London: Burns and Oates, 1968.

Leduc, R., *L'Eglise et la Sexualité d'après les Pénitentiels*. Lille, 1980.

Leech, K., *Soul Friend: A Study of Spirituality*. London: Sheldon, 1977.

Lejeune, R., *Jeûner guérison et fite du corps et de l'esprit*. Hauteville: Editions Du Parvis, 1988.

Lobo, George B., *Renewal of the Sacrament of Reconciliation*. Bangalore: Asian Trading Corporation, 1981.

Loewe, H., ed., *Die Iren und Europa in früheren Mittelalter*. Stuttgart, 1982.

Macintyre, Alasdair, *After Virtue: A Study in Moral Theory*. London: Duckworth, 1981.

Mackey, J.P., ed., *An Introduction to Celtic Christianity*. Edinburgh: T&T Clark, 1989.

MacNeill, Eoin, *Phases of Irish History*. ed. John Ryan, Dublin Clonmore and Reynolds; London: Burns and Oates, 1964.

Macquarrie, J., *Pathways in Spirituality*. London: S.C.M. 1973.

Maher, Michael, ed., *Irish Spirituality*. Dublin: Veritas, 1981.

Manselli, R., 'Il matrimonio nei penitenziali.' *Il matrimonio nella società altomedievale*, Settimane di studio del centro italiano di studi sull'alto medievo 24. 287–315. Spoleto:1977.

Marlangeas, B., *Réconciliation Aujourd'hui, Perspectives théologiques et pastorales*. Paris: Editions Ouvrières, 1989.

McCone, K., *Pagan Past and Christian Present in Early Irish Literature*. Maynooth: An Sagart, 1990.

McNeill, John T., *The Celtic Penitentials and Their Influence on Continental Christianity*. Paris: 1923.

——, *A History of the Cure of Souls*. New York: Harper and Row, 1977.

——, *The Celtic Churches; A History A.D. 200–1200*. Chicago: University of Chicago Press, 1974.

Mélanges Colombaniens Actes du Congrès international de Luxeuil 20–23 Juillet, 1950, Paris : Editions Alsatia, 1951.

Mellet, M., *La Pénitence, Sacrement d'Amitié*. Bruxelles: Pensée Catholique, 1961.

Menninger, Karl, *Whatever Became of Sin?* New York: Hawthorn Books, 1973.

Meyer, Kuno, *Learning in Ireland in the Fifth Century and the Transmission of Letters*. Dublin: Dublin Institute of Advanced Studies, 1961.

Mick, Lawrence E., *Penance: The Once and Future Sacrament*. Collegeville: The Liturgical Press, 1987.

Mirgeler, A., *Mutations of Western Christianity*. London: Burns and Oates, 1964. (Orig. *Rückblick auf das abenländische Christentum* Matthias Grünewald Verlag, Mainz, 1961).

Mortimer, R.C., *The Origins of Private Penance*. Oxford: University Press, 1939.

Murray, Donal, *Life and Sacrament. Reflections on the Catholic Vision*. Delaware: Michael Glazier, 1983.

Muzzarelli, M., *Una Componente della Mentalità Occidentale: I Penitenziali Nell'Alto Medio Evo*. Bologna: Mondo Medievale, 1980.

Ní Chatháin, and Richter, eds., *Irland und Europa die Kirche im Frühmittelalter*. Stuttgart: Klett-Cotta, 1984.

Nocent, Adrien, *Le Sacrement de la Réconciliation dans l'Eglise d'Occident*. Rome: Institut Pontifical De Liturgie S. Anselme, 1972.

O'Callaghan, Denis, ed., *Sin and Repentance*. Dublin: Gill and Son, 1967.

Ó Corráin, Breathnach and McCone, *Sages, Saints and Storytellers, Celtic Studies in Honour of Professor James Carney*. Maynooth: An Sagart, 1989.

O'Donoghue, Noel, Dermot, *Aristocracy of Soul: Patrick of Ireland*. London: Darton Longman and Todd, 1987.

O'Dwyer, P., *Céili Dé: Spiritual Reform in Ireland 750–900*, Dublin: 1981.

O'Rahilly, Thomas F., *Early Irish History and Mythology*. Dublin: Dublin Institute of Advanced Studies, 1946.

O'Riordán, J.J., ed., *Irish Catholics: Tradition and Transistion*. Dublin: Veritas 1980.

Orsy, L., *The Evolving Church and the Sacrament of Penance*. New Jersey: Dimension Books, 1978.

Payer, P., *Sex and the Penitentials*. Toronto: University Press, 1984.

Peschke, C.H., *Christian Ethics*. II. Dublin: Goodliffe and Neale, 1978.

Picasso, Piana, and Motta, *A Pane e Acqua: Peccati e Penitenze nel Medioevo*. Novara: Europa, 1986.

Pinckaers, Servais, *Les sources de la morale chrétienne. Sa méthode, son contenu, son histoire*. Fribourg : Ed. Universitaires, 1985.

Plummer, Charles, *Vitae Sanctorum Hiberniae*. 2 vols, Oxford: Clarendon Press, 1910.

——. *Irish Litanies*. London: Henry Bradshaw Society, 1925.

Pochin Mould, Daphne, *The Irish Saints*. Dublin: Clonmore and Reynolds, 1964.

Poschmann, B., *Penance and the Anointing of the Sick*. trans. rev. F. Courtney, New York: 1964.

Powell, Thomas, *The Celts*. London: Thames and Hudson, 1958.

Ramos-Regidor, J., *El Sacramento de la Penitencia; Reflexión teológica a la Luz de la Biblia, la Historia y la Pastoral*. Salamanca, Ed. Sígueme, 1975.

Quasten, J., *Patrology*. 3 vols. Maryland: Newman Press, 1963.

Rossi, Leandro et al., *La Crisi della Confessione*. Bologna: EDB, 1974.

Richter, M., *Medieval Ireland, the Enduring Tradition*, Dublin: Gill and Macmillan, 1988.

Ricoeur, Paul, *Finitude et Culpabilité*. 2 vols. Paris: Aubier, 1960.

——, *Le Conflit des Interpretations. Essais d'ermeneutique*. Paris: Gallimard, 1969.

Ryan, John, *Irish Monasticism: Origins and Early Development*. Dublin: The Talbot Press, 1931; reprint Dublin: Four Courts Press, 1933.

——, ed., *Irish Monks in the Golden Age*. Dublin: Clonmore and Reynolds, 1963; London: Burns and Oates, 1964.

——, ed., *Essays and Studies Presented to Professor Eoin MacNeill . . .* 1938. Dublin: The Sign of the Three Candles, 1940.

——, *Ireland from the earliest times to A.D. 800*. Dublin: Browne and Nolan.

——, *The Monastic Institute*. Dublin: Gill and Macmillan, 1972.

Seebass, Otto, *Über Columba von Luxeils Klosterregal und Bussbüch*. Dresden: 1883

Sesboüé, B., *Riconciliati in Cristo*. Brescia: Queriniana, 1990.
Skene, W.F., *Celtic Scotland*. Edinburgh: 1877.
——, *Chronicles of the Picts, Chronicles of the Scots and Other Early Memorials of Scottish History*. Edinburgh: 1867.
Tentler, T., *Sin and Confession on the Eve of the Reformation*. Princeton: Princeton University Press, 1977.
Teetaert, A., *La Confession aux laïques dans l'Église latine depuis le 8e jusqu'au 14e siècle*. Wettern: De Meester, 1926.
Tierney, Clement, *The Sacrament of Repentance and Reconciliation*. Dublin: Dominican Publications, 1983.
Vogel, C., *Le Pécheur et la Pénitence au Moyen Age*. Paris: Pastorale du Péché, 1961.
Watkins, Oscar D. *A History of Penance, being a Study of Authorities for the Whole Church to A.D. 450, for the Western Church from A.D. 450 to A.D. 1215*. 2 vols. London and New York: Longmans, Green and Co., 1920.
Watt, J.A. et al., eds., *Medieval Studies Presented to Aubrey Gwynn*. Dublin: O'Lochlainn, 1961.
——, *The Church and the two nations in medieval Ireland. Dublin, 1972.*
——, *The Church in medieval Ireland. Dublin 1972.*
——, ed. *The Churches, Ireland and the Irish*. London: Blackwells, 1988.
Weatherhead, D., *Psychology, Religion and Healing*. New York/Abingdon: Cokesbury Press, 1930.
Whitaker, McKetterich, and Dumville, 'Ireland in early medieval Europe.' *Studies in Memory of Kathleen Hughes*, Cambridge, 1982.
Wilson, A., *Pardon and Peace*. London /New York: Sheed and Ward, 1961.
Zöckler, *Askese und Mönchtum*, Frankfurt, 1897.

(B) Articles

Amann, E., 'Pénitence-Sacrement II. La pénitence privée; son organisation, premières spéculations à son sujet.' *DTC* 12 (1933) : 845–948.
Baumgartner, Konrad, 'The Process of Conversion and its Ministries.' *Concilium* 190 (1987) : 41–51.
Bieler, L., 'The Irish Penitentials, Their Religious and Social Background.' *Studia Patristica* 82 (1966): 329–39.
Billy, D., 'The Penitentials and 'The Making of Moral Theology'.' *Studia Moralia* 28 (1990): 143–51.
Binchy, D., 'Patrick and His Biographers, Ancient and Modern.' *Studia Hibernica* 2 (1962): 7–173.
Bonet-Maury, G., 'Columban et la fondation des Monastères Irlandais en Brie au VII siècle.' *Revue Historique* LXXXIII (1903): 277–99.
Callewaert, R.S., 'Les pénitentiels du moyen âge et les pratiques anticonceptionelles.' *La Vie Spirituelle. Supplément* 18 (1965): 339–66.
Cambiaso, D., 'San Colombano sua opera e suo culto in Liguria.' *Rivista Diocesana Genovese* VI (1916).
Clancy, Finbarr, 'The Irish Penitentials.' *Milltown Studies* 21 (1988): 87–109.
Debarge, L., 'Le Syncrétisme Religieux: Druidisme et Christianisme.' *MSR* 46 (1989): 5–21.

De Bhaldraithe, E., 'Obedience: The Doctrine of the Irish Monastic Rules.' *Monastic Studies* 14 (1981): 63–81.

De Clerc, B., 'Célébrer la pénitence, ou la réconciliation? Essai de discernement théologique à propos du nouveau rituel.' *Revue Théologique de Louvain* 13 (1982): 387–424.

Díaz y Díaz, 'Para un estudio de los penitenciales hispanos.' *Mélanges offerts à Edmond-René Labande, Etudes de Civilisation Médiévale (IXe–XIIe siècles)*, 217–22, Poitiers, 1974.

Dooley, Kate, 'From Penance to Confession.' *Bijdragen* 43 (1982): 390–411.

——. 'Development of the Practice of Devotional Confession.' *Questions Liturgiques* 64 (1983): 89–117.

Esposito, Mario, 'A bibliography of the Latin writers of medieval Ireland.' *Studies* II (1913).

Fahey, P., 'Reconciliation: Retrospect and Prospect.' *Angelicum* 62 (1985): 168–93.

Fournier, P., 'De l'influence de la collection irlandaise sur la formation des collection canoniques.' *NRHDFE* 23 (1899): 27–78.

——, 'Etudes sur les pénitentiels.' *RHLR* 6 (1901): 289–317; 7 (1902): 59–70, 121–27; 8 (1903): 528–53; 9 (1904): 97–103.

Frantzen, A., 'The Significance of the Frankish penitentials.' *JEH* 30 (1979): 409–21.

Fuchs, E., 'Confession du péché et responsabilité éthique' *Lumière et Vie* 185 (1987): 31–40.

Galtier, Pierre, 'Les Origines de la Pénitence Irlandaise.' *Recherche des Sciences Religieuses* 42 (1954): 58–85 and 204–25.

Gervais, P., 'Le Sacrement de la réconciliation selon le Nouveau Rituel.' *Nouvelle Revue Théologique* 112 (1980): 879–99.

Gougaud, Louis, 'Les conceptions du martyre chez les Irlandais.' *Revue Bénédictine* (1907).

——, 'Inventaire des Règles Monastiques Irlandaises.' *Revue Bénédictine* XXV (1908): 167–84, 321–33.

——, 'L'oeuvre des Scotti dans l'Europe Continentale.' *Revue d'Histoire Ecclesiastique* IX (1908): 21–37 and 255–77.

Hauck, A., 'Über die sogenannten Instructiones Columbani.' *Zeitschrift für Kirchliche Wissenschaft* VI (1885).

Hertel, 'Über des h. Columba Leben und Schriften.' *Zeitschrift für Historische Theologie* (1875).

Hughes, D., 'From Brideprice to Dowry in Mediterranean Europe.' *Journal of Family History* 3 (1978): 262–96.

Lahache, J., 'Pénitentiels.' *Dictionnaire de Droit Canonique* VI col. 1337–43 Paris, 1957.

Le Bras, G., 'Pénitentiels.' *DTC* 12 1160–79.

Leclerq, H., 'Pénitentiels.' *DACL* 14 (1939): 215–51.

Ledoyen, H., 'Saint Basile dans la tradition monastique occidentale.' *Irénikon* 53 (1980): 30–45.

Levison, Wilhelm, 'Die Iren und die Frankische Kirche.' *Historische Zeitschrift* 109 (1912): 1–22.

Lorenzetti, L., 'Un etica di riconciliazione.' *Rivista di Teologia Morale* 17 (1985): 123–30.

McNamara, M., 'Celtic Christianity, Creation and Apocalypse, Christ and Antichrist.' *Milltown Studies* 23 (1989): 5–39.

Mitchell, Gerard, 'St Columbanus on Penance.' *I.T.Q.* 18 (1951): 43–54.
——, 'The Origins of Irish Penance.' *I.T.Q.* 22 (1955): 1–14.
Muzzarelli, M.G., 'Norme di comportamento alimentare nei libri penitenziali.' *Quaderni Medievali* 13 (1982): 45–80.
Moitel, Pierre, 'Le langage sur le péche depuis un siècle.' *Lumière et Vie* 185 (1987): 5–18.
Noonan, J.T., 'The Lessons of the Penitentials' in *Contraception: A History of its Treatment by the Catholic Theologians and Canonists.* Cambridge, Mass. Harvard Press, 1965.
Oakley, Thomas P., 'Celtic Penance: Its Sources Affiliations and Influence.' *I.E.R.* LII (1938): 147–64. and 581–601.
——, ' Commutations and redemptions of penance in the Penitentials.' *CHR* 18 (1932): 341–51
——, 'The Cooperation of Medieval Penance and Secular Law.' *Speculum* 7 (1932): 515–24.
——, 'The Origins of Irish Penitential Discipline.' *CHR* 19 (1933):320–332.
——, 'Cultural Affiliations of Early Ireland in the Penitentials.' *Speculum* 8 (1933) 489–500.
——, 'The Penitentials as Sources for Medieval History.' *Speculum* 15 (1940): 210–23.
O'Briain, F., 'The expansion of Irish Christianity to 1200; an historiographical study.' *Irish Historical Studies* 3 (1942–1943): 241–66 and 4 (1944–1945): 131–3.
Ó Duinn, S., 'Liodán na Faoistine.' *Irisleabhar Mhá Nuad* (1988): 190–202.
——, 'Celtic Christianity.' *Cistercian Studies* 20 (1985): 249–61.
——, 'The Trinity in the Early Irish Church.' *Monastic Studies* 19 (1986): 121–42.
Ó Fiaich, T., 'The Monastic Life in Early Christian Ireland.' *Capuchin Annual* 36 (1969): 116–34.
Ó hAinle, C., 'Irish Spirituality.' *The Furrow* 27 (1976): 583–96.
O'Laoghaire, Diarmuid, 'Early Irish Spirituality.' *Capuchin Annual* 36 (1969): 135–47.
——, 'Daily Intimacy with God — an Ever New Aspect of Celtic Worship.' *Studia Liturgica* 13 (1979): 46–56.
——, 'The Celtic Monk at Prayer.' *Monastic Studies* 14 (1986): 123–43.
——, 'Jesus Christ in Irish Spirituality.' *The Furrow* 32 (1981): 627–38.
——, 'Being Part of God's Family An Aspect of Irish Spirituality.' *Doctrine and Life* 32 (1983): 24–34.
——, 'Bibliography of Early Celtic Sprituality A.D. 400–1300.' *Milltown Studies* 12 (1983): 87–92.
——, 'Traditions of Spiritual Guidance: Soul Friendship.' *The Way* 25 (1985): 149–58.
O'Leary, P., 'An Irish Theology?' *Doctrine and Life* 27 (1977): 97–100.
Ó Maidín, V., 'The Monastic Rules of Ireland.' *Cistercian Studies* 15 (1980): 27–40.
Paganini, C., 'Presenza dei Penitenziali Irlandesi nel Pensiero Medievale.' *Studia et Documenta Historiae Et Iuris* 33 (1967) 359–66.
Payer, P., 'Early Medieval Regulations concerning Marital Sexual Relations.' *Journal of Medieval History* 6 (1980):353–76.
——, 'The Humanism of the Penitentials and the Continuity of the Penitential Tradition.' *Medieval Studies* 46 (1984): 340–54.

Rahner, K., 'Forgotten Truths Concerning the Sacrament of Penance.' *Theological Investigations* V.II London: D.L.T., 1963, 135–74.
——, 'Guilt And Its Remission: The Borderland Between Theology And Psychotherapy.' *Theological Investigations* II, 265–82.
——, 'Problems Concerning Confession.' *Theological Investigations* III, 190–206.
——, 'The Sinful Church in the Decrees of Vatican II.' *Theological Investigations* VI, 273–92.
Ramshaw Schmidt, Gail, 'Sin: One Image of Human Limitation.' *Concilium* 190 (1987): 3–10.
Seebass, Otto, 'Über die Handschriften der Sermonen und Briefe Columbas von Luxeuil.' *Neues Archiv der Gesellschaft für altere Geschichteskunde* 17 (1990).
——, 'Über die sogenannten Instructiones Columbani.' *Zeitschrift für Kirchengeschichte* XIII.
Sellar, W., 'Marriage, Divorce and Concubinage in Gaelic Scotland.' *Transactions of the Gaelic Society of Inverness* 51 (1978–1980): 464–93.
Valsecchi, A., 'I Libri Penitenziali e la Morale Cristiana. Alcuni Studi Recenti.' *La Scuola Cattolica* Supp. Biblio. 3 (1966): 260–68.
Vogel, C., 'Bussbücher.' *Lexikon für Theologie und Kirche*, II 1958 col. 802–5.
——, 'Composition légale et commutations dans le système de la pénitence tarifée.' *Revue de droit canonique* 8 (1958): 289–318, 9 (1959): 1–38, 341–59.
——, 'La Discipline Pénitentielle en Gaule des Origines au IXe Siècle.' *Revue des Sciences Religieuses* 30 (1956): 1–26.

INDEX